I0752717

IMAGES
of America

PERRY TOWNSHIP

On the Cover: The Longacre Lagoon. The lagoon at Longacre pool was a popular spot for high school students during the summer months. The man-made waterway, located north of Thompson Road, east of Madison Avenue, served as an area for paddle boating and swimming. (Perry Township/Southport Historical Society.)

IMAGES
of America

PERRY TOWNSHIP

Casey A. Smith with the
Perry Township/Southport Historical Society

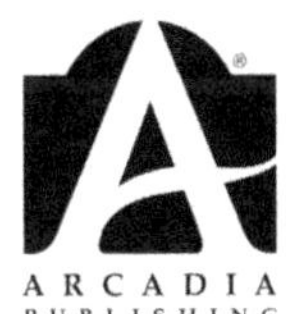

ISBN 9781540235428

Published by Arcadia Publishing
Charleston, South Carolina

Library of Congress Control Number: 2018934185

For all general information, please contact Arcadia Publishing:
Telephone 843-853-2070
Fax 843-853-0044
E-mail sales@arcadiapublishing.com
For customer service and orders:
Toll-Free 1-888-313-2665

Visit us on the Internet at www.arcadiapublishing.com

To David Sr. and Linda and David Jr., Chad, and Ryan:
May we continue to always appreciate history

Contents

Acknowledgments 6
Introduction 7
1. Early Perry Township 11
2. Founding of Southport 29
3. Time to Eat 45
4. Perry Township Schools 55
5. Life and Recreation 97

Acknowledgments

The author gratefully acknowledges the help of many individuals and resources, including the Perry Township/Southport Historical Society, Diane Saari, Michael Thrall, Judy Elder, Barry Browning, Fred Shonk, Janet Isaac, Jan and Jim Cooney, Jerry Brown, Rick Shaffer, and the Southport mayor's office.

Background for these photographs is drawn from information in the *Southside Times*, the *Southsider Voice*, *Indianapolis Star* and *Indianapolis News*, the *Encyclopedia of Indianapolis*, the *History of Indianapolis and Marion County*, *Hail, Hail Our Southport!*, eyewitness stories and accounts, and Internet research.

Introduction

Before the early 1800s, southeastern Marion County was nothing more than prairie fields and wooded forests. Bordering the southern banks or the White River, farmsteads didn't become permanent in the area until the early 19th century.

In 1822, Perry Township—one of nine in Marion County—was laid out by the US Army Corps of Engineers and named after Oliver Hazard Perry, a War of 1812 hero. County records indicate that a "lack of population" induced the combination of Perry, Decatur, and Franklin Townships into one, known as "Decatur-Perry-Franklin" Township. By the early 1820s, 81 entries of land were recorded in Perry Township.

In 1827, residents of Perry Township petitioned the separation of the township, which was promptly granted by the county board.

Soon after, Samuel and Mary Bryan, two of the townships now-notable residents, moved into the neighborhood known as Southport in the early 1830s. Perry Township historians note that Samuel and Mary Bryan are regarded as relatives of Daniel Boone, the famous Kentucky pioneer, with Samuel's mother being Daniel Boone's sister. Samuel had served in the Continental Army and was married just before heading to battle.

The Bryans started their journey in North Carolina in 1779 and headed toward Kentucky on horseback and with pack horses. When they came to the Cumberland River, their belongings were transported on a raft. Local folklore suggests that Mary was the first white woman who set foot north of the Cumberland River in Kentucky, although this story is hard to prove for sure.

The Bryans settled in Campbell County, Kentucky, where they started their family. Luke, a farmer and the son of Mary and Samuel, brought his parents to Southport around 1830. Samuel Bryan died in 1837 at 83, and his wife died in 1840 in Perry Township. They were buried on Luke's farm, but were taken to the Southport Cemetery afterwards, where other pioneers during their time were also buried.

As settlers moved west and made the outskirts of Indianapolis their home, agriculture dominated the land with dense fields of corn and soybeans spanning for miles. Prominent farmers, including Jacob Smock and Abraham Lemaster, settled and began farming around 1822. Smock, another notable resident of the area, was born in Kentucky in 1797 and moved to Indiana in the early 1820s. The town of Southport—established in 1832 and the first to be incorporated in Marion county in 1853—was platted on the original quarter-section that Smock settled on, which was then an unbroken forest. Township records suggest that is also where the first Presbyterian preacher, Rev. John M. Dickey, first preached in the township.

Around this time, another small "village" or community, Glenn's Valley, was taking shape in the southwest part of the township on the Bluff road, three-fourths of a mile north of the Johnson

County line. The community, named for Archibald Glenn, one of the earliest settlers in the township was laid out partly on land of John Smart and partly on land of Robert Burns. The first house on the village site was built by Burns in the winter of 1830–1831. Nearly a century later in 1920, the community recorded around 80 residents and a number of businesses.

The first schoolhouse was a log building erected on Jacob Smock's farm north of Buck Creek. A second location, known as the Mud Schoolhouse, also served as a church.

The pioneer schoolhouses of Perry Township—and others nearby—were small, low structures built of logs with puncheon floors, seats, and writing benches. There was a large fireplace of stones and mud and a log cut out from two sides for windows; the openings were covered with greased paper in place of glass, and there were no appliances of other more modern schoolhouses. The teachers were men who farmed throughout the spring, summer, and autumn. In winter, they taught school for terms of six weeks to three months. Teachers were required to teach reading, spelling, and writing, and they received a small wage for their services.

Frame schoolhouses later took the places of the old log buildings, in addition to the implementation of longer school terms and stricter teacher requirements.

By 1883, Perry Township had 14 school districts and the same number of schoolhouses—2 frame schoolhouses and 12 brick schoolhouses. The average daily student attendance was 446, while the total number of students admitted to the schools was 662. By this time, Marion County's African American population was also growing. A small population of African Americans lived in Perry Township, although students attended separate schools. Two black teachers taught 31 black male students and 42 female students. There was also one private school taught in the township at that time, with an average attendance of 84 in 1883.

The separate school that had been constructed for African American students—which was located at the intersection of Epler Avenue and Belmont Road—was built by a large landowner, Allen Fletcher, for the children of his employees, as he wanted to ensure their children had the opportunity to be educated. This being said, Perry Township schools were never purposefully segregated, according to local historians. The school located at Epler and Belmont was predominately black because they were children of Fletcher's African American employees, and Fletcher built the school because there were none others close enough for children to walk to. After Fletcher sold his farm, most of the African American families moved, and the school was then known as Township School 14. Because of the township's small overall African American student population moving forward, though, the students were later assimilated to other public schools.

In 1891, the township opened its first high school, located at what is now Madison Avenue and Southport Road. The new, and original, Southport High School was less than a mile from the Smock farm—a testament to how small the township still was at that time.

The first mill in the township was built around 1827 by William Arnold on Lick Creek, three-quarters of a mile west of the eastern boundary of the township. It was used a few years and then abandoned because of water supply failure. The next year, Jacob Smock built a gristmill on Buck Creek, which operated for several years until it was also abandoned due to water shortage. Other mills were built throughout the course of the 19th century in the area, and when steam engines on the Madison & Indianapolis Railroad began servicing the area around the 1850s, shops, factories, and immigrant workers were attracted to the Perry Township area.

In the years following, immigration grew, but by the early 1900s, much of Perry Township was still undeveloped, and it remained that way until part-way into the 20th century when the population slowly began increasing throughout Indianapolis and in the township. Electric cars on Indianapolis's interurban railway boomed at the turn of the century, and by 1910, dozens of railcars were making stops around Perry Township each day, many headed to and from downtown Indianapolis. Those living farther away from the city center were now able to travel with far more ease.

German immigrants also helped develop more businesses, building greenhouses, nurseries and truck farms along Bluff Road and South Meridian Street. The town of Homecroft was laid out in 1923, and bungalow-style homes became popular between 1930 and 1950.

Following World War II, suburban development spanned across Marion County. Older Perry Township neighborhoods, including University Heights, Homecroft, and Edgewood, attracted a number of new residents.

The enlargement of Madison Avenue in the 1960s further increased accessibility to the south side, and access to and from Indianapolis was further aided by the construction of Interstates 465 and 65.

By this time, the educational needs of the township had grown as well. Southport High School's original 1891 building took only 18 years to outgrow, and it was replaced by a new structure at the same location. Just 20 years after that, a third iteration of the building was constructed at the corner of Banta Road and Orinoco Avenue. By the 1950s, a fourth building was erected and—after serving a brief stint as a township junior high school—served as the fourth official Southport High School and still does today at 971 East Banta Road. As the population continued to grow in Perry Township, Southport was joined by another high school, Perry Meridian, and more businesses—like restaurants, groceries and department stores—continued to pop up.

Perry Township has had its fair share of recreational activities, too. One of the most popular, Longacre Pool, opened to the public in 1927. Attorney Edwin Thompson created the south-side park after developing a nearby subdivision between the areas of University Heights and Edgewood east of Madison Avenue in 1913. The pool grew substantially over the next four decades, with the park being popularized by its acre-size pool, baseball fields, putt-putt areas, and bathhouse during the summer months. Longacre was sold in 1946 to Rufus Dodrill Jr., whose family operated it until 1972.

Aside from swimming, local restaurants like Southern Circle were frequent spots for Perry Township residents during the 1940s and 1950s, predating the area now known as Southern Plaza. Those were the days when carhops would serve patrons from car windows, and a hamburger cost less than a quarter.

When Southern Plaza—the first major shopping center on Indianapolis's Southside — celebrated its grand opening in April 1961, stores like The Kroger Co., Hook Drugs Inc., Kay Jewelry, The Pet House, J.C. Penney Co., Kimmel Shoe Repair, and many more made shopping centralized and easier to do in one trip out.

This book, although not a complete history of the township, further explores prominent parts of Perry Township's history from the days of its pioneer settlers. Although the area has a long history of serving farmers and their families, the township today thrives with a population of more than 100,000 residents. Township schools have continued to expand, and although many iconic pieces of the Perry Township's past no longer exist, memories of their existence still remain. The stories that form Perry Township and the city of Southport are evidence that the people who have lived in on Indianapolis's southeast side have influenced those who still reside in the area today, nearly two centuries later.

One

Early Perry Township

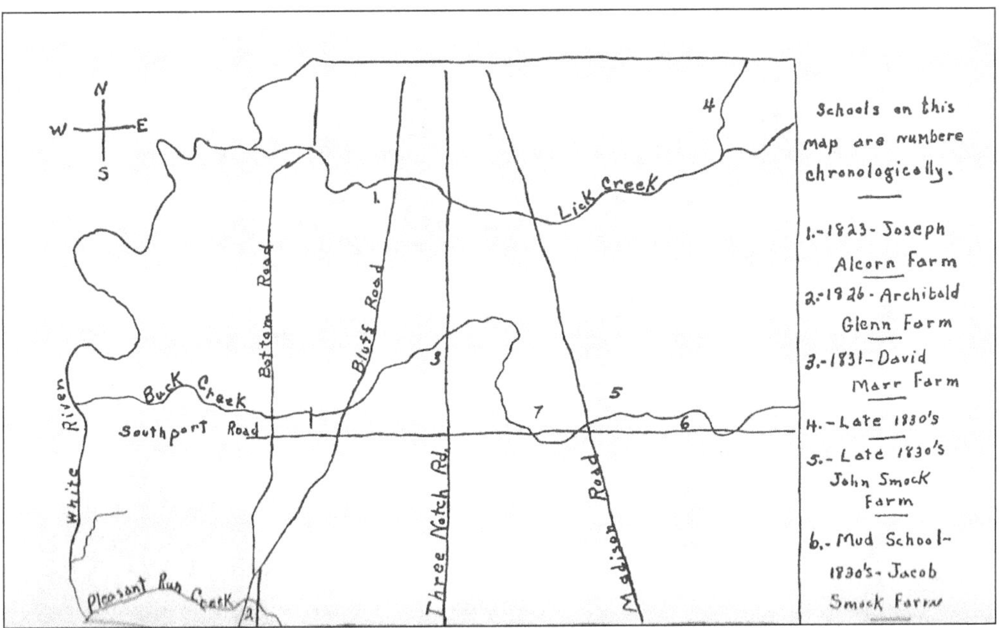

Early Township Map. Southport was established in 1832, and Jacob Smock of Kentucky is considered to be one of its founding fathers. The Smocks purchased the first land in Southport in May 1822, and many of those plots can be seen above. Jacob cleared the land and built a cabin in the summer of 1823. He also built one of the earliest gristmills in present-day Perry Township on Buck Creek. Oliver Hazard Perry was an American naval commander most notable for his heroic role in the War of 1812 during the 1813 Battle of Lake Erie. During the war against Britain, Perry supervised the building of a fleet at Erie, Pennsylvania. He earned the title "Hero of Lake Erie" for leading American forces in a decisive naval victory at the Battle of Lake Erie, receiving a Congressional Gold Medal and the Thanks of Congress. Although it is not clear why, Perry Township was named after Perry when it was laid out in 1822. (Perry Township/Southport Historical Society.)

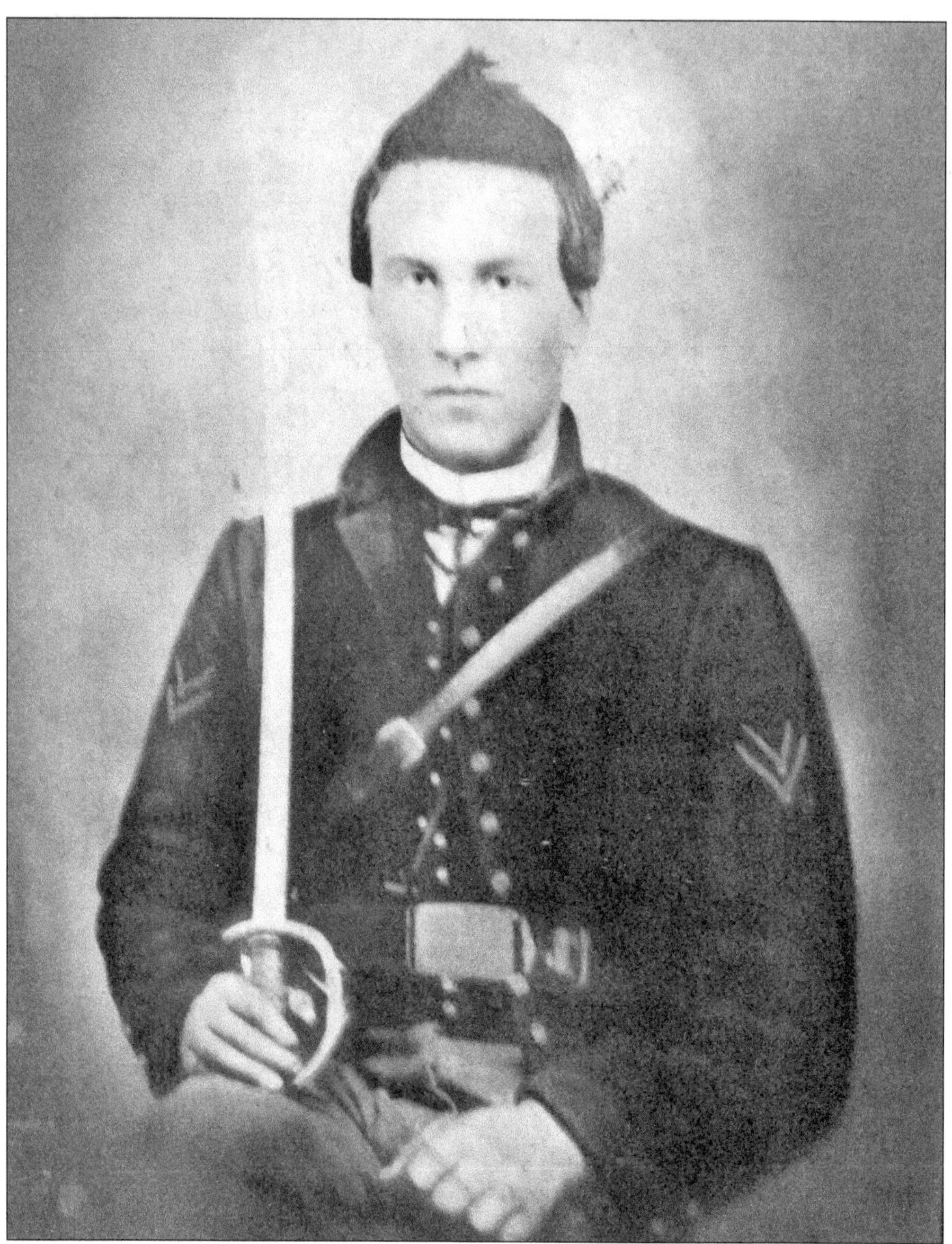

Civil War Soldier. John Smith, pictured in a painting here, was a resident of Southport in the mid-19th century, living on Union Street. During the Civil War, Smith fought for the Union. Today, some of his decedents can still be found living in Southport and the surrounding Perry Township area. (Perry Township/Southport Historical Society.)

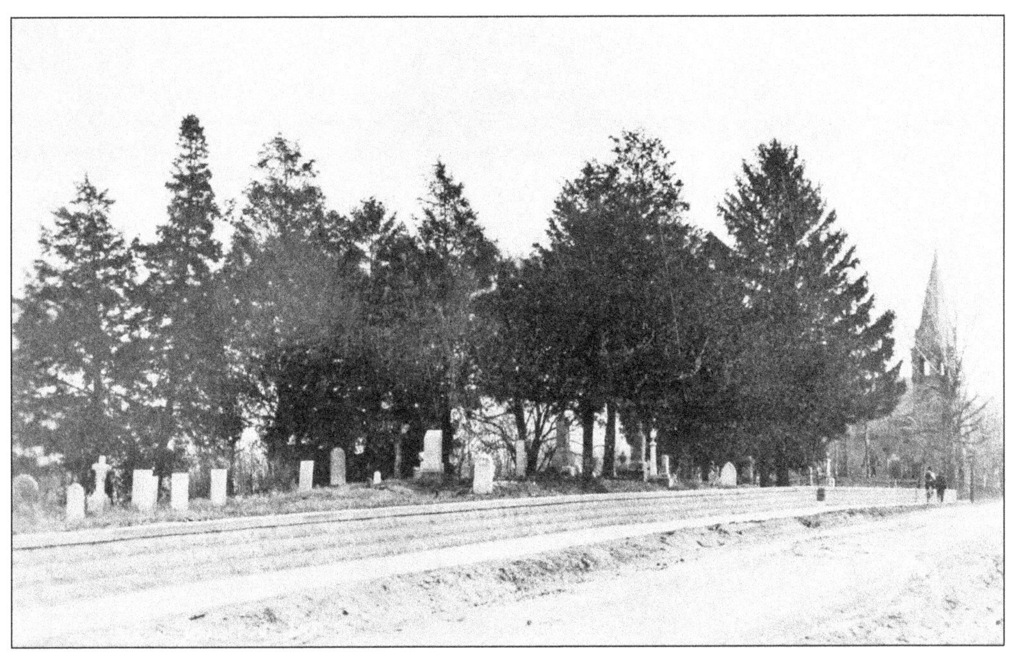

Southport Cemetery. This 1914 photograph depicts the Southport Baptist Cemetery, located on Union Street (now Southport Road). The cemetery is located on what was once Jacob Smock's farm, and the Southport Baptist Church, which was built in 1896, can be seen in the background. The sidewalk next to the cemetery had been recently constructed, and excavated dirt was placed in the middle of the street to be hauled away later. (Perry Township/Southport Historical Society.)

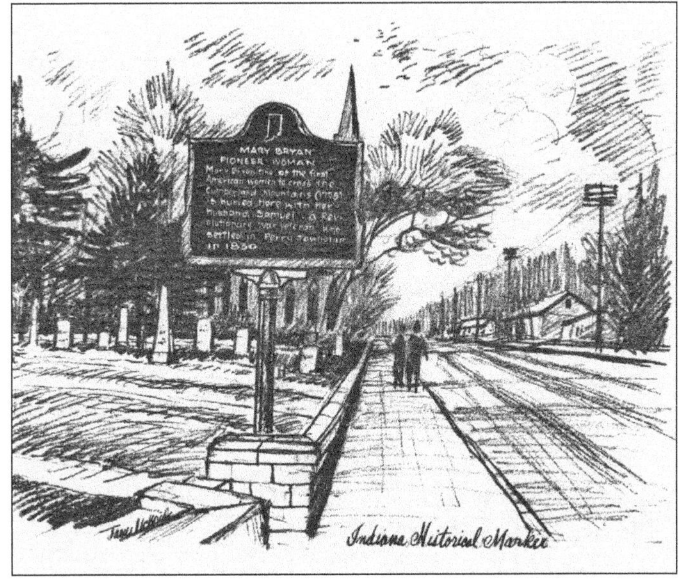

Cemetery Historical Marker. Today, the cemetery is located just west of Bethel Memorial Church and is also known as the Mary Bryan Cemetery. Here, pioneer woman Mary Bryan and her husband, Samuel, a Revolutionary War veteran, are buried. Early Perry Township residents began burying relatives in the cemetery in as early as the 1810s, and more than 120 individuals have been identified both with and without grave markers. (Perry Township/Southport Historical Society.)

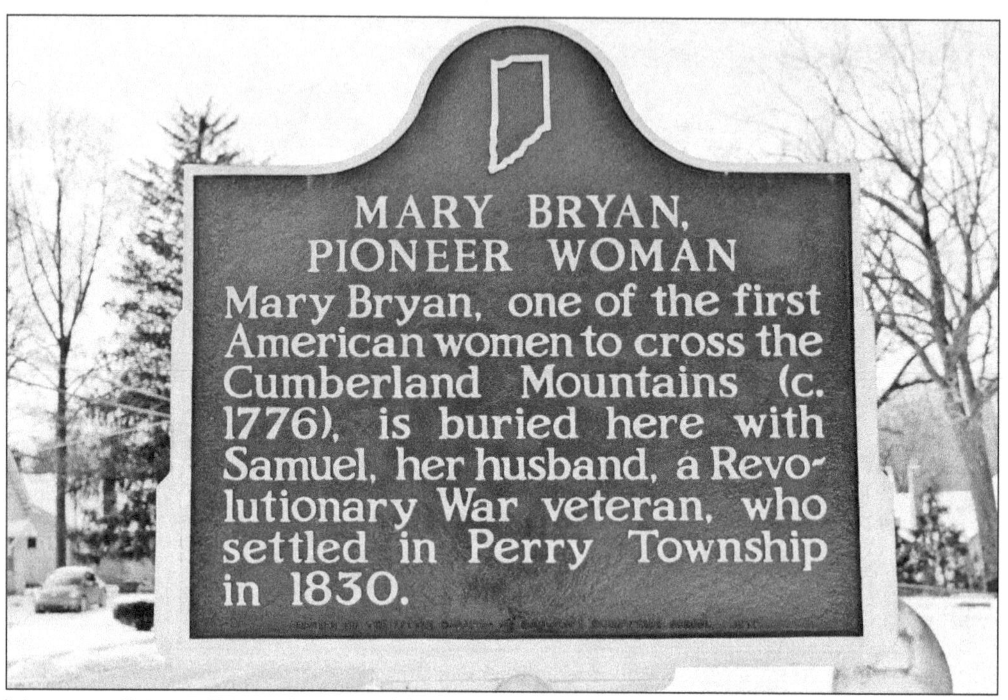

Mary and Samuel Bryan. Now-notable residents Mary, a supposed decent of Daniel Boone, and Samuel Bryan, a member of the Continental Army, migrated from North Carolina to Kentucky and later Southport in April 1825. The couple had two sons, Thomas and Luke, who both married and raised their families in the area as well. Samuel died in 1837 and was buried in the Southport Cemetery, located at 2700 East Southport Road. Mary passed away three years later and was also buried in the cemetery. Both sons were later buried next to their parents in 1857. The family's plot remains at the cemetery today. (Photograph by Casey Smith.)

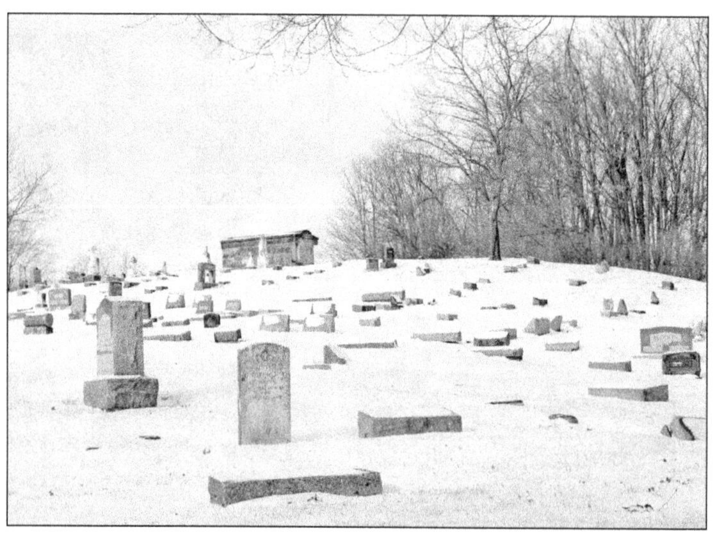

Round Hill Cemetery. Located on the corner of Old Meridian Street and Epler Avenue, this small cemetery was once home to two cemeteries—the corner of Epler is the previous location of the older Union Cemetery. First established by a Methodist priest in 1830, Round Hill is home to graves ranging from the 1830s through the present day. (Photograph by Casey Smith.)

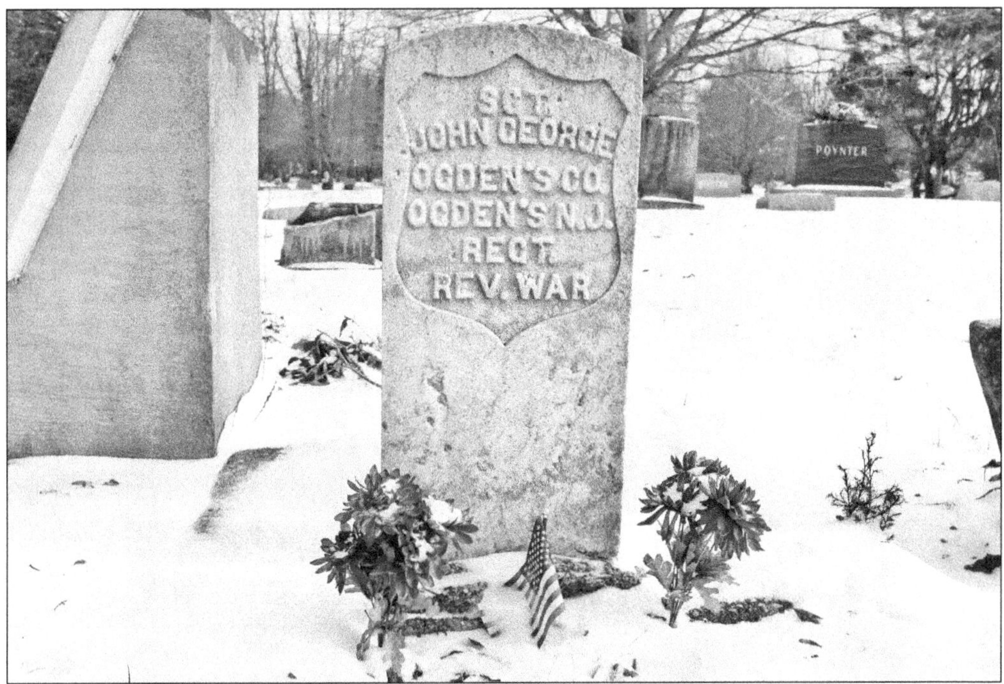

George Washington's Drummer Boy. The cemetery contains a popular grave belonging to that of George Washington's drummer boy, Sgt. John George. He was a Revolutionary War veteran of the First Battalion of the New Jersey Continental Line and likely served as the personal drummer boy of Washington's headquarters guard during a large portion of the Revolution. George moved to Indiana in the 1830s, and following his death in 1847, his daughter buried him at Round Hill. George's grave can still be seen today toward near the center of the cemetery. (Photographs by Casey Smith.)

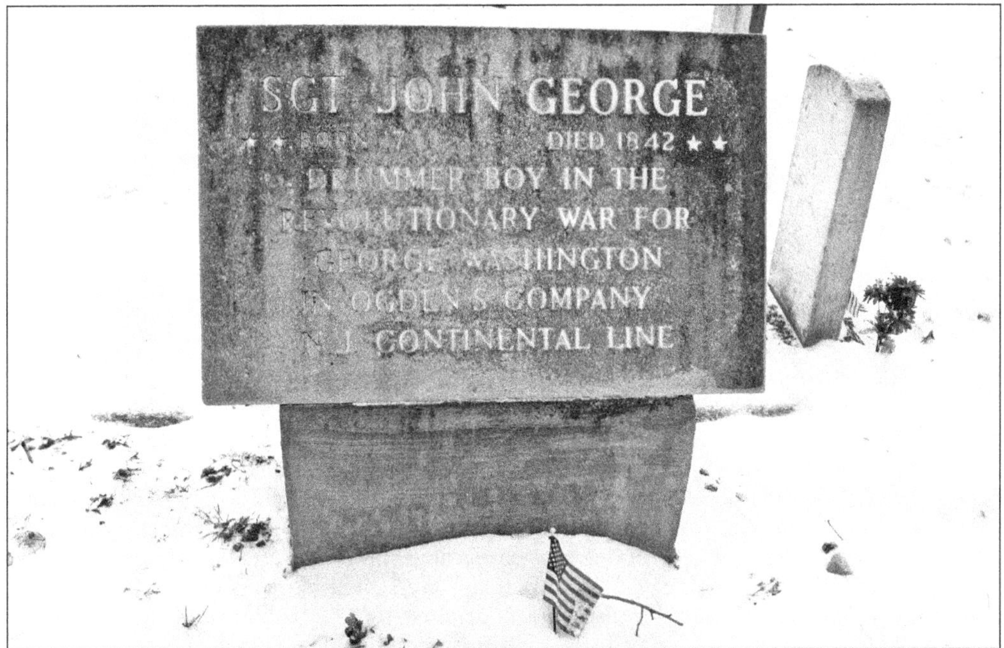

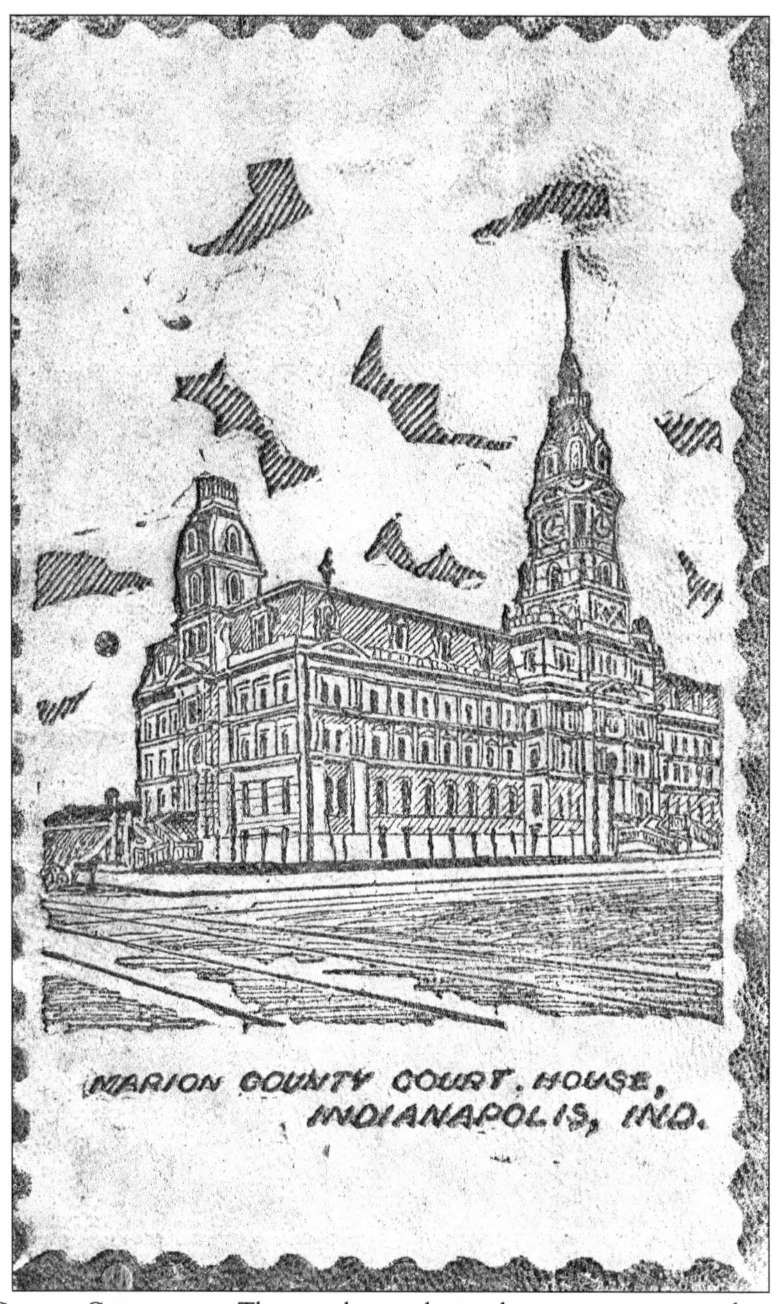

Marion County Courthouse. The courthouse, depicted on a vintage postcard, was designed by Isaac Hodgson and built in 1876. The courthouse occupied the block between Delaware and Alabama Streets in downtown Indianapolis and faced East Washington Street. It was a French Second Empire building of brick and limestone. Outside of the Perry Township Small Claims Court, residents who needed to conduct business would have traveled to the county courthouse. The building was razed in June 1962 due to overcrowding and because it was considered ugly by some. It was replaced by the new City-County Building on the same block but facing Market Street. Eight stone ladies were brought down from their perches atop the building and were auctioned off for a grand total of $2,150. (Perry Township/Southport Historical Society.)

UNION STREET IN SOUTHPORT. This drawing by James McBride was sketched from an original photograph to depict the old Southport business district in the early 1900s. The street-scene image looks west and provides a view of Union Street. The original Southport Post Office and train depot can be seen on the south side (left) of the road. (Perry Township/Southport Historical Society.)

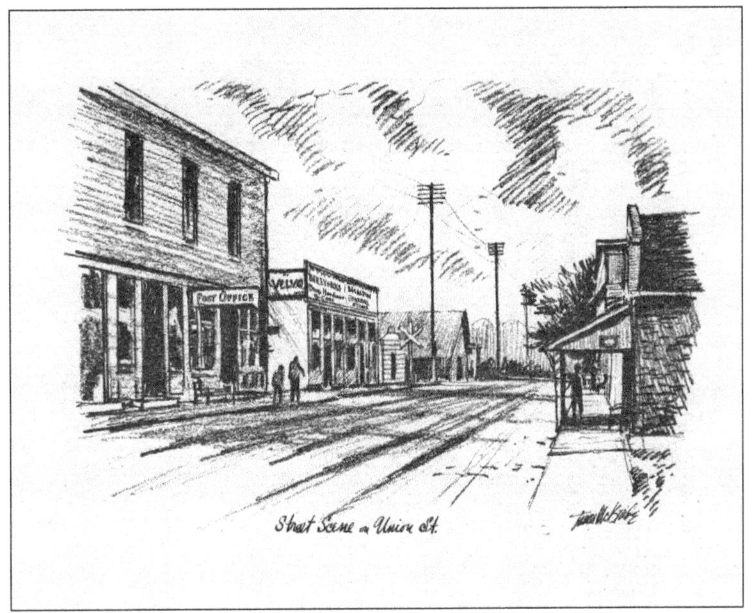

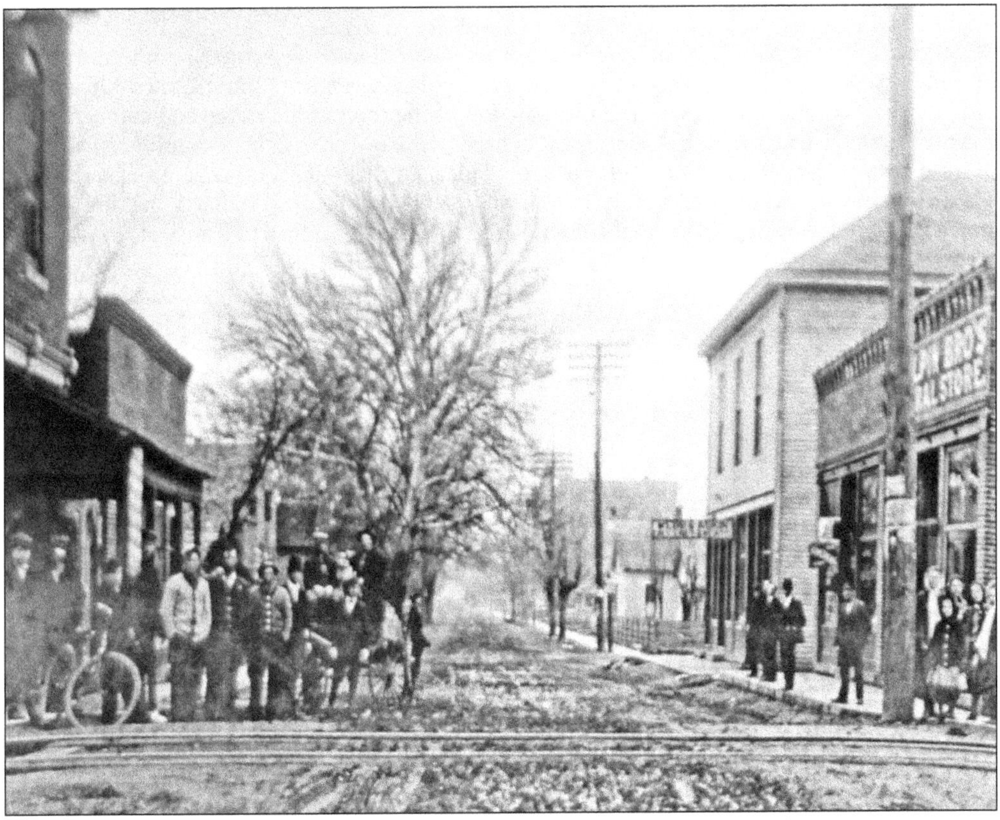

SOUTHPORT STREET SCENE. Looking east again down Union Street, this early-1900s image is one of few that capture the original Southport Odd Fellows Lodge while still active (in the distance, on the right). At the time this photograph was taken, sidewalks had been paved, but the road had not. (Perry Township/Southport Historical Society.)

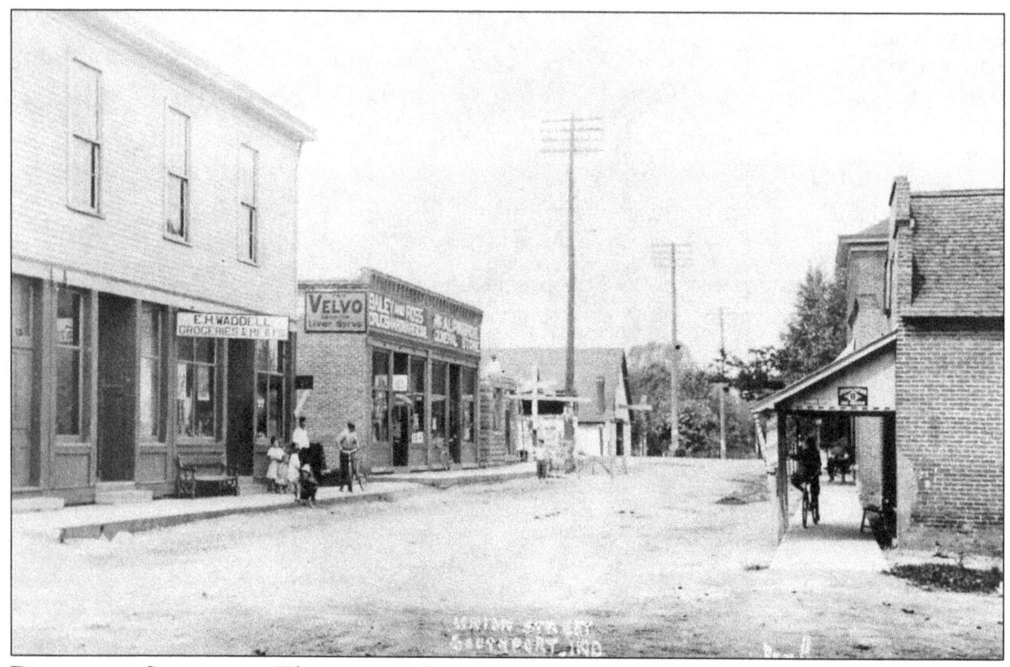

DOWNTOWN SOUTHPORT. This image offers another view of Union Street in Southport. In 1903, around the time this photo was taken, Southport had only 400 residents and the township in total had between 800 and 1,000. With the introduction of the interurban, however, people in Perry Township found it easier to go to and from other local municipalities, and Southport itself also saw an influx in visitation, business, and church attendance. At the time, Southport also had the only full-fledged interurban railroad station in Marion County and Central Indiana, making it even more attractive for those coming and going. (Perry Township/Southport Historical Society.)

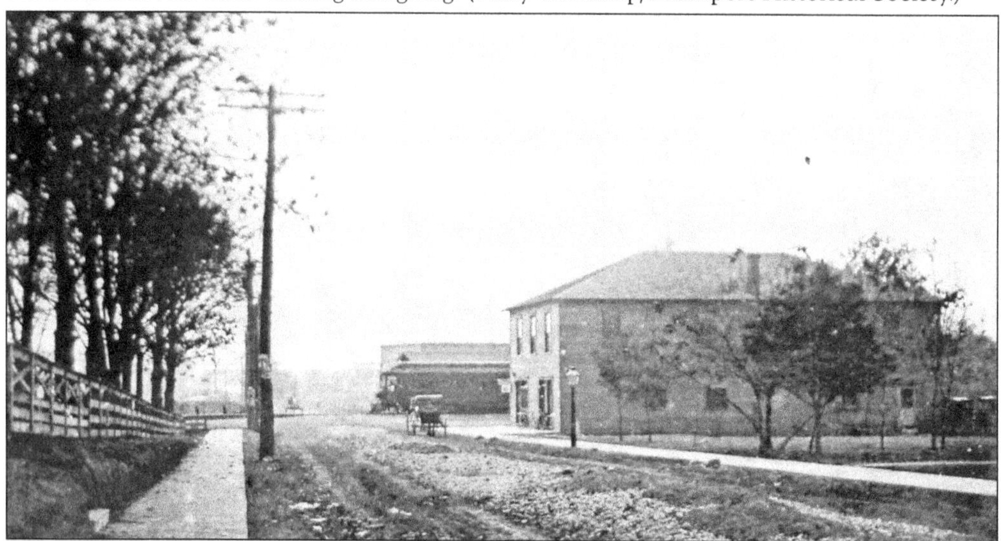

UNION STREET AND MADISON AVENUE. Taken between 1900 and 1908, this image faces west down Union Street toward the intersection with Madison Avenue. Wooden fencing surrounds the original Southport High School building to the left, and an interurban car is making its way south down Madison Avenue near the center of the image. (Perry Township/Southport Historical Society.)

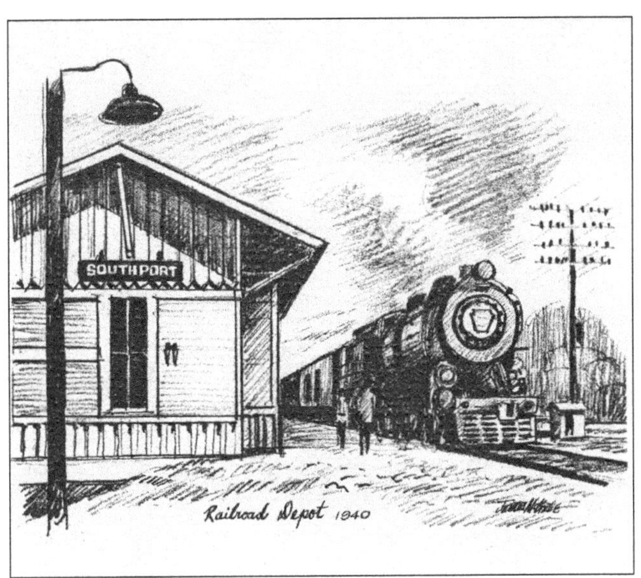

Southport Railroad Depot, 1940. This drawing by James McBride depicts the Southport Railroad Depot, which stood alongside the railroads tracks on Southport Road east of Madison Avenue. Different from the interurban line, the railroad brought shipments—mainly wood and other building materials—from across the country to Southport and other parts of Perry Township on the Louisville & Indiana (L&I) Railroad route, formerly known as the JM&I Railroad, and later the Pennsylvania Railroad. (Perry Township/ Southport Historical Society.)

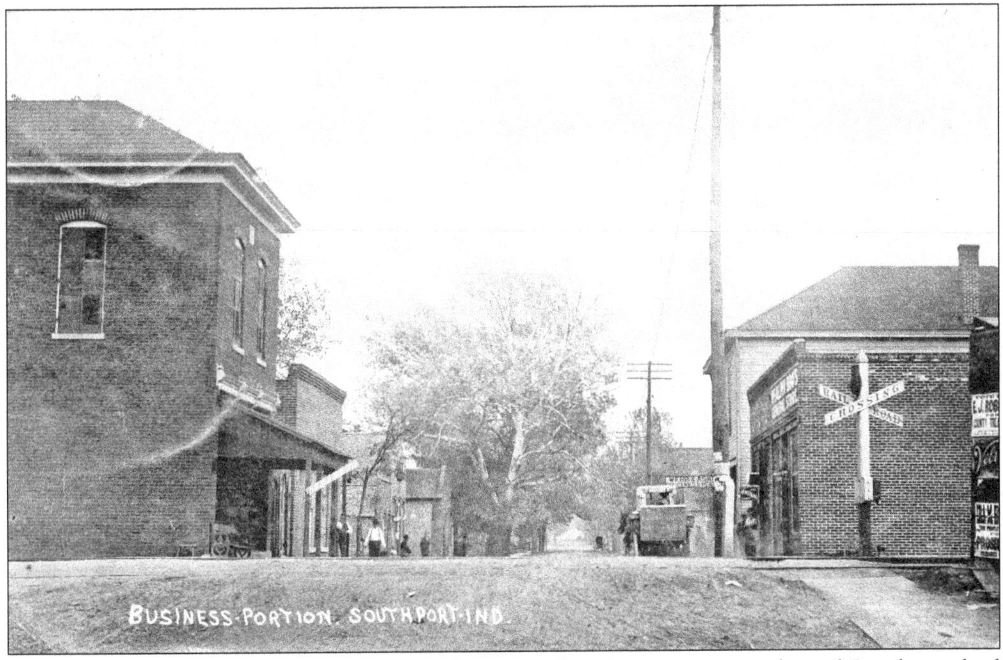

Southport Trains. By 1876, Perry Township started to show more growth, and Southport had developed a station along the rail line connecting to Union Terminal in downtown Indianapolis. The railroad line which intersects Perry Township connects Indianapolis to Louisville. Two to three trains still currently travel the Louisville & Indiana Railroad's tracks on a direct north–south route from Indianapolis to Louisville each day at speeds of up to 25 miles per hour. (Perry Township/ Southport Historical Society.)

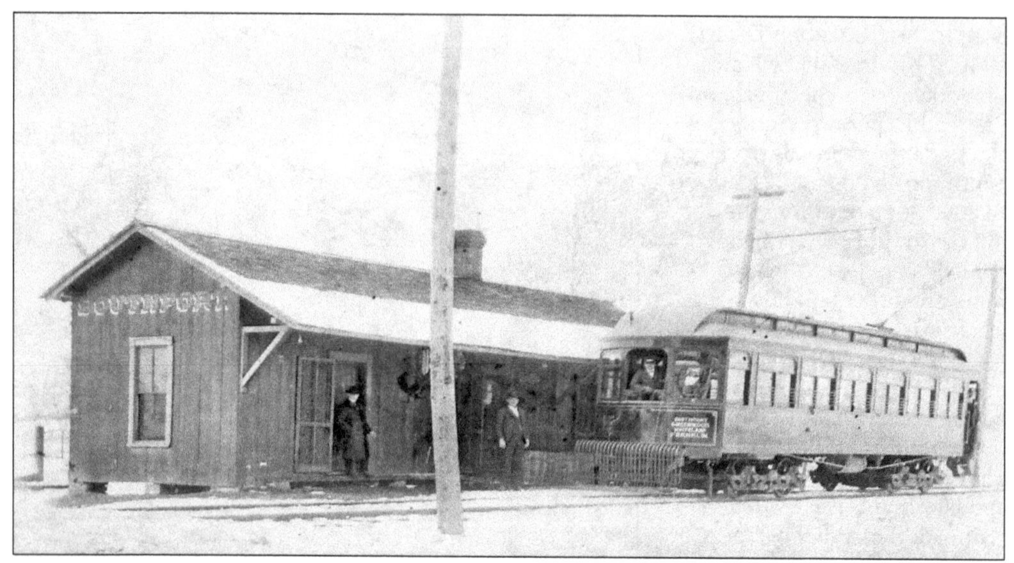

SOUTHPORT INTERURBAN STATION. In addition to the railroad line that connected Indianapolis to Louisville, there was also the interurban that connected various communities to Indianapolis. Madison Avenue is to the right of the train that is stopped at Southport's station en route to Greenwood, Franklin, Edinburg, Columbus, and Seymour. (Perry Township/Southport Historical Society.)

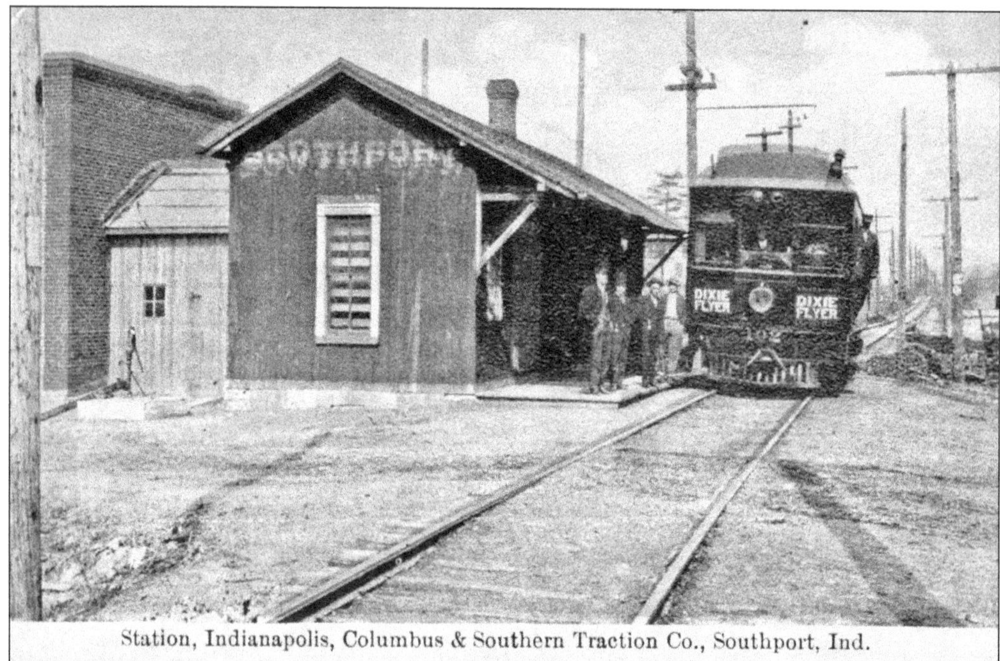

Station, Indianapolis, Columbus & Southern Traction Co., Southport, Ind.

THE INTERURBAN. Between 1900 and the mid-1930s, the best way to get from city to city in Indiana was the interurban rail car. After departing from the Indianapolis Terminal Traction station at Illinois and West Market Streets, the electric rail cars traveled to and from suburbs around the city, including Southport. The interurban ran south of downtown alongside Madison Avenue. Here, Southport's interurban depot is seen at its Southport Road/Madison Avenue location. (Perry Township/Southport Historical Society.)

SOUTHPORT & INDIANAPOLIS GRAVEL ROAD.

RATES OF TOLL, AND REGULATIONS,

For Persons Traveling on the Road.

1st. No person shall horse race on said road, nor shoot across or along said road.

2d. The driver of any wagon, cart, carriage, sleigh, or other vehicle, on said road, when met or overtaken by any other wagon, cart, carriage sleigh, or other vehicle, shall keep to the right, so as to allow such other wagon, cart, carriage, or other vehicle meeting or overtaken as aforesaid, to pass freely, and without obstruction or hindrance.

3d. The following are hereby declared to be the tolls, chargeable on the said road, to-wit:

For every sled, sleigh, carriage, or other vehicle, drawn by one horse, 2 cents per mile, and for every animal in addition thereto, three-fourths of a cent per mile.

For every horse and rider, or led horse, one and a half cents per mile.

For every score of sheep or swine, five cents per mile, and in the same ratio for a greater or less number.

For every score of nett cattle, mules, or asses, ten cents per mile, and in the same ratio for a greater or less number.

For every vehicle drawn by oxen, the same rate as is allowed on carriages drawn by horses.

At the above rates of toll, the following will be the charges to and from the different points named along the road.

	No. of Miles.	For One Horse and Wagon.	For Two Horses and Wagon.	For One Horse and Rider.
From Toll Gate to Indianapolis,	½	1	1½	¾
" Pennsman's to Indianapolis,	¾	1½	2	1
" Cross Roads at Myers's to Indianapolis,	1	2	2½	1½
" Hoefgan's to Indianapolis,	1½	3	4	2
" Weaver's to Indianapolis,	1¾	3½	5½	2½
" D. W. Noble's to Indianapolis,	2½	5	8	3½
" A. M. Hannah's to Indianapolis,	3	6	9	4½
" Jasper Wright's to Indianapolis,	3½	7	10½	5
" Eli Haverick's to Indianapolis,	4	8	11	6
" Morris Howland's to Indianapolis,	4¼	8½		
" Road intersecting North of T. C. Brock's to Indianapolis,	4½	9	12½	7
" Wm. Wallace's, and Road South of his Farm, to Indianapolis,	5¼	10½	15	8
" Lower Toll Gate to Indianapolis,	6	12	16½	9
" Southport to Indianapolis,	6½	13	19	10

December 19, 1864. **MORRIS HOWLAND, [illegible]**

GRAVEL ROAD TOLL, 1864. This toll notice was used for travel between Southport and Indianapolis by carriage. For several decades, new gravel roads required toll payment, seen here. To travel from Indianapolis to Southport (or vice versa), the toll varied between one and twenty cents, depending on the number of horses and occupants. (Perry Township/Southport Historical Society.)

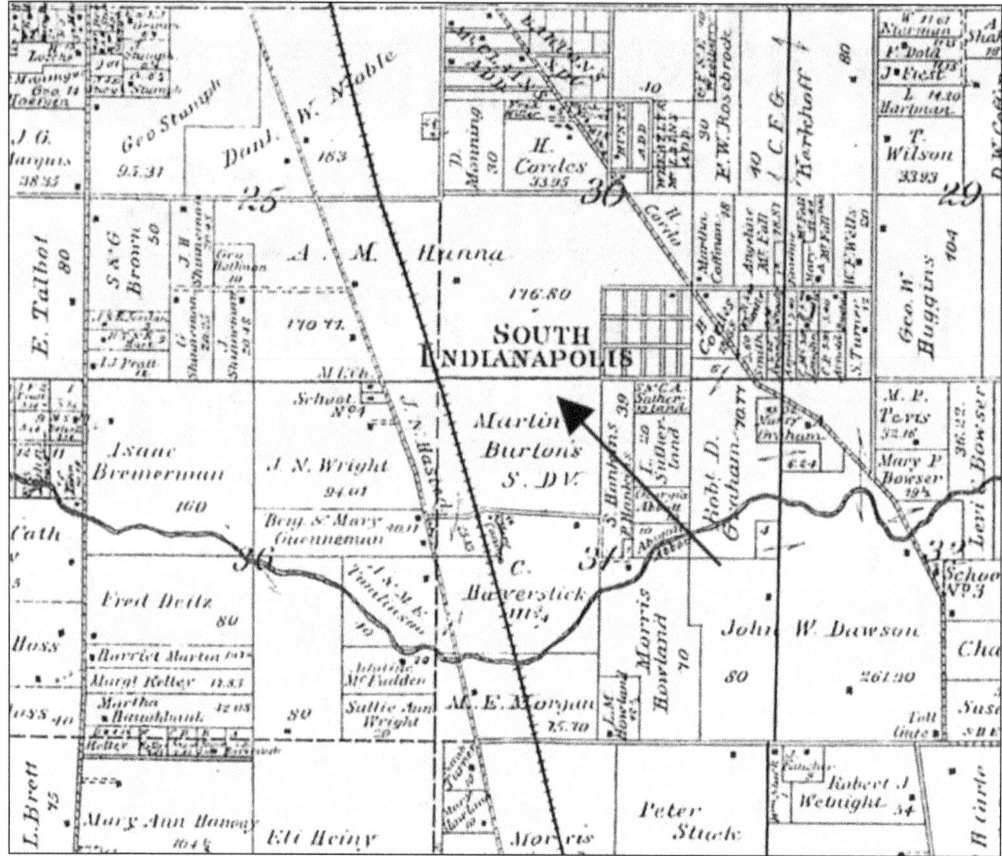

UNIVERSITY OF INDIANAPOLIS. Formerly known as Indiana Central College and Indiana Central University, the University of Indianapolis is located on East Hanna Avenue, just east of Shelby Street. The campus straddles the Carson Heights and University Heights neighborhoods. In the early 20th century, William L. Elder, an Indianapolis real estate developer, offered the Church of the United Brethren in Christ eight acres of real estate southeast of downtown Indianapolis to establish a college in exchange for help selling 446 parcels of land around the donated acreage. Indiana Central University was chartered in 1902, but instruction did not start until 1905 when the first building, Good Hall, was completed. The school opened its doors for students in September 1905. (Perry Township/Southport Historical Society.)

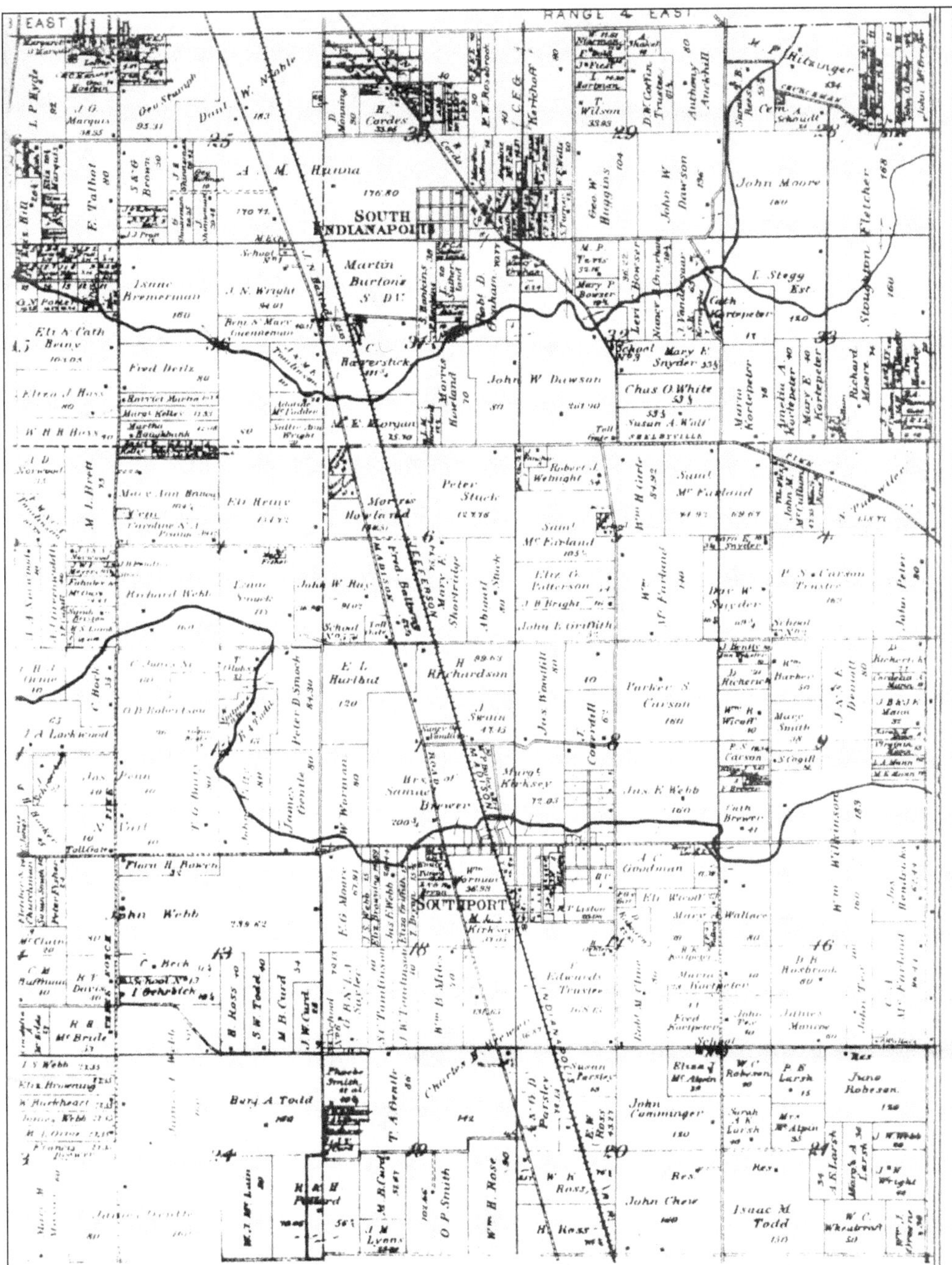

Perry Township Plat Map. This later 19th-century map of Perry Township indicates land parcels and their owners. Madison Avenue (previously Madison Road) runs adjacent north and south along the center of the map. Excluding Southport proper, labeled on this map, much of Perry Township consisted of farmland at the time this map was created. (Perry Township/Southport Historical Society.)

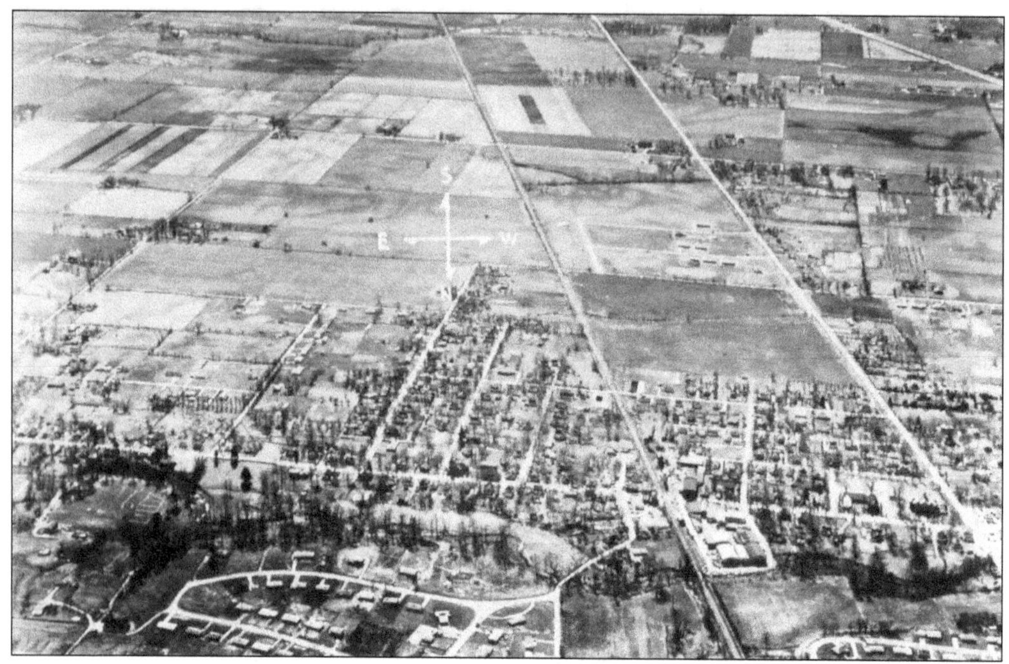

Map of Perry Township. This 1958 aerial map depicts the southern side of Perry Township, facing south toward Southport. Madison Avenue is the main road running north and south down the center of the image. Near the lower right-hand corner of the image is the second Southport High School building, which was located at the intersection of now Southport Road and Madison Avenue. (Perry Township/Southport Historical Society.)

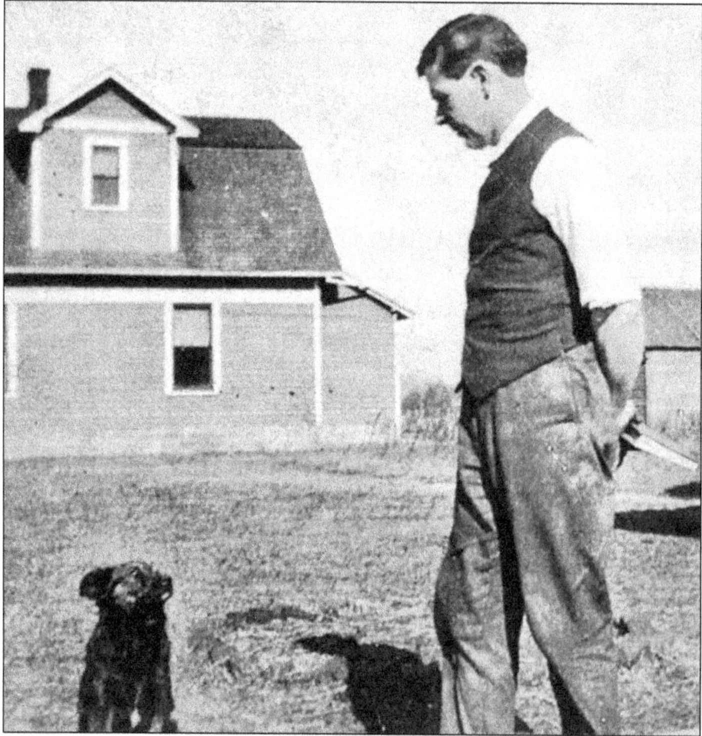

J.T. Zufall. John Theodore "J.T." Zufall, although born near Dephi, Indiana, was a resident of the Indianapolis area for 38 years. A cabinet maker who operated a shop from his home, Zufall also constructed the limestone arches over the doors at Edgewood Grade School. That school building was later demolished in 1980. Zufall was also a member of the Southport Masonic lodge before he passed away in 1958 at the age of 76. (Perry Township/Southport Historical Society.)

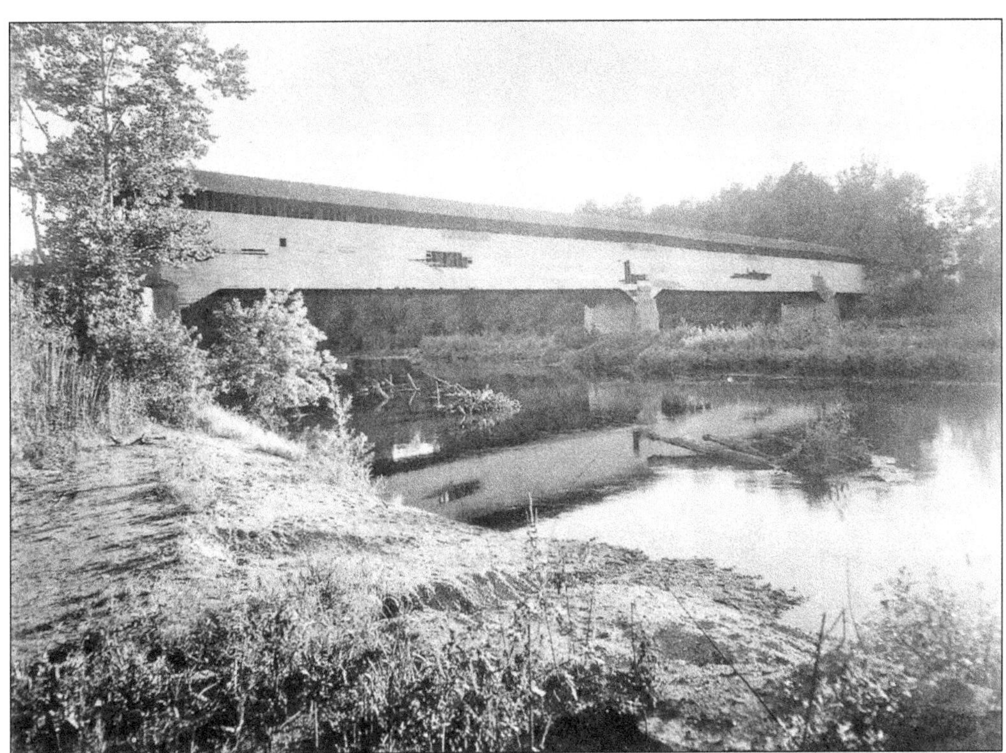

Southport Road Bridge. Indiana's White River was the reason that many bridges were constructed throughout central and southern Indiana. The Southport Road Bridge, seen here, was built in 1883. This three-lane bridge was built by the Kennedy family of Rushville and was one of the longest wooden bridges in the state around the time it was completed. It was rebuilt once again with cement in the 1950s due to old age. (Perry Township/Southport Historical Society.)

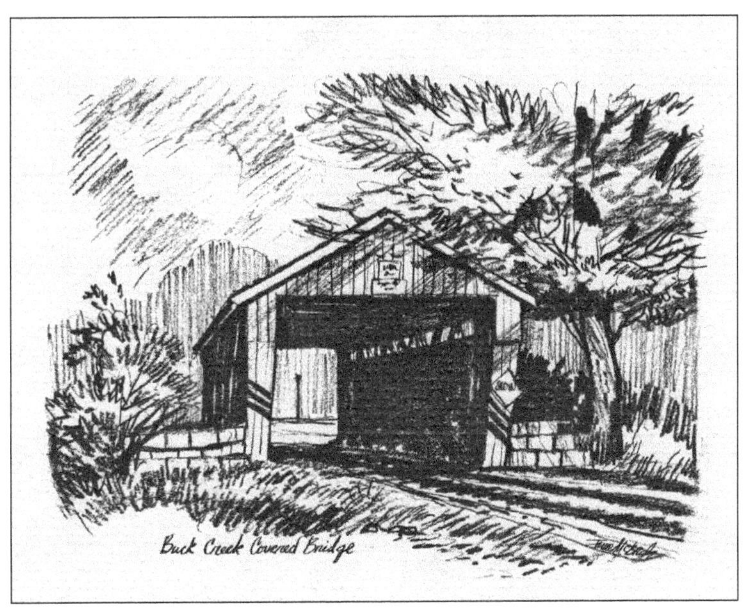

Buck Creek Covered Bridge. This sketch of a covered bridge near Southport Road predates the first brick school building in the area by two years. Built in 1881, the total cost to build the bridge was just $1,680. The bridge crossed Little Buck Creek just east of what is now the intersection of Southport Road and Gray Road. (Perry Township/Southport Historical Society.)

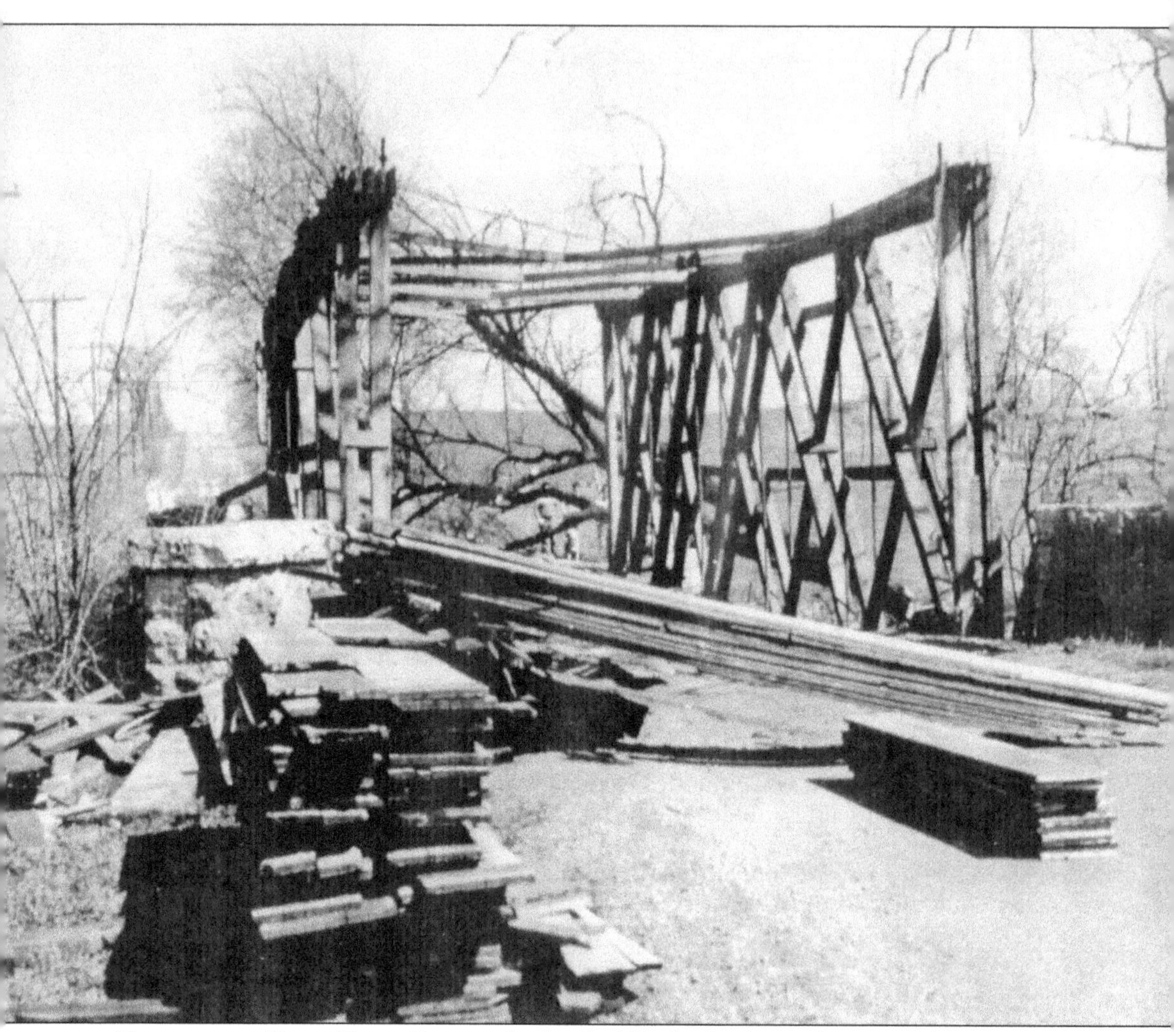

DISMANTLING BUCK CREEK BRIDGE. In April 1955, the Buck Creek covered bridge was razed. County commissioners awarded a contract to Sparks Construction Inc. of Evansville, Indiana, to build a new bridge for just under $53,000. Construction of the bridge took place later that month, just days after the previous wood structure was removed. Before it was dismantled, the Buck Creek bridge was one of the last five covered bridges that remained in Marion County at that time. (Perry Township/Southport Historical Society.)

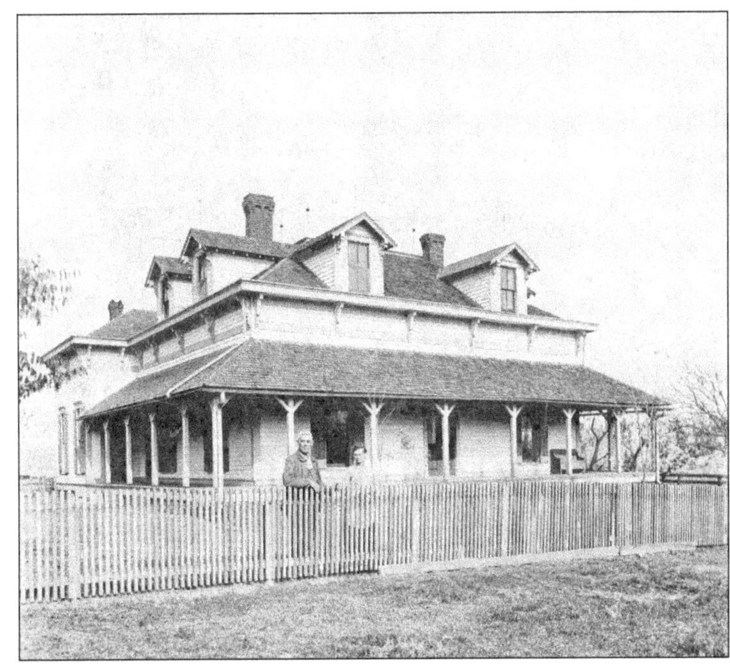

Chas and Etta McLain. At their farm located near Bluff and Southport Roads, Charles "Chas" and Etta McLain tended land and raised a family. Charles, a lifelong Perry Township resident, was a founder of the Farmers' Cooperative and the Southport State Bank. He died in June 1946 at the age of 82. (Perry Township/Southport Historical Society.)

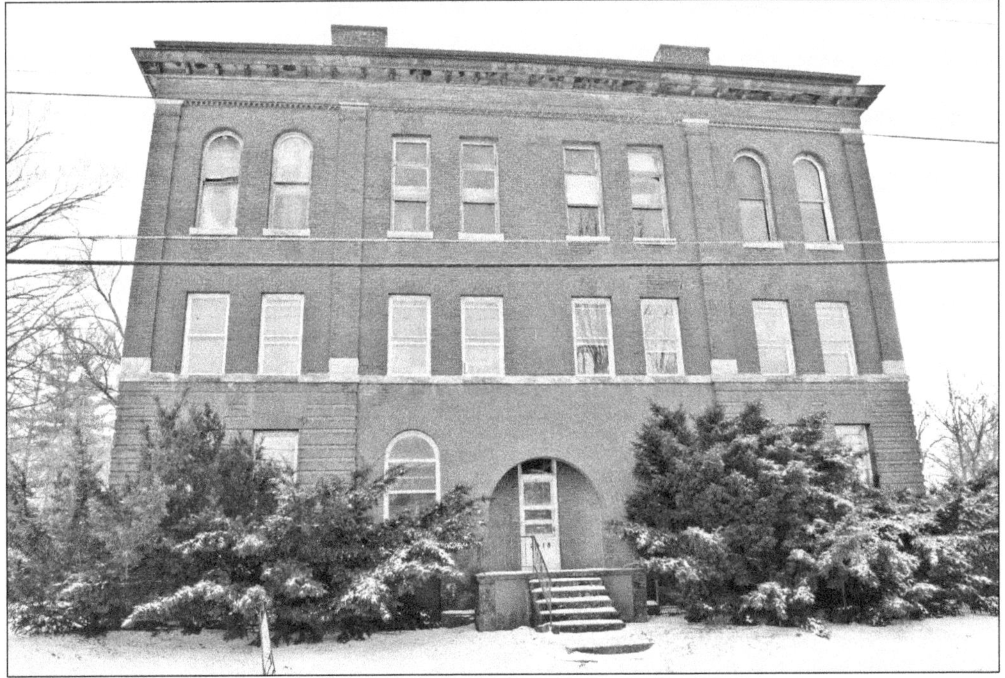

The Odd Fellows Lodge. Although this building at the corner of Southport Road and Church Street was built in 1899 by local Masons, it was taken over by the International Order of Odd Fellows in 1908. Though vacant now, it still stands today. On the first level, there are two lodge rooms and ample storage space. The second has four lodge rooms, and the third floor has a high-ceiling ballroom. Visitors in the early 20th century would come to dance and attend get-togethers, and for many years the ballroom space would also serve as the site for several Southport High School proms. (Photograph by Casey Smith.)

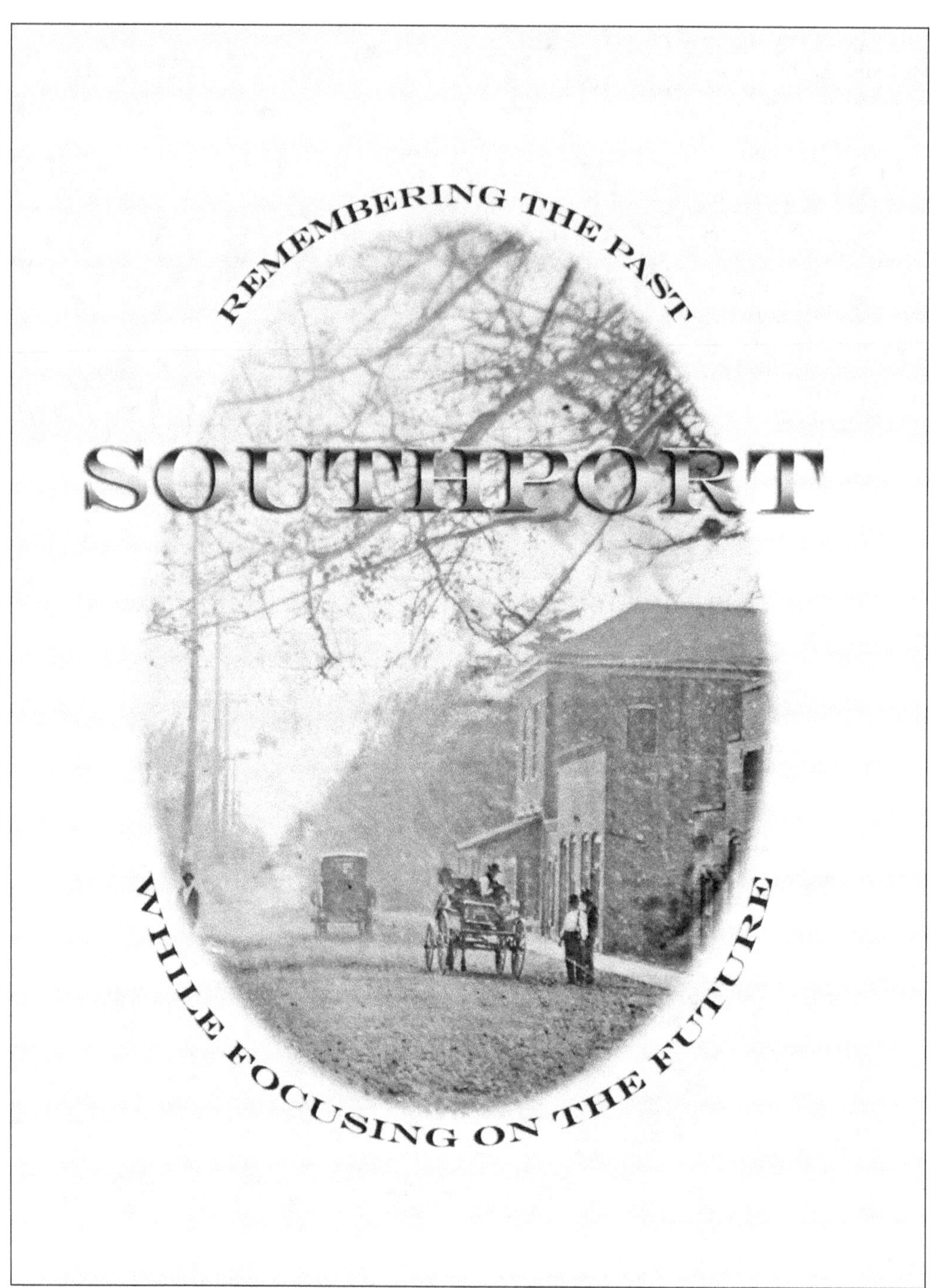

Celebrating the Centuries. In 2007, the Southport community celebrated the city's 175th anniversary. Since then, the Southport City Council and the Southport Business Alliance have worked together to reintegrate businesses into Southport's business district, despite building vacancies that began in the 1990s. Since 2007, the city has plans to build up parts of the business district again and welcome new ownership to empty storefronts. (Perry Township/Southport Historical Society.)

Two

FOUNDING OF SOUTHPORT

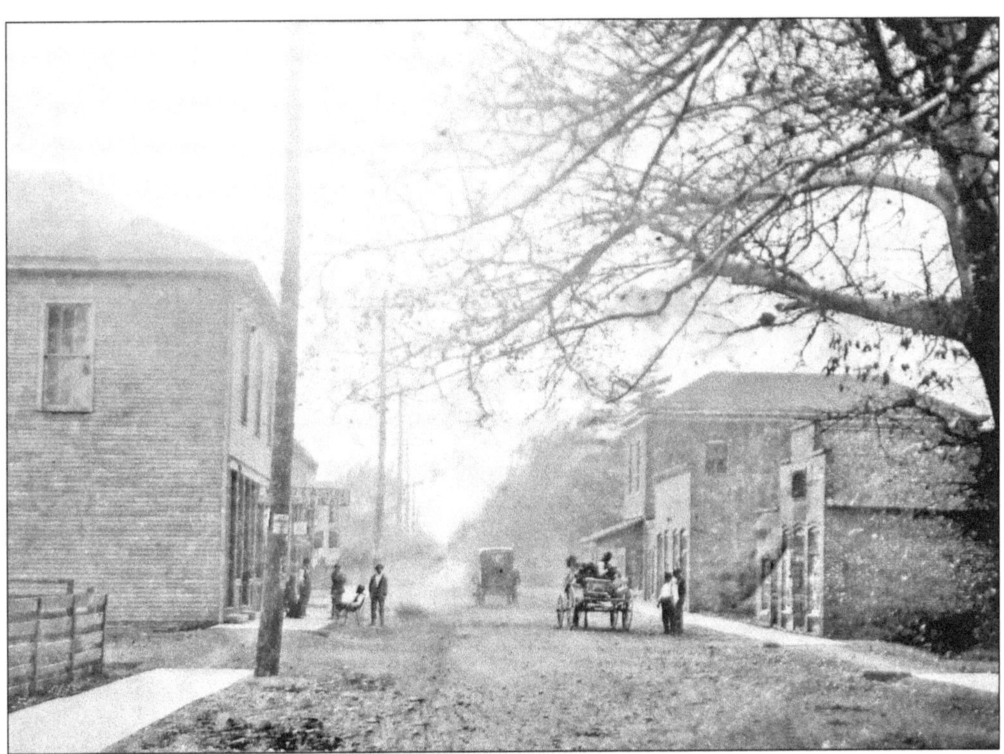

SOUTHPORT BUSINESS DISTRICT. Taken around 1908, this photograph looks west down Union Street in Southport toward the business portion of the area, near the intersection with the railroad. In the early 1900s, Southport's business district, which sits along a one-mile stretch of Southport Road, was comprised of more than a dozen businesses and a post office. (Perry Township/Southport Historical Society.)

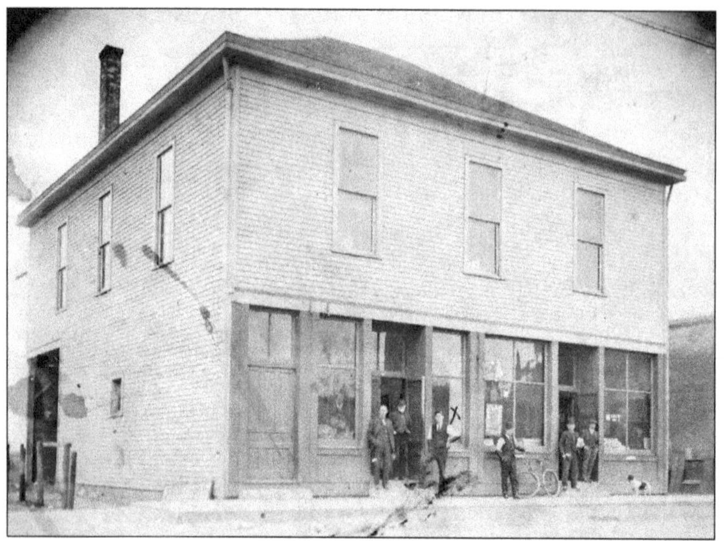

WADDELL'S HALL. Owned by Edward H. Waddell, the hall was housed in the two-story structure in Southport and was adjoined to the Daley & Rose Drug Store, as well as the Central Union Telephone Company. Entertainment was frequently offered here—such as music and plays—and basic foods and goods could be purchased there as well. In November 1914, a fire destroyed the hall and damaged several other surrounding buildings, causing $10,000 in damages. Because the town had no water system, volunteer firefighters could only use a bucket brigade to attempt to fight the flames, and the building was destroyed. (Perry Township/Southport Historical Society.)

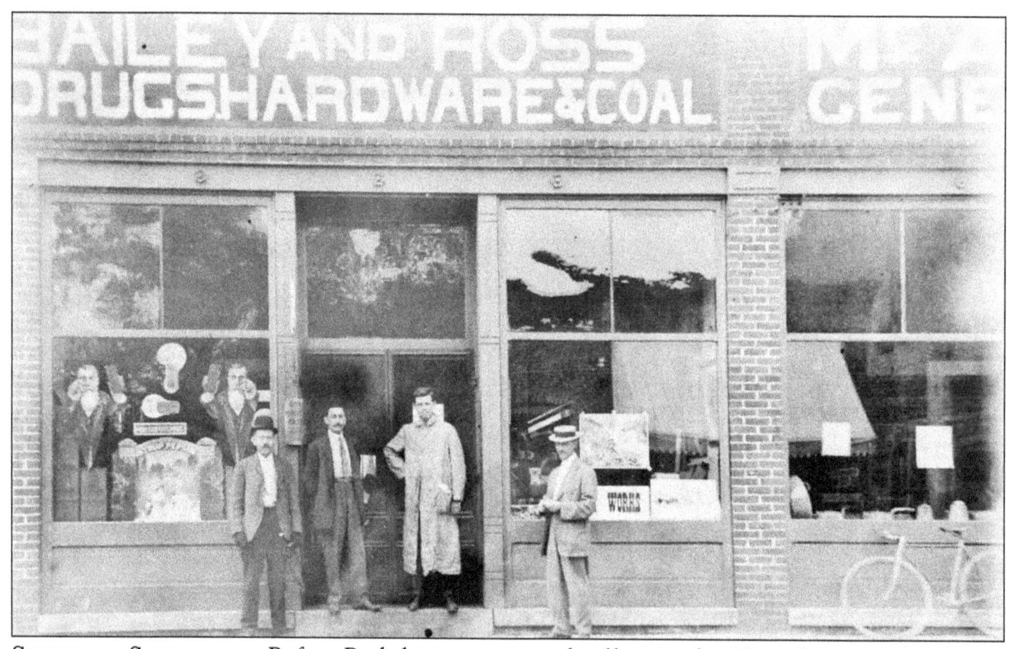

STORES IN SOUTHPORT. Before Prohibition even took effect in the United States, Southport operated under local laws prohibiting the sale of alcohol or opening saloons. Instead, local stores and businesses and attractions consisted of groceries, drugstores, lodges, churches, and schools. All were attractive to Hoosiers around the turn of the 20th century, and according to the *Indianapolis News* in 1899, Southport was "one of the prettiest villages a poet ever sung about." In the months approaching 1900, none of the homes in Southport were vacant, and real estate continued to grow in the area as more people moved South from Indianapolis to live in the suburbs. (Perry Township/Southport Historical Society.)

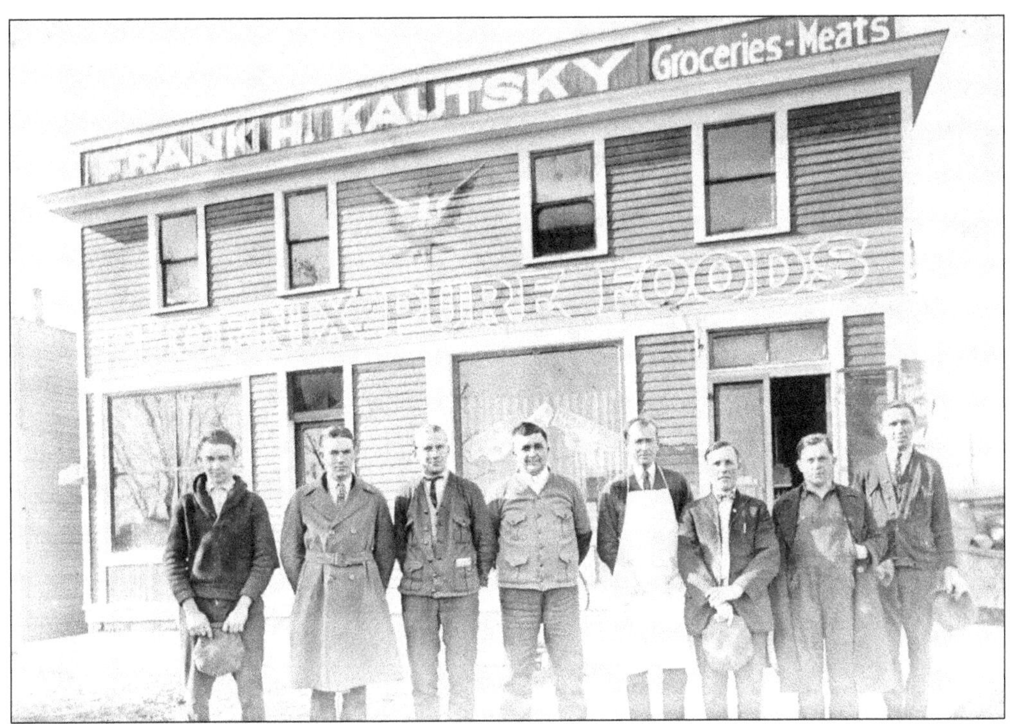

THE KAUTSKY'S GROCERY STORE. In 1923, Frank H. Kautsky bought the Waddell store, which had originally opened around 1907, at the southwest corner of Madison and Epler Avenues. The picture above, taken around 1925, includes Frank (fourth from left), butcher Ernest Harsin (in a white apron), bookkeeper Ish Young (far right), three clerks (left to right: Bruce and Price Robinson and Harmon Lee), as well as Charlie Benner and Herb Zufall, who were not employees. After World War II, Frank built a new supermarket at 5501 Madison Avenue, and Kautsky's stayed open until 1970. (Perry Township/Southport Historical Society.)

KAUTSKY and SONS

SUPER MARKET

Serving the Southside for 36 Years

5501 Madison Ave.

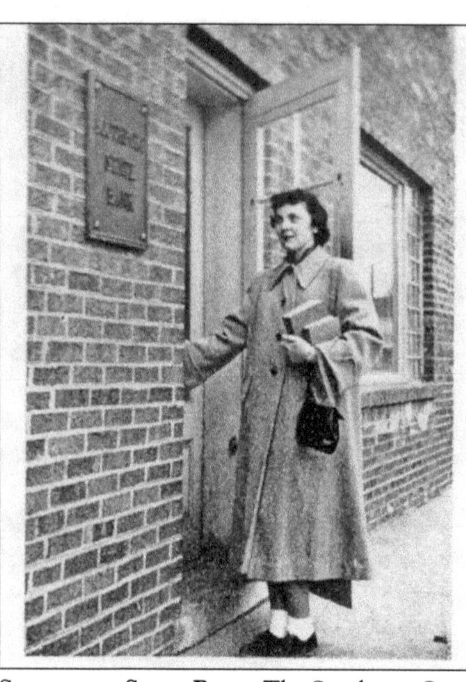

Southport State Bank. The Southport State Bank, seen here in an advertisement image, began servicing Perry Township residents in 1928 before merging with other banks in 1957, although its original address was 2201 East Southport Road. Perry Township resident Jack Whalen originally owned the bank. Around 2:00 a.m. on June 11, 1956, Whalen and his wife were awakened in their home by an armed intruder who demanded they drive to the bank and give him access to the vault. Once there, the robber pulled out a pillowcase and took nearly $70,000—the second-largest robbery in Indiana at the time—before taking the keys to the Whalen's car and fleeing to New Orleans. Roy Rudolph Drake was arrested two days later. (Perry Township/Southport Historical Society.)

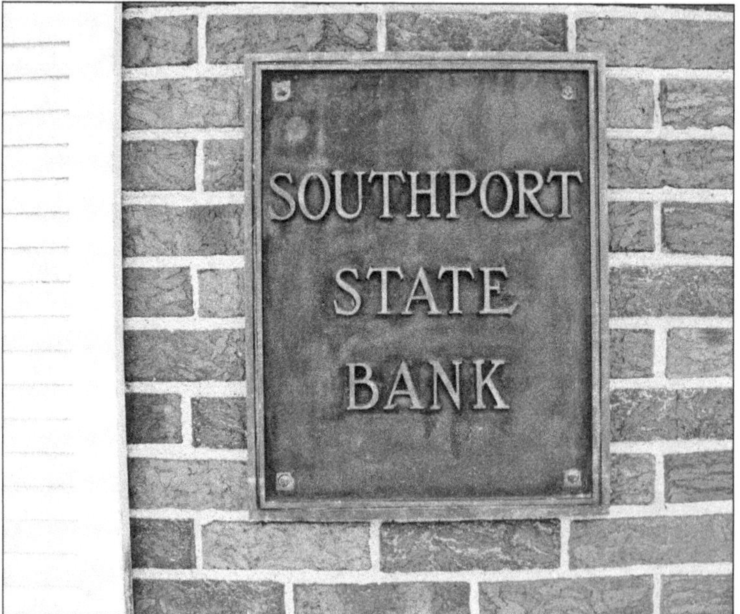

Southport Bank Plaque. The bronze Southport State Bank plaque was returned to its original location at 2201 East Southport Road in April 2015 after it was discovered at an auction at Christys of Indiana earlier in 2014. Located outside of what is now the EM Company, the plaque is visible from the street and sidewalk. (Photograph by Casey Smith.)

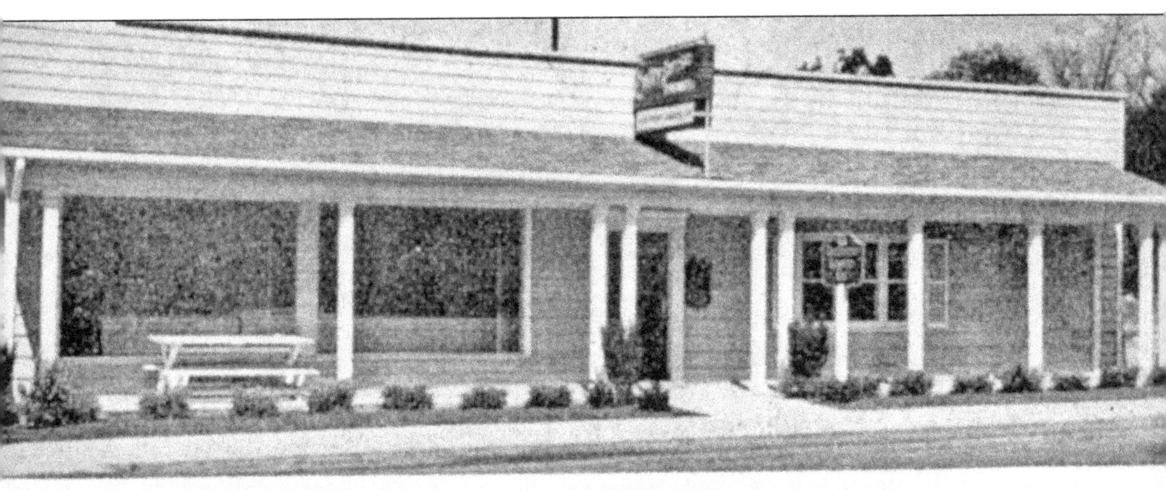

SOUTHPORT LUMBER COMPANY

"Builders Department Store"

JOHNS-MANVILLE INSULATION—ROOFING—CABINETS
STORM SASH—BASEMENT WATERPROOFING—PLASTIC TILE

Let Us Help You With Your Building Problems

GA. 2431 Financing Arranged

Southport Lumber Co. The Southport Lumber Co. was a sawmill operation situated in a complex just west of the railroad tracks and north of Union Street. In January 1925, the Davidson family acquired the company, but because of the Great Depression in the early to mid-1930s, business was almost nonexistent. Sales picked up in the 1940s, however, the housing boom of the mid-1950s to mid-1960s was a profitable time for the company, and in the 1960s and 1970s, they were one of the first to build roof and floor trusses and wall panels in Indiana. (Perry Township/Southport Historical Society.)

LUMBER

WE CAN HELP YOU WITH
YOUR
BUILDING PROBLEMS

We Offer Complete Service
Planning, Estimating and
Assistance in Arranging
Financing

BUDGET PLAN FOR REMODELING
& MODERNIZING

CALL • ST. 4-2451 • CALL

SOUTHPORT
LUMBER CO.

7000 So. on Madison Ave. to 108 Union in Southport

Davidson Lumber Inc. In the late 1970s, the name was changed to Davidson Industries, Inc., and by the 1990s the administrative offices were relocated to Franklin and the Southport property was sold. By the early 2000s, Davidson Industries employed over 400 people (the family business had long been known for retaining long term employees) and housed a fleet of 35 to 40 trucks. Since 2008, the lumber yard has been abandoned, and in 2016, it the Southport Redevelopment Commission announced plans to build a 95-unit apartment complex in its place. (Perry Township/Southport Historical Society.)

Compliments of

SHONK'S
SUNOCO SERVICE

TIRES, BATTERIES AND ACCESSORIES
ROAD SERVICE
BRAKE SERVICE—TUNE-UP

5335 Madison Ave. ST. 4-0795

Shonk's Sunoco. Floyd D. Shonk, a local Sunoco dealer in Perry Township, operated a station at 5335 Madison Avenue. Shonk started operating the station in 1956 and was also a member of the Perry Township Volunteer Fire Department. In 1960, Shonk was also one of four Sunoco dealers in Indianapolis elected to the newly-created Dealer Advisory Council, which strove to improve teamwork between the company and Sunoco dealers. (Perry Township/Southport Historical Society.)

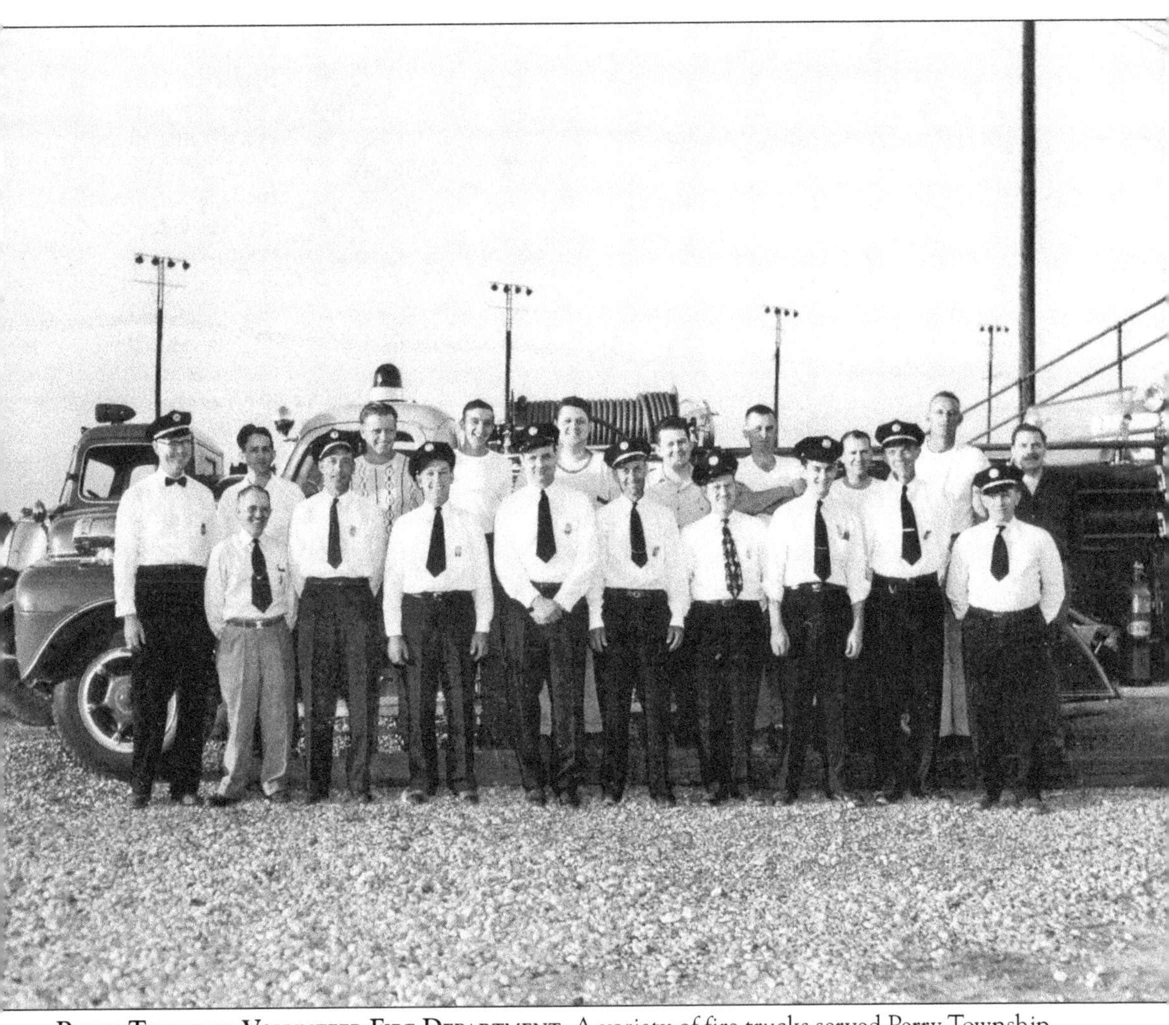

PERRY TOWNSHIP VOLUNTEER FIRE DEPARTMENT. A variety of fire trucks served Perry Township since the volunteer department became officially established in 1940. Before then, volunteers would take turns making runs to and from different fires with their own vehicles and equipment, lending to many elongated arrival times for the firefighters. This photograph was taken at the Southport High School football stadium. At the time, the fire engine was housed under the grandstand. (Perry Township/Southport Historical Society.)

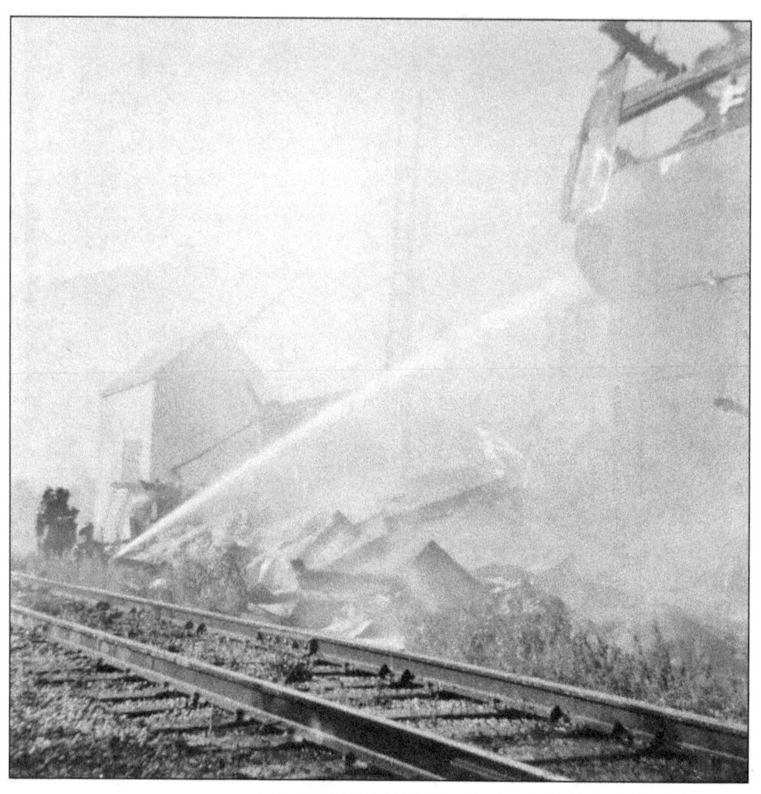

Southport Grain Elevator Fire. Although it was not the first time this happened, the Farmers' Cooperative grain elevator in Southport went up in flames on August 31, 1955. The elevator, which was located in the heart of the business district, was 100 feet tall, storing grain for local farmers. The structure—and $50,000 worth of grain inside—caught fire around 4:00 a.m. before a local resident alerted Southport town marshal Leon Sullivan. (Perry Township/Southport Historical Society.)

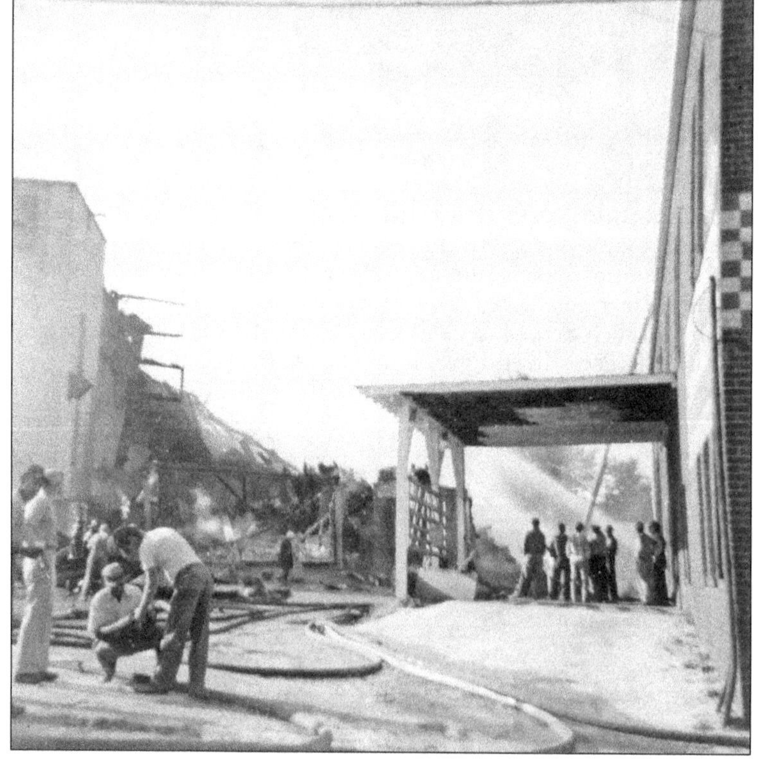

The Farmers' Cooperative. The 1955 fire was the third major blaze at the elevator since it was completed in 1919. By 1930—when an earlier fire destroyed 3,000 bushels of grain—240 farmers in Marion and Johnson counties owned the elevator. Once rebuilt, another fire broke out in 1938, causing more than $40,000 in damages to the elevator, which was again covered by insurance and rebuilt. (Perry Township/Southport Historical Society.)

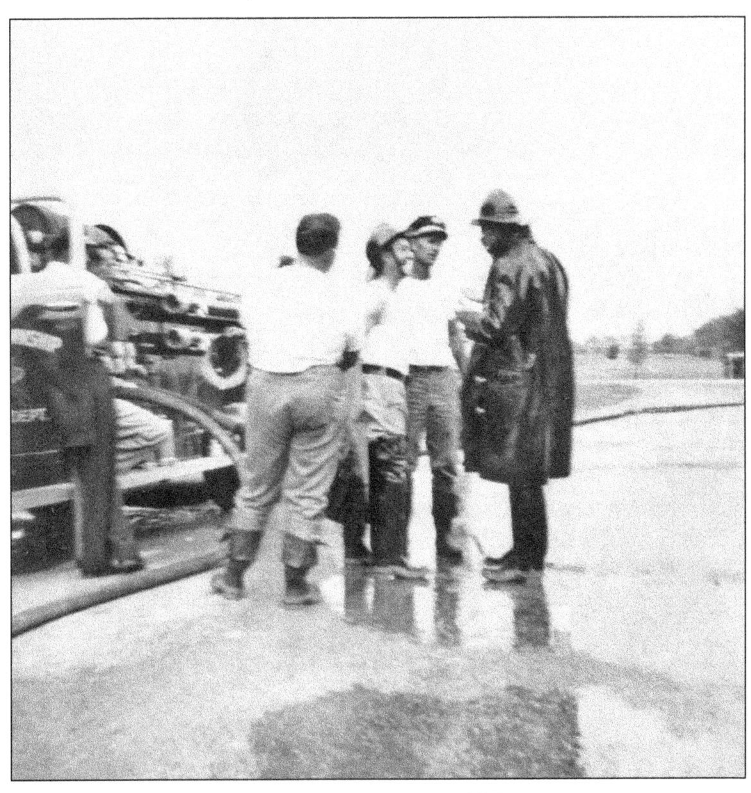

Putting out the Flames. Firemen from Perry Township were the first to respond to the alarm. They were also assisted by numerous surrounding fire-fighting units, including those from Lawrence Township, Bargersville, Smith Valley, Franklin, Greenwood, and engine houses Nos. 3, 17, and 26 from Indianapolis. The flames shot hundreds of feet into the air at the height of the fire and could be seen as far south as Franklin. (Perry Township/Southport Historical Society.)

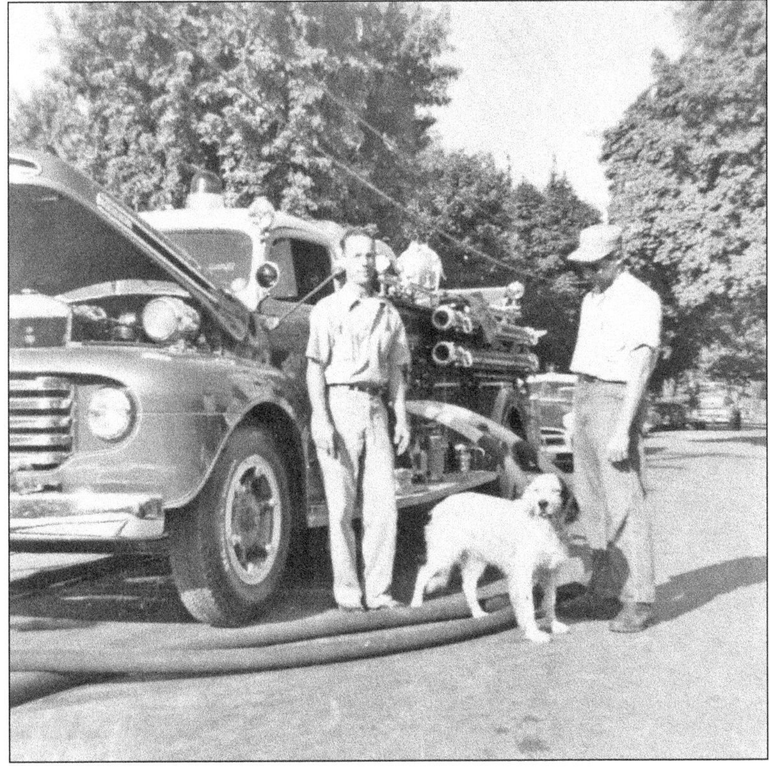

Firefighters on the Scene. At the height of the blaze, there were more than 125 firemen from seven cities and towns in south Marion County—in addition to three Indianapolis fire companies—fighting 200-foot flames. Firefighters worked through the early daylight hours and into the morning to keep flames from spreading. Remains of the building smoldered for more than 12 hours after the fire was put out. (Perry Township/Southport Historical Society.)

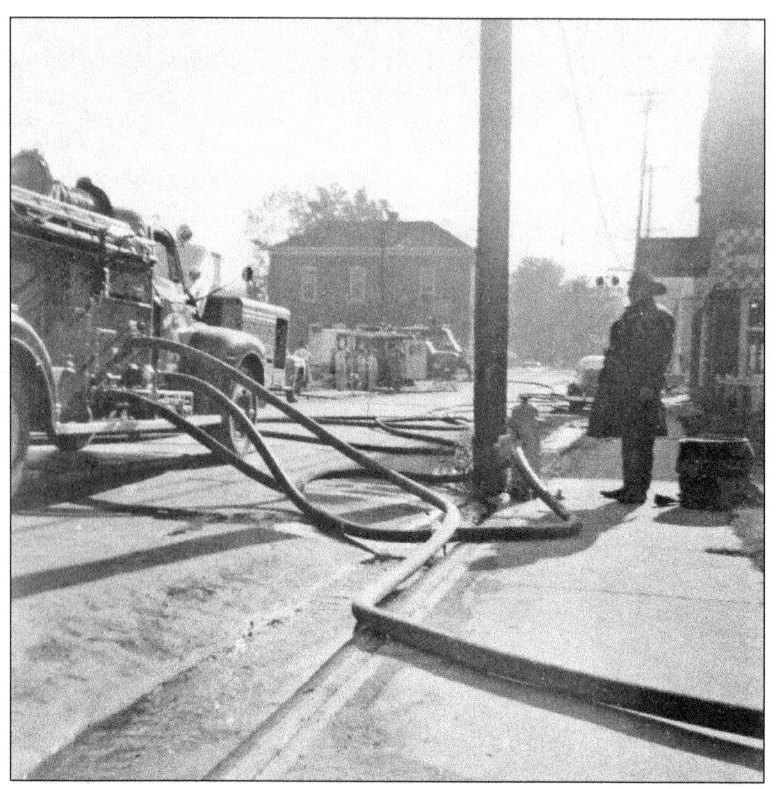

Perry Township Firefighters. It was not until 1950 that the township fire department purchased its first fire truck, a new 1950 Ford. Because the township had no place to house the truck, it was parked at Bob Boggs's automotive garage. The volunteer on duty as the driver would get a call at his house and then drive to the garage to get the truck. After closing time at the garage, Boggs would also get a call. (Perry Township/ Southport Historical Society.)

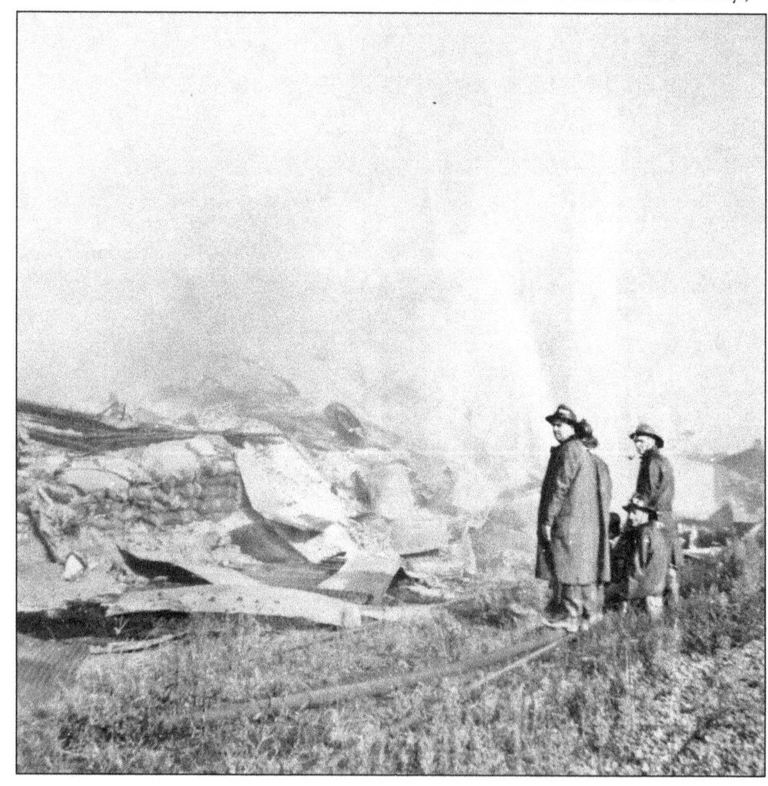

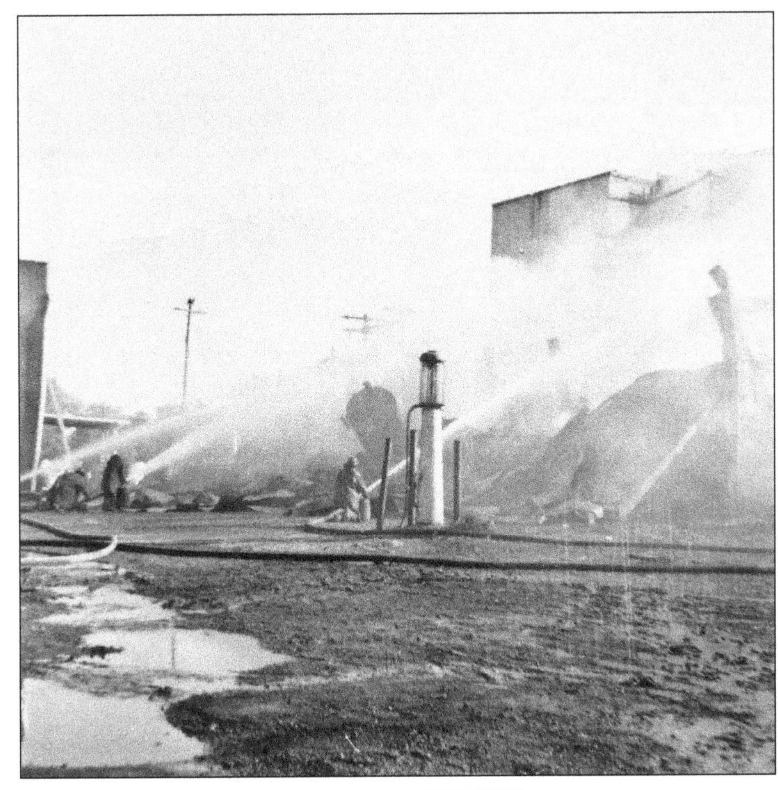

Protecting the Business District. Due to the elevator's close proximity to businesses in the area, firefighters were especially concerned about containing the fire. Had the fire continued to spread, it could have engulfed a nearby farm implement store, storage sheds, and businesses across the railroad tracks. Nearby neighborhoods were also in danger of being consumed by the massive fire. (Perry Township/Southport Historical Society.)

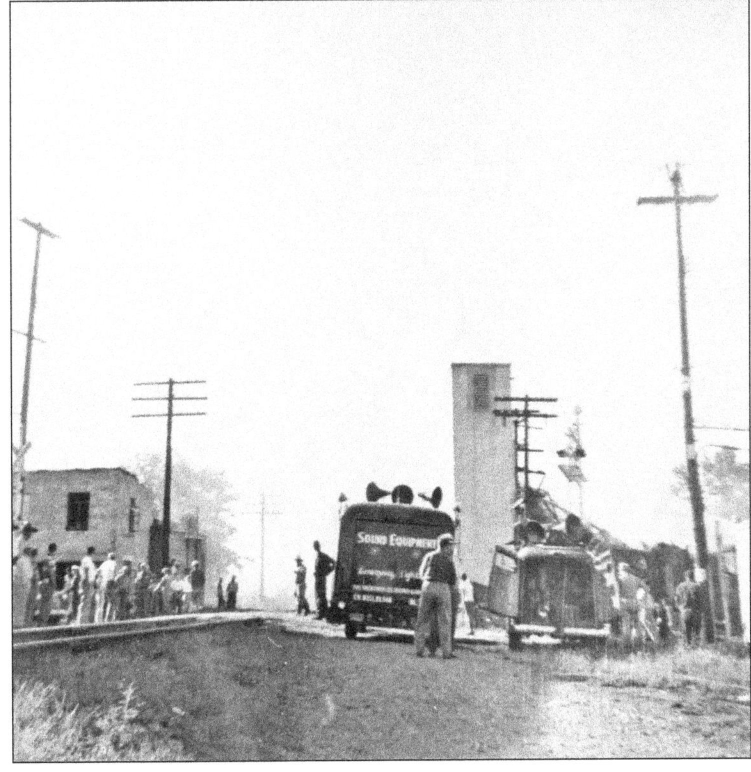

Onlookers at the Fire. The spectacular blaze attracted dozens of people, and crowds of onlookers even came out to see the flames in their nightclothes. When morning came around, some nearby residents brought coffee and breakfast to the firefighters as they continued efforts to extinguish the fire. (Perry Township/Southport Historical Society.)

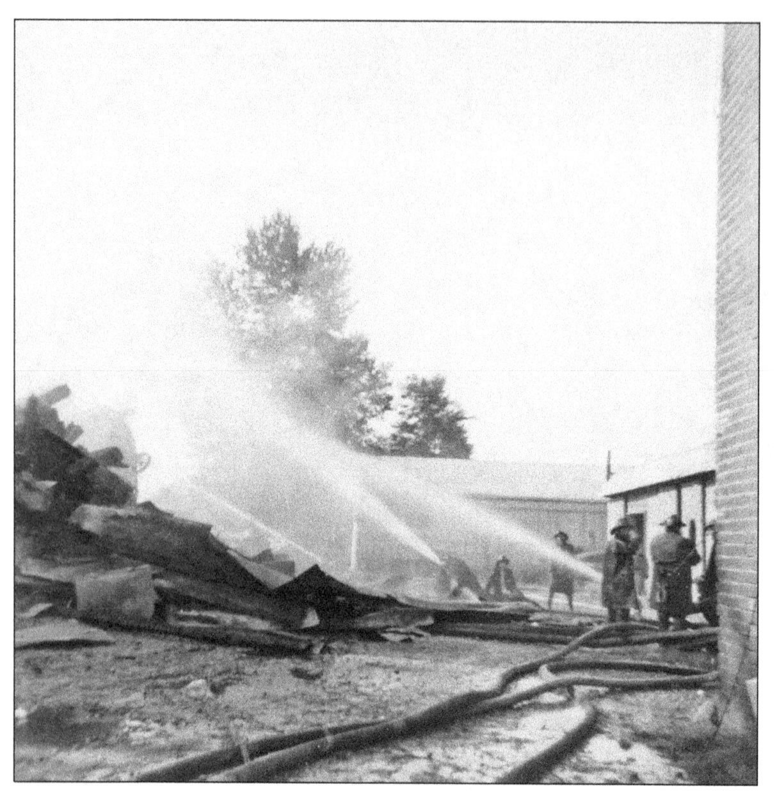

Controlling the Fire. Firefighters worked for hours to confine the flames to the elevator. A civil defense sound truck and a privately owned amplifying system (pictured at left) were used to direct the fighting efforts. (Perry Township/Southport Historical Society.)

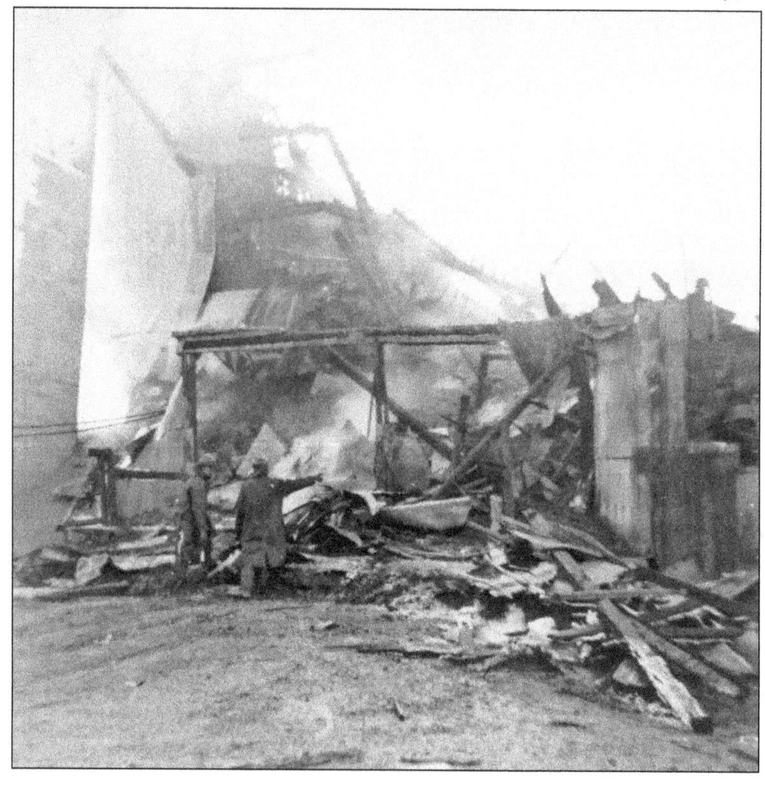

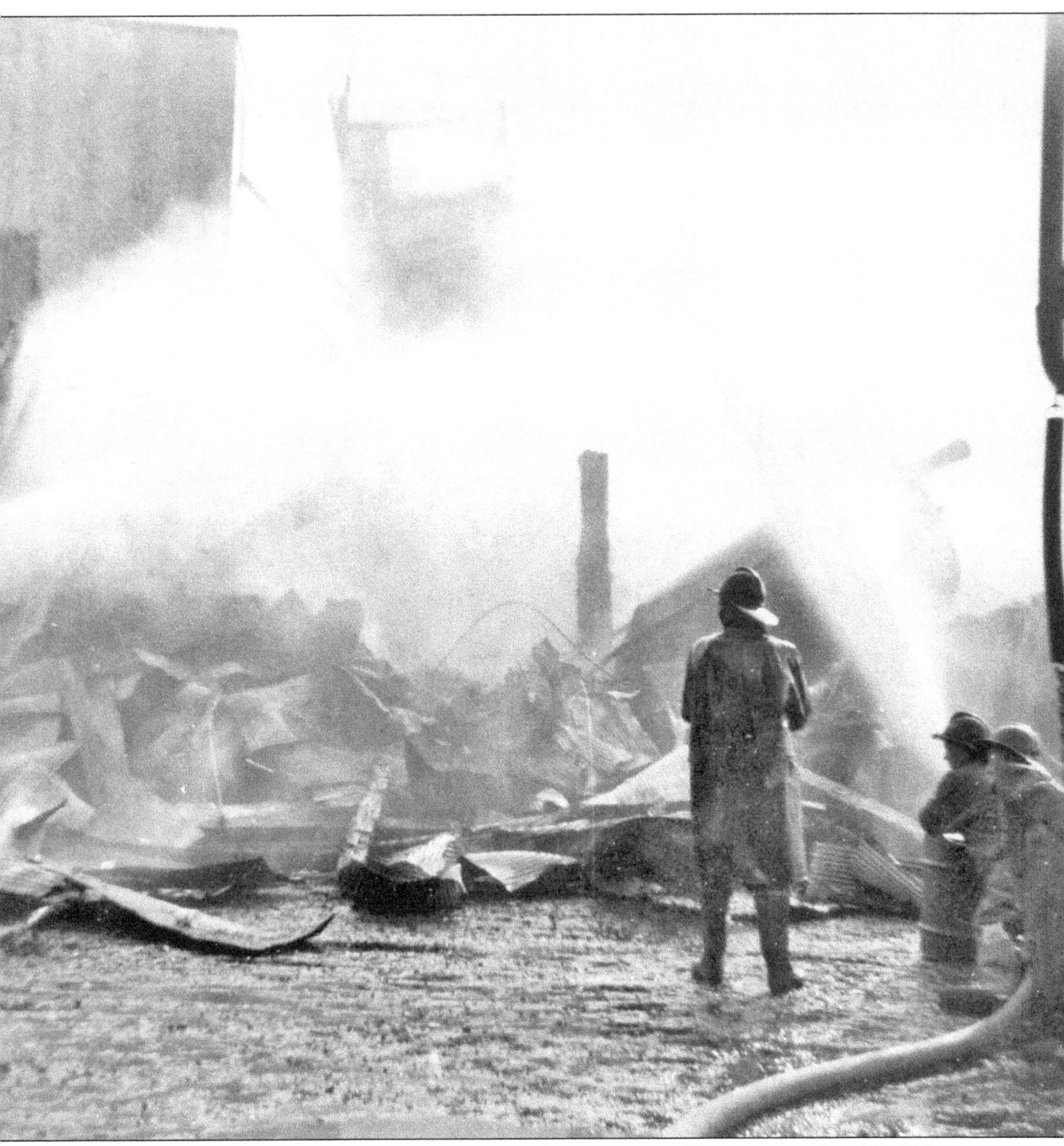

Costly Blaze. The building loss was estimated at $300,000, in addition to another $50,000 in damages to a capacity load of wheat, oats, corn, and soybeans stored in the elevator. Two half-ton electric motors and a one-and-a-half-ton truck inside the elevator were also lost in the fire. Although the exact cause of the fire was not determined, representatives from the Perry Township Fire Department at the time hypothesized the blaze could have been the result of spontaneous combustion of the stored grain. (Perry Township/Southport Historical Society.)

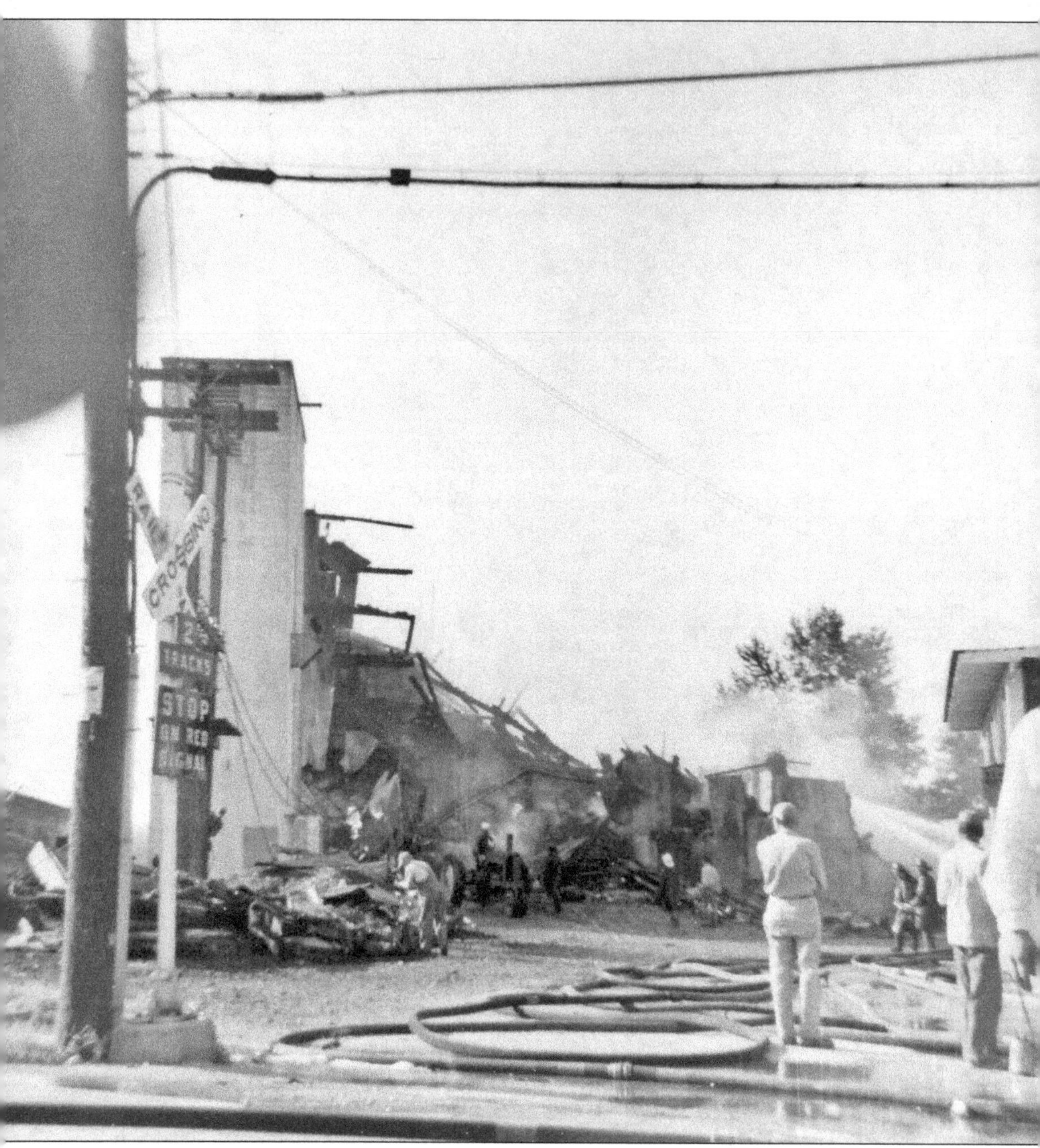

GRAIN ELEVATOR DESTROYED. Once the fire was put out, all that remained of the six-story elevator was charred ruins and a 75-foot concrete block dryer that was inside. Although the elevator had been destroyed and rebuilt 17 years earlier, the grain elevator was not rebuilt again after the 1955 fire. (Perry Township/Southport Historical Society.)

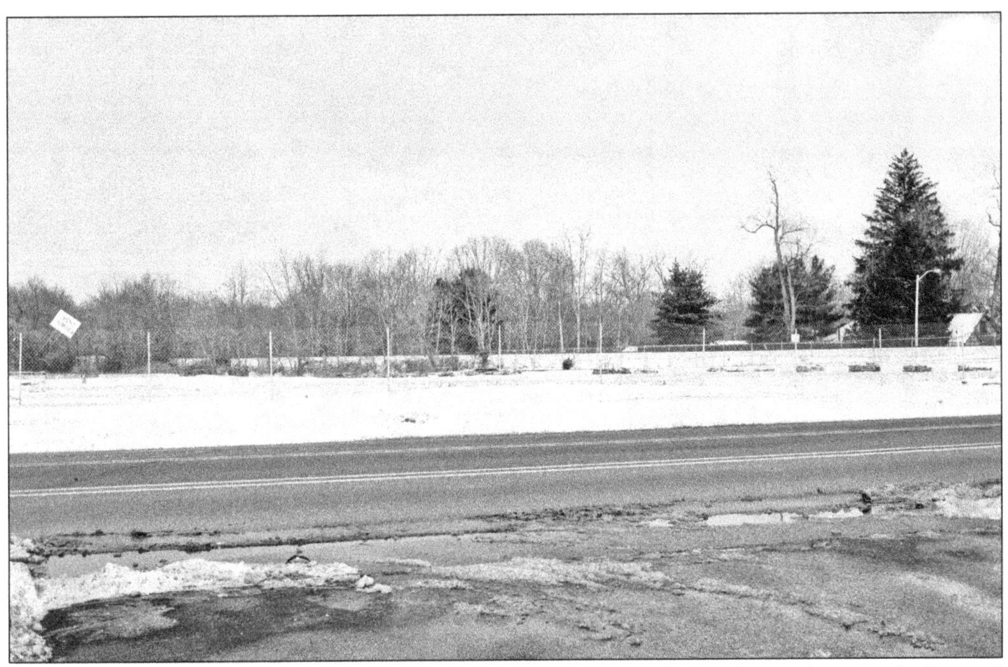

Abandon Land. On the north side of Southport Road, where the lumberyard used to be located next to the railroad tracks, an empty lot is all that remains. However, the City of Southport is hoping to change that soon. In 2016, city officials announced hopeful plans that would make way for more than 90 apartments catering to the 55-and-over crowd, as well as retail. (Photograph by Casey Smith.)

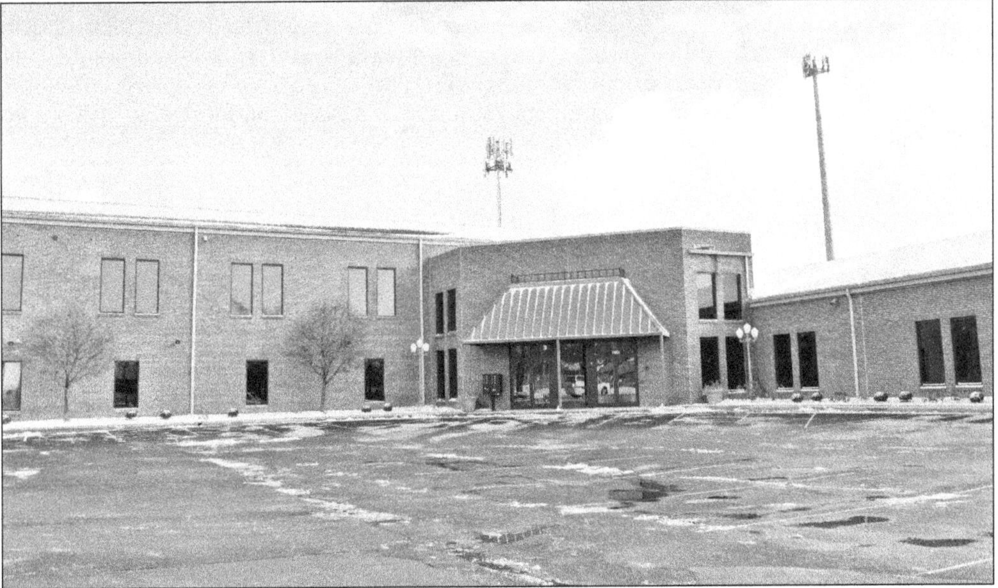

Gerdt Furniture. Edward Gerdt, a detective for the City of Indianapolis in the 1950s, opened the Southport Gerdt Furniture store in 1959 after saving enough money to realize his dream of operating his own business. The Gerdt store, at 2115 East Southport Road, was housed in a 66,000-square-foot building. In 2012, the store closed its Southport location following the closures of additional locations in Avon and Castelton. (Perry Township/Southport Historical Society.)

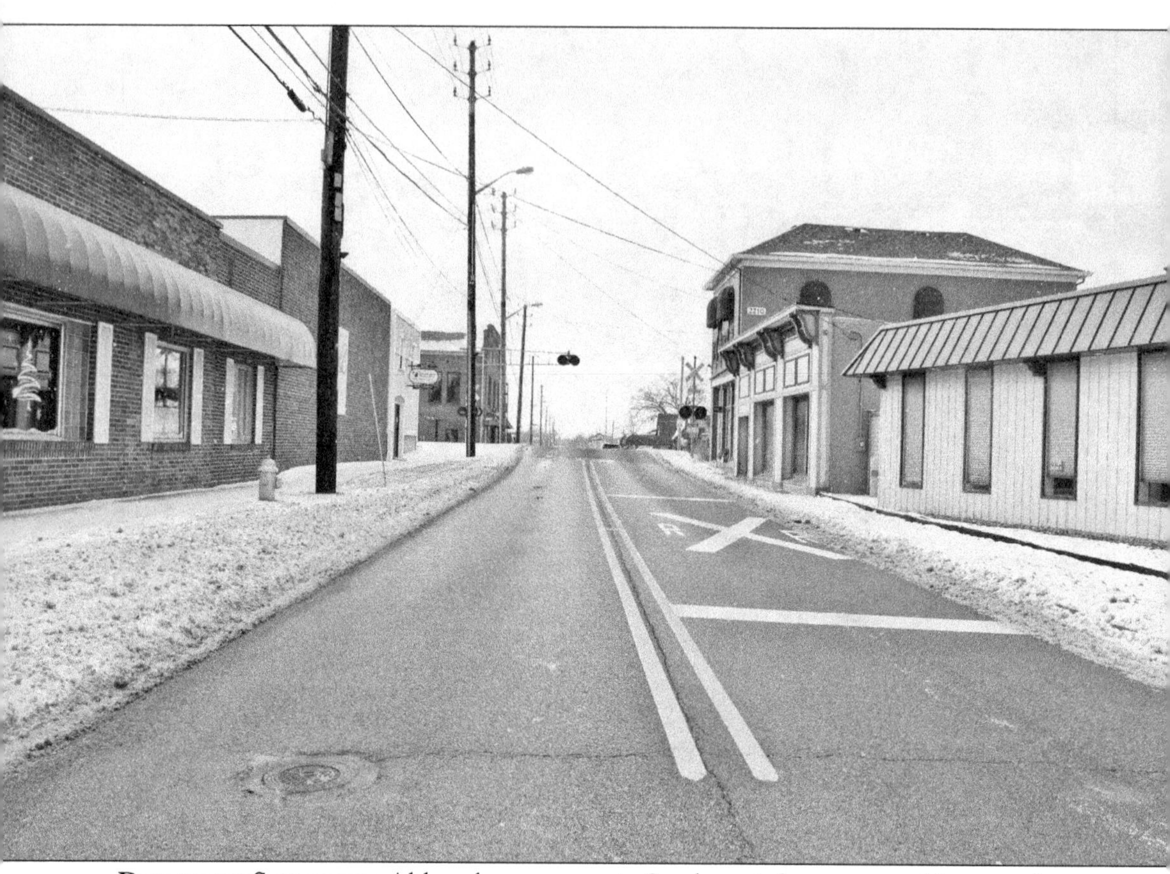

Downtown Southport. Although some areas in Southport's downtown and business districts have been vacant or inactive for several decades, the city announced plans to construct a 95-unit apartment complex, new restaurants, and retail as a part of an overhaul for the city. (Photo by Casey Smith.)

Three

TIME TO EAT

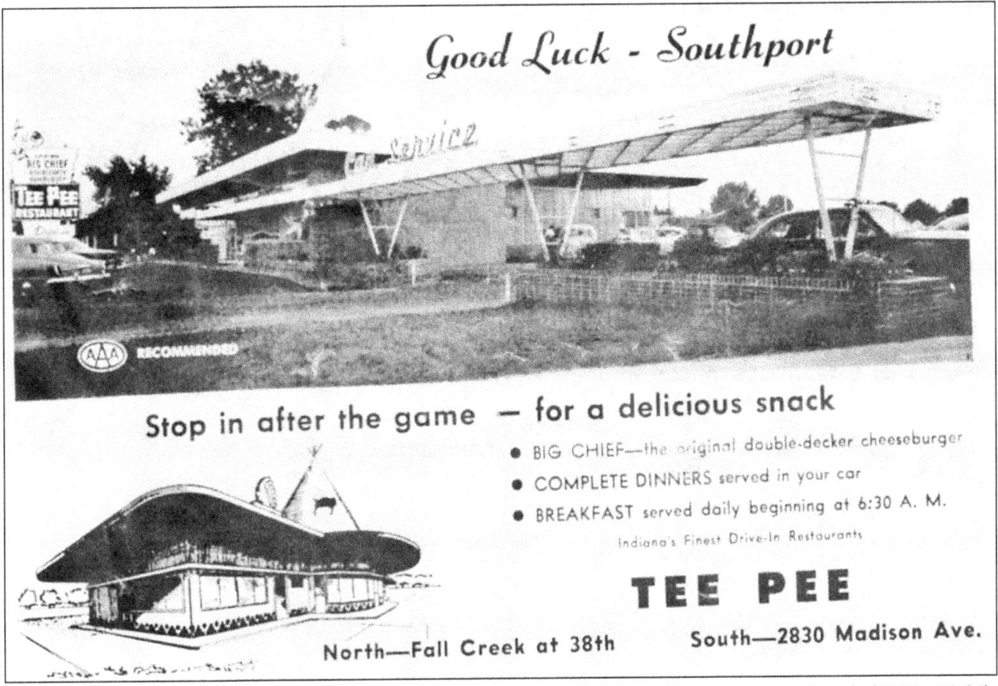

SOUTHSIDE TEE PEE. The Tee Pee restaurants were founded by Albert Ray McComb (1892–1964), a Terre Haute native who later moved to Indianapolis. The automobile-friendly restaurant was open for breakfast, lunch and dinner every day of the week and allowed customers could get the same meals delivered to them in their cars as they could if they went inside and sat at a table. After the success of the first Tee Pee on the north side of Indianapolis, McComb sought a location for a second Tee Pee on the south side. In 1954, he opened another Tee Pee at 2830 Madison Avenue, a few miles north of Southport High School. In 1978, when the carhop faze was dying out, the widowed Dorothy McComb sold the Madison Avenue Tee Pee to McDonald's. Within days, the Tee Pee was demolished, and within weeks, a golden arch beckoned its first customers. (Perry Township/Southport Historical Society.)

STOP IN AFTER THE GAME — FOR A DELICIOUS SNACK

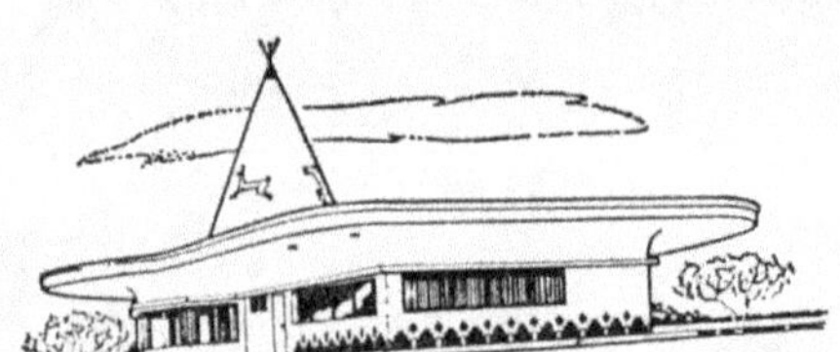

- BIG CHIEF — the original double-decker cheeseburger
- COMPLETE DINNERS served in your car
- BREAKFAST served daily beginning at 6:30 A.M.

Indiana's Finest Drive-In Restaurants

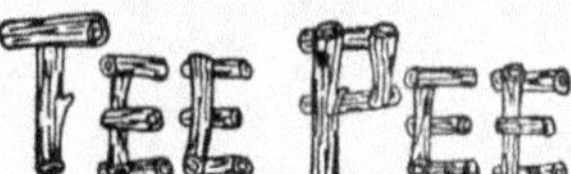

North — Fall Creek at 38th   South — 2830 Madison Ave.

1.50

TEE PEE

- Big Chief — F. F. Onions
- Big Teep — F. F. Potatoes
- Tee Pee
- Cheese B
- Pork Tend.
- Barbecue
- Baked Ham
- Grill Cheese
- Steak
- Salad
- Bacon & Tom.
- Fish
- F. F. Shrimp
- B. Q. Ribs
- B. Q. Chicken
- Fish & Chips
- Pot. Chips — Pretzels

Choc.	Van.			Malts
Choc.	Stra.	Pine.		Shakes
Oran.	Lem.	Lime		Ades
Choc.	Stra.	Pine.		Sodas
Choc.	Stra.	Pine.		Sundaes
Bd.	Wd.	Bu.	Wu.	Custard
Lime	Lem.	Cher.		Phos.

Plain	Lem.	Cher.	Choc.	M M	Coke
F. Li.	F. Le.	Mint	Van.		

Coffee	Tea	Milk	H. Choc.
O. Juice	Root Beer	T. Juice	B'milk

31A870

License No.

No. 17 CHECK No. 20121

A Popular Spot. The Tee Pee, a popular restaurant, with only one south-side location along Madison Avenue, was built in 1954. It became a popular cruising spot and, within three years, expanded to twice its size. The building was sold to McDonald's in the late 1970s and demolished. Today, the former Tee Pee location is still home to a McDonald's. (Perry Township/Southport Historical Society.)

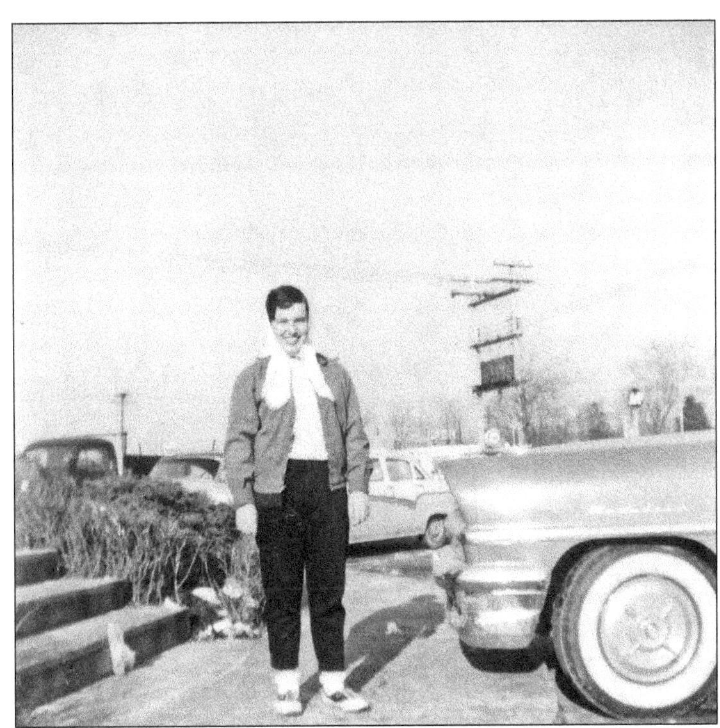

Carhops. Before ordering and dining in fast food restaurants was the norm, carhops would provide curbside service to customers in their cars. A tray would be placed in the window of the car, and food would be ordered, delivered, and eaten without patrons ever stepping outside. At Southern Circle, carhops were typically high school females. Although the base pay for the workers was below minimum wage, carhops could make more than $100 with tips on busy weekends. Pictured here is Janet Isaac, carhop at Southern Circle in 1959. (Janet Isaac.)

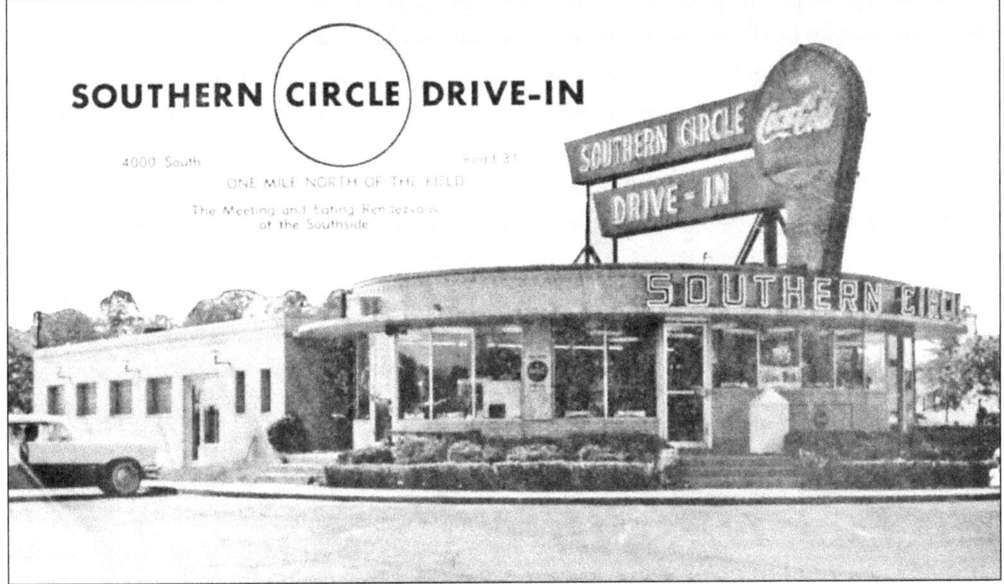

Southern Circle Drive-In. Southern Circle, a well-known spot for eating, shopping and leisure driving, was developed by siblings Frank Bixler and George Bixler Jr,, Emma Meadows, and Ruth Hoffmann. The Bixler family has a long history in development; their father, George Bixler, constructed most of the two-bedroom homes on Edwards, Mills, Markwood, and Lawrence Avenues just before World War II. Southern Plaza celebrated its grand opening in April 1961 with stores such as the Kroger Co., Hook Drugs Inc, Kay Jewelry, the Pet House, J.C. Penney Co., Kimmel Shoe Repair, and many more. Frank and George operated Southern Circle and Southern Triangle restaurants. (Janet Isaac.)

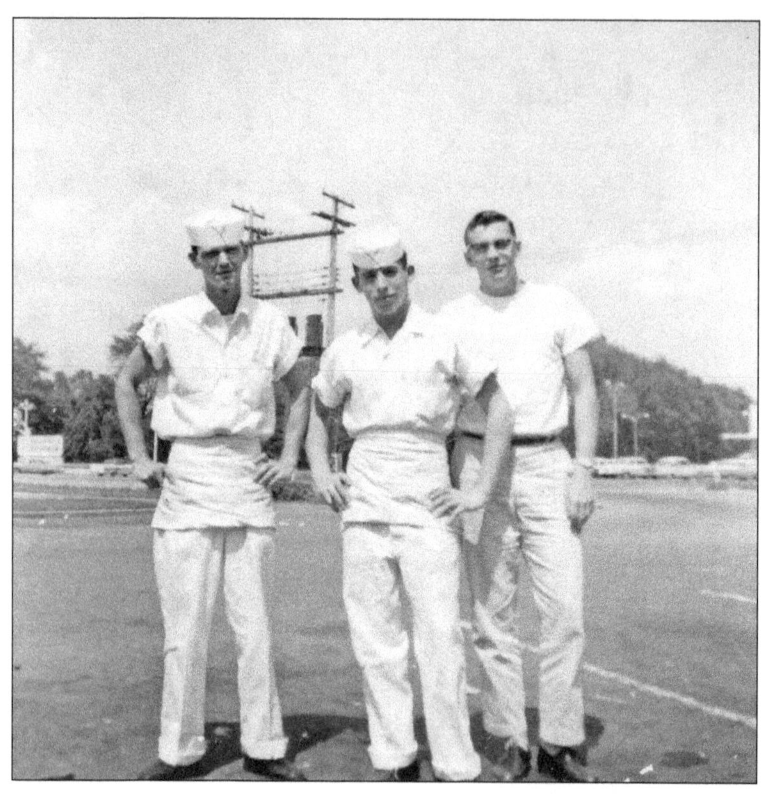

Order's Up. The Southern Circle Drive-in Restaurant, located at 4000 South East Street, offered a variety of options on the menu. Hamburgers and french fries were popular on the curbside menu, and inside, other home-style dishes like steak and vegetables were also available. When it came to desserts and sweet treats, Southern Circle was known for its soda fountain. Three cooks and a carhop, Betsy, are pictured here. (Janet Isaac.)

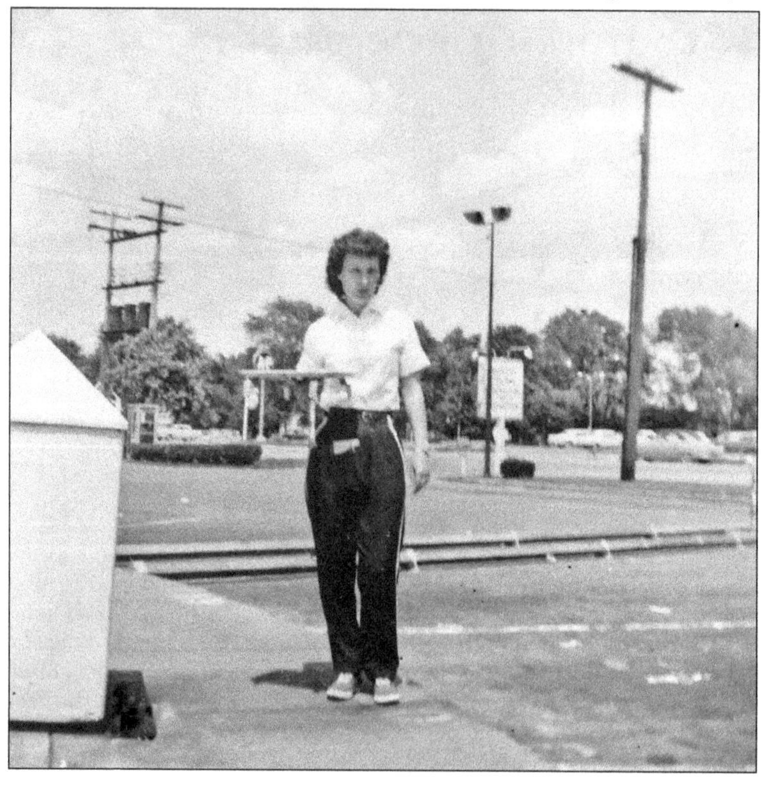

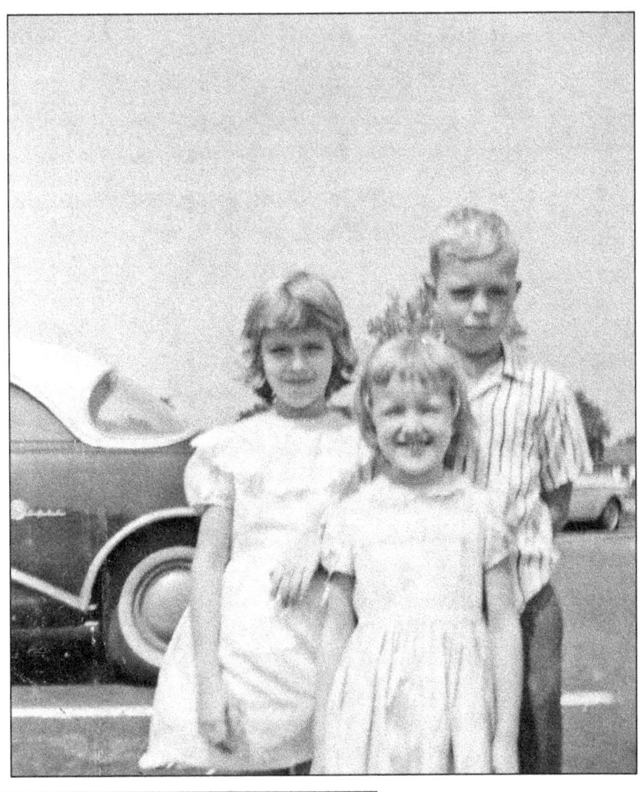

THE BIXLERS. Southern Plaza was developed by siblings Frank Bixler and George Bixler Jr., Emma Meadows and Ruth Hoffmann. Frank and George handled the daily operations. The Bixler family has a long history in development. Their father, George Bixler, constructed most of the two-bedroom homes on Edwards, Mills, Markwood, and Lawrence Avenues just before World War II. Frank and George operated Southern Circle and Southern Triangle restaurants. The Bixler family farm was located on US Route 31, roughly between Thompson Road and Hanna Avenue. They had purchased more acreage with the idea to build a shopping complex. Three of the Bixler children, from left to right, Carol, Mary, and Kenny, are photographed here. (Janet Isaac.)

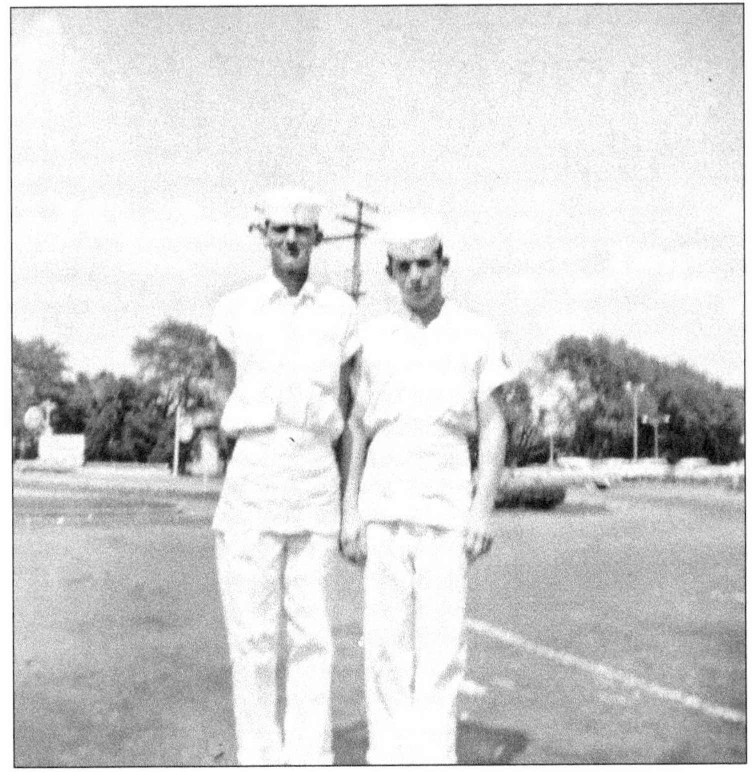

ICE CREAM ON THE MENU. In 1954, the restaurant also gained popularity for its Bing Crosby ice cream formula. The Bixler brothers signed an agreement with the entertainer and businessman in January 1954, and later that year, Crosby's famous ice cream was served at Southern Circle in chocolate, vanilla, strawberry, and "flavor of the month." (Janet Isaac.)

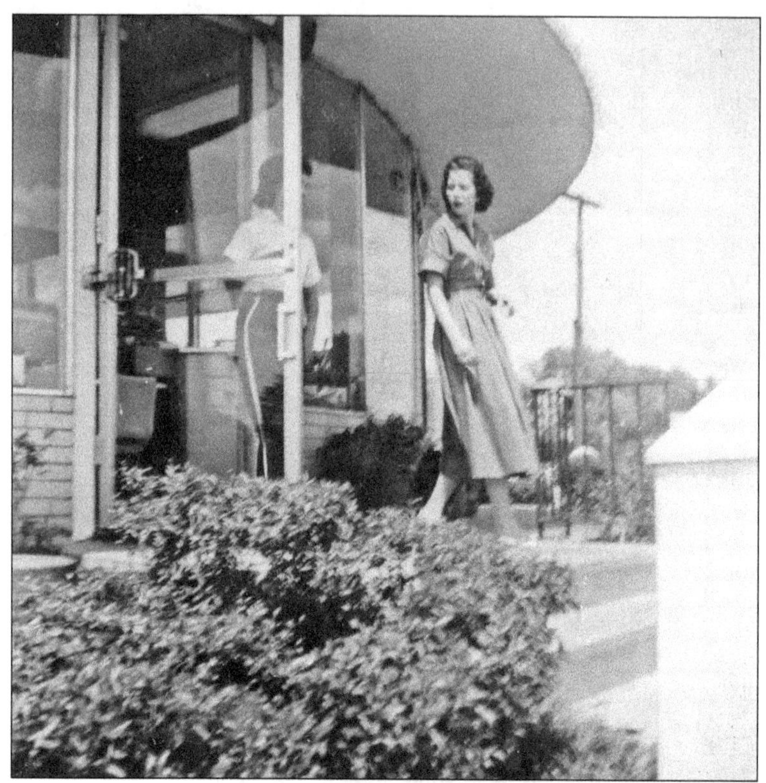

Where to Eat and What's Around. Before Southern Plaza opened several years later, Southern Circle was nearly by itself in what George Bixler Jr. later called "the boondocks." Pictures from the 1950s, like these, show that the Southern Circle, Sport Bowl bowling lanes (which went in around 1943), and acres of corn were all that was around. (Janet Isaac.)

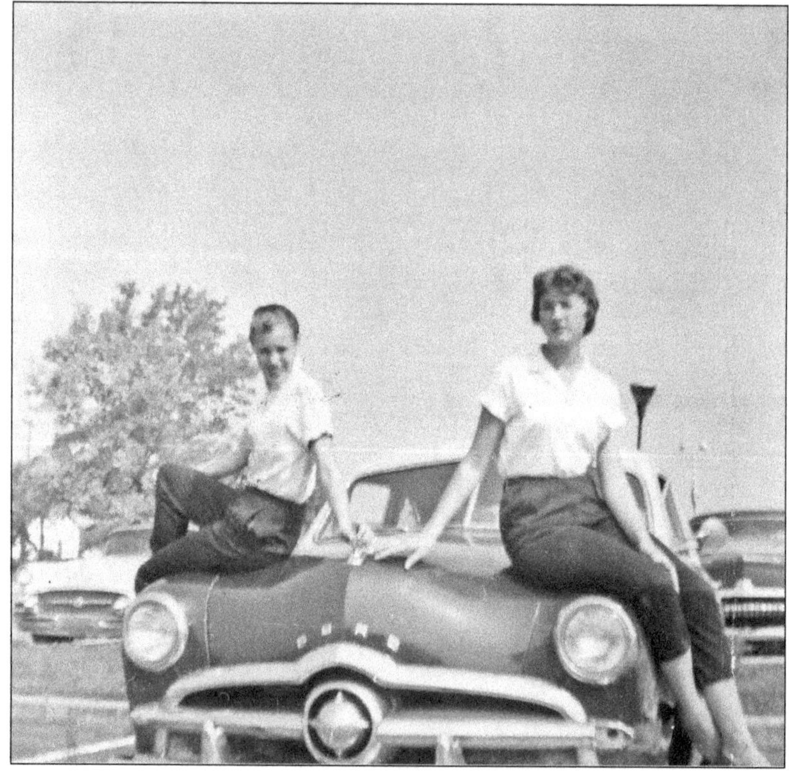

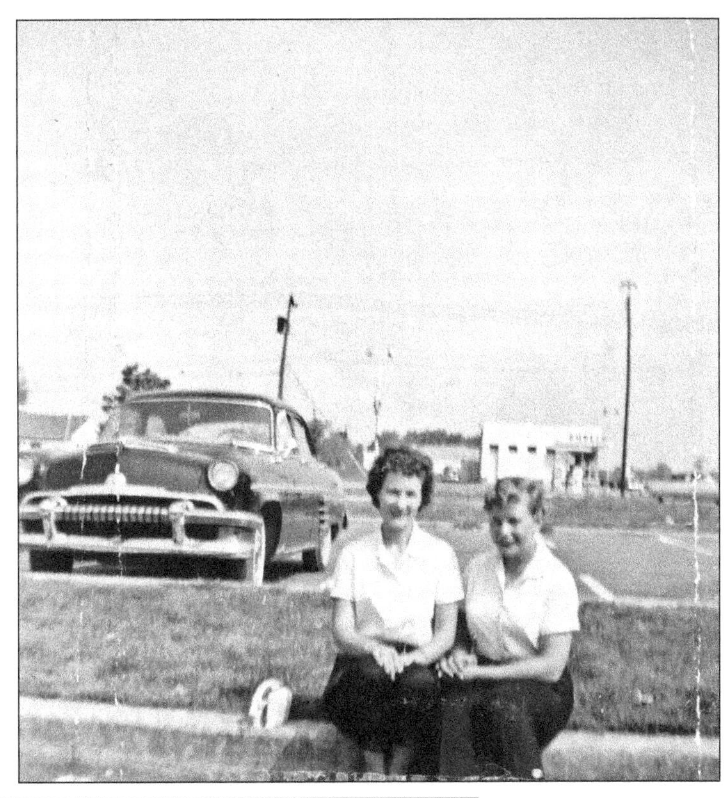

Before Southern Plaza. Southern Plaza was the first shopping center on Indianapolis's south side. Southern Plaza celebrated its grand opening in April 1961 with stores such as the Kroger Co., Hook Drugs Inc, Kay Jewelry, the Pet House, J.C. Penney Co., Kimmel Shoe Repair, and more. Advertisements boasted that there was ample parking for 2,000 cars and bus service that runs on the hour. All stores were ready for the opening except WM. H. Block Co., which insisted on buying its own land under the store and opened in the fall. Kroger now occupies that space. (Janet Isaac.)

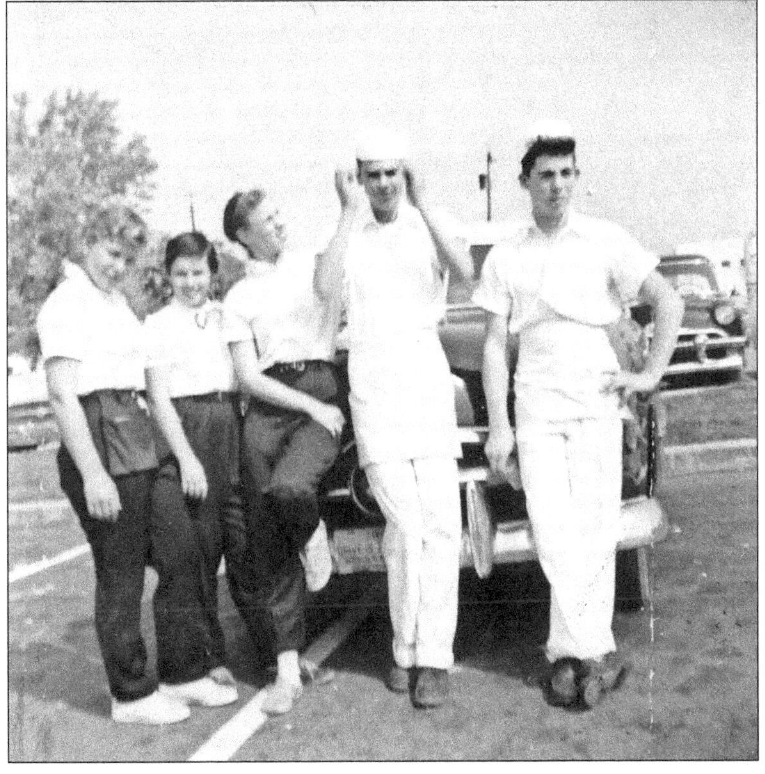

Students at Work. The primary employees at Southern Circle consisted of local high school and college students. Women typically worked as carhops and as waitresses, and men were usually hired for cooking positions where they would be responsible for operating the soda fountain, grills, and sandwich block. (Janet Isaac.)

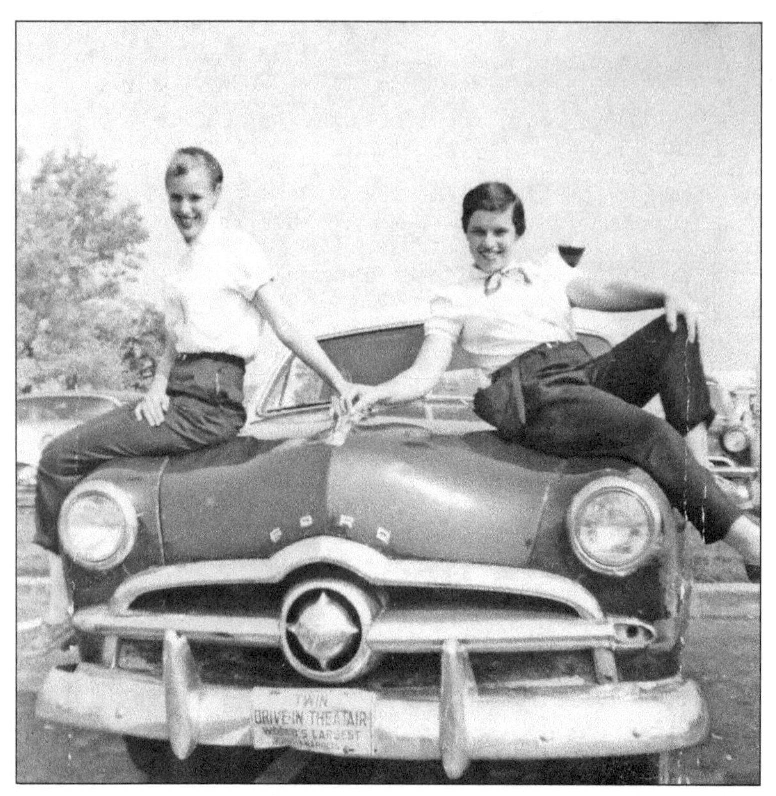

DRIVING AROUND. For local students, especially, cruising from the South Circle Drive-In (Hanna Avenue and East Street, the now location of a Steak & Shake) to the Triangle Restaurant to the Tee Pee Restaurant (East Street) and to Southern Plaza was a popular route to take in the 1940s, 1950s, and 1960s and a way to socialize with friends. (Janet Isaac.)

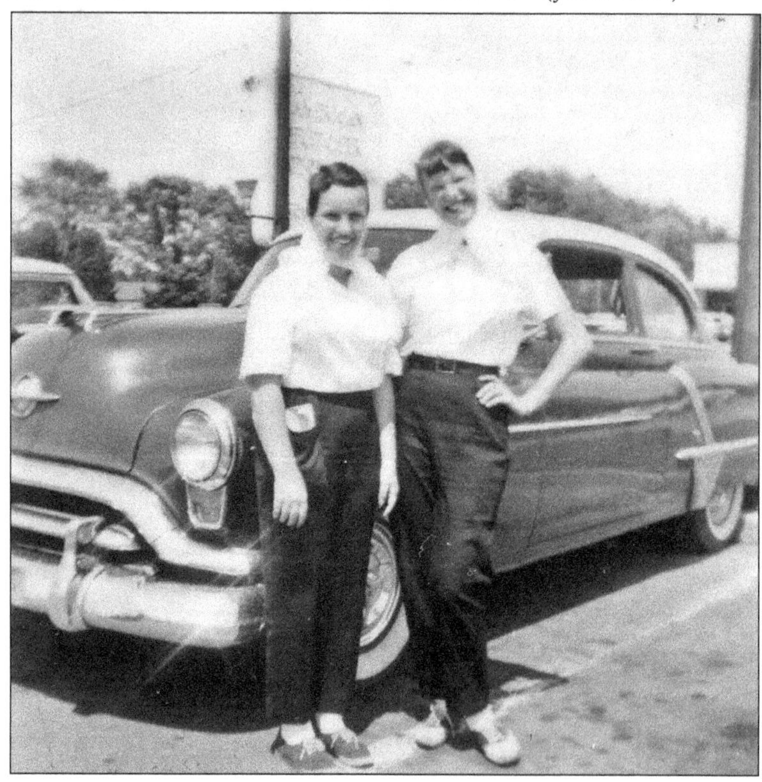

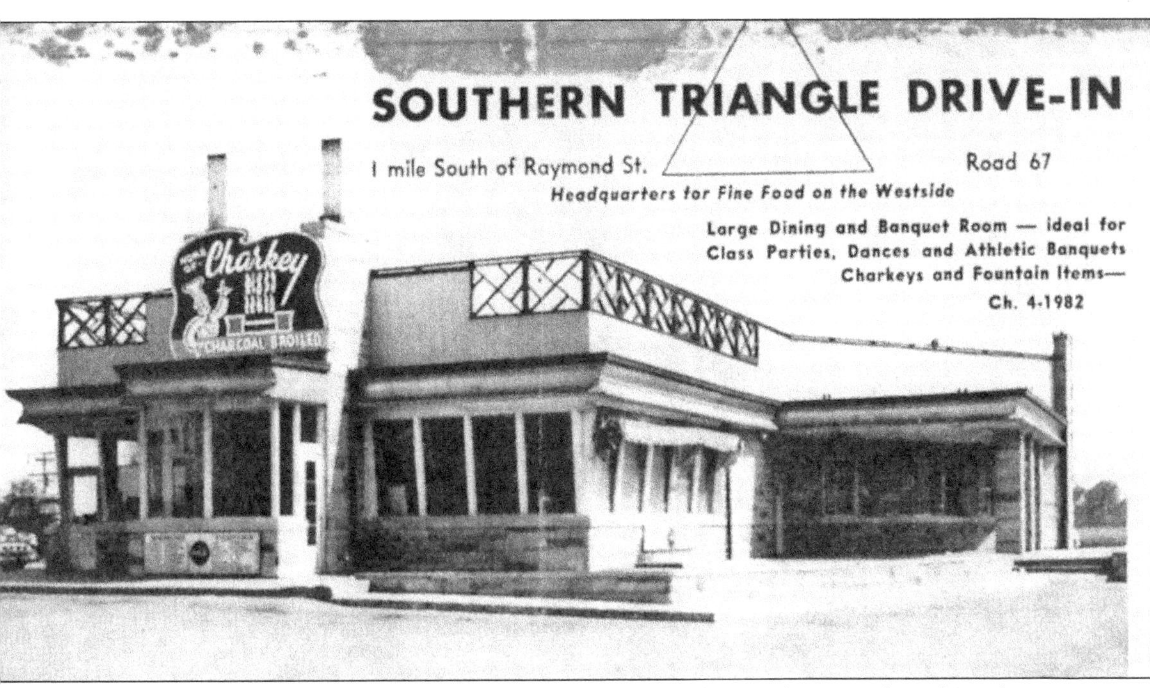

THE SOUTHERN TRIANGLE. Frank and George operated both the Southern Circle and Southern Triangle restaurants. Seen here, the Southern Triangle, located at Tibbs Avenue, and Ind. 67 (Kentucky Avenue), was an early fast food restaurant, which opened at in April 1952. Curb service was available every day from 11:00 a.m. to 12:30 a.m., and an air-conditioned banquet room was also open from 11:00 a.m. to 2:00 p.m. and again from 5:00 p.m. to 9:00 p.m. (Janet Isaac.)

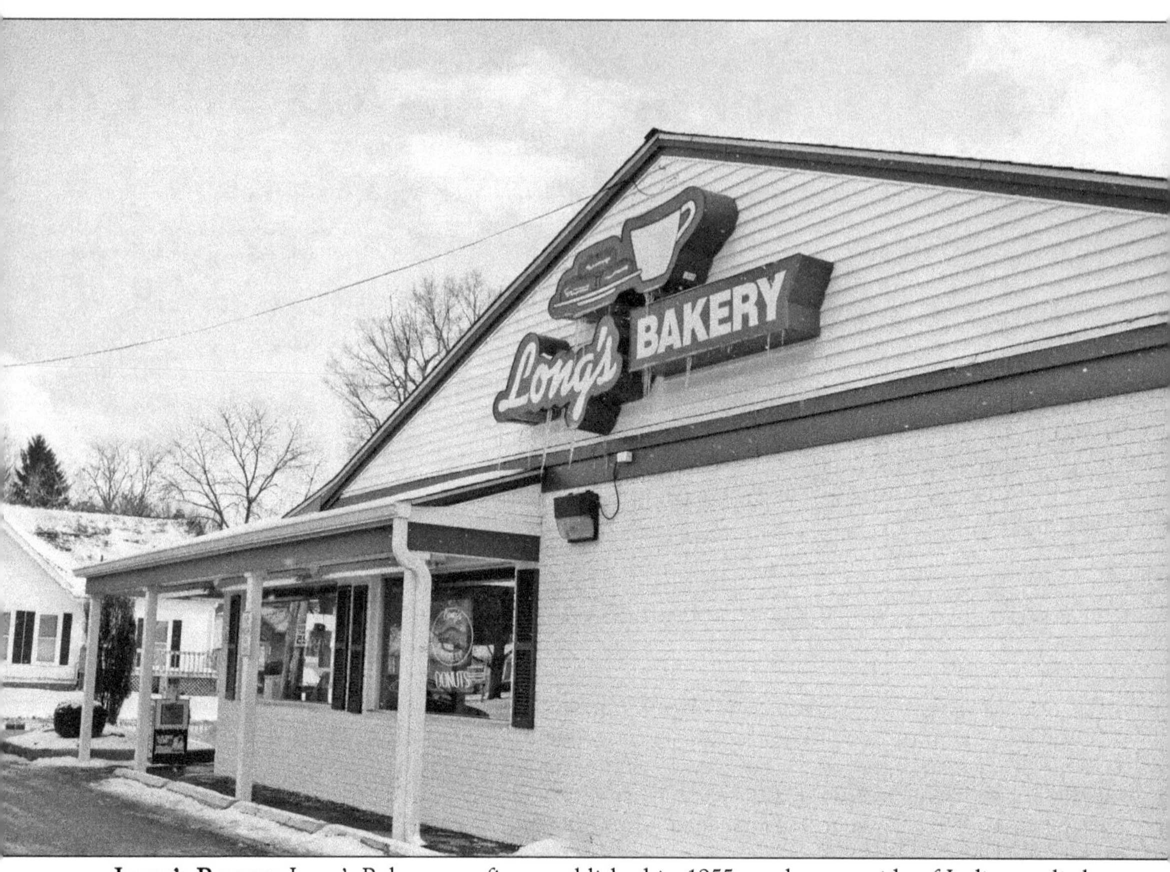

LONG'S BAKERY. Long's Bakery was first established in 1955 on the west side of Indianapolis by Mike Long. There are currently two locations on the west side—one on Tremont Street and another on West Sixteenth Street—and a third on the south side along Southport Road. The Southport location, pictured here, has remained a popular spot in Perry Township since it opened in 1987. Long's moved from its Union Station store to the Southport location; the building used to be the home of the Bi Rite Grocery but was converted into a 41,000-square-feet bakery. (Photograph by Casey Smith.)

Four

Perry Township Schools

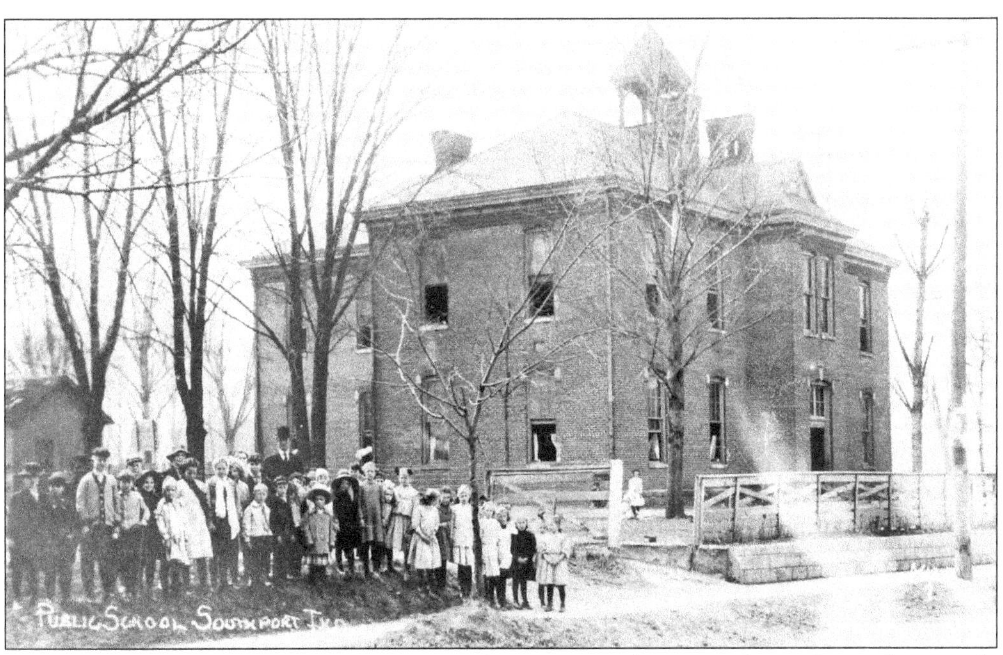

The Original Southport High School. Elementary students stand outside in what is only one of two known photographs of the original Southport High School, located on what is now near the southeast corner of Southport Road and Madison Avenue. Built in 1883, the upper level housed the high school in 1891, while elementary students met on the second floor of the brick structure. (Perry Township/Southport Historical Society.)

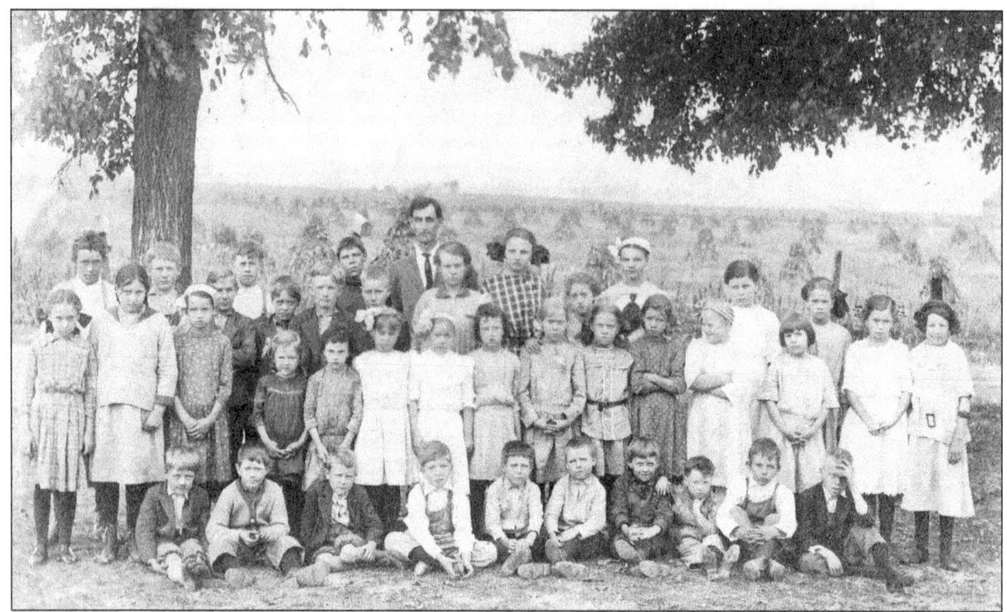

Perry Township Schoolchildren. Pictured here are students in front of Old School No. 14 at the northeast corner of Epler and Belmont Avenues, looking to the farm field to the west, across Belmont Avenue. Southport's first schools provided a poor learning community for students—the school year was normally three months in length as a result of farming in the area—but they were later improved following new state laws and became models for schools in nearby townships. (Perry Township/Southport Historical Society.)

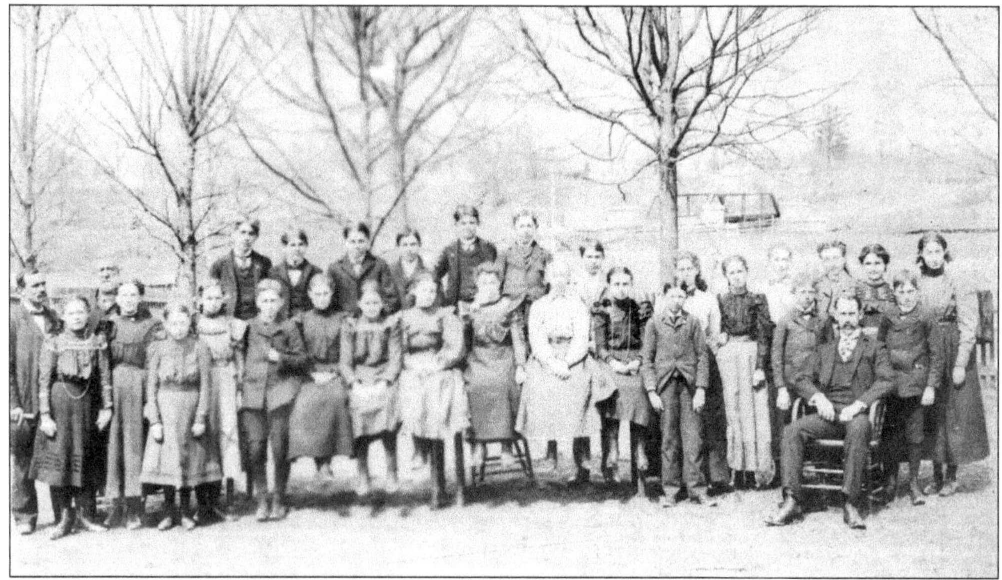

Early Southport High School Students. Toward the start of the 20th century, there were a number of changes at the helm of Southport High School. Josiah Puett, who had been principal since 1891, decided to retire and peruse a career in 1904. He was succeeded by C.E. Cline, pictured here with students, before F.E. Cline became principal in 1907. From 1909 to 1910, Maude Likenhoker became principal and was the first woman to serve in the position. (Perry Township/Southport Historical Society.)

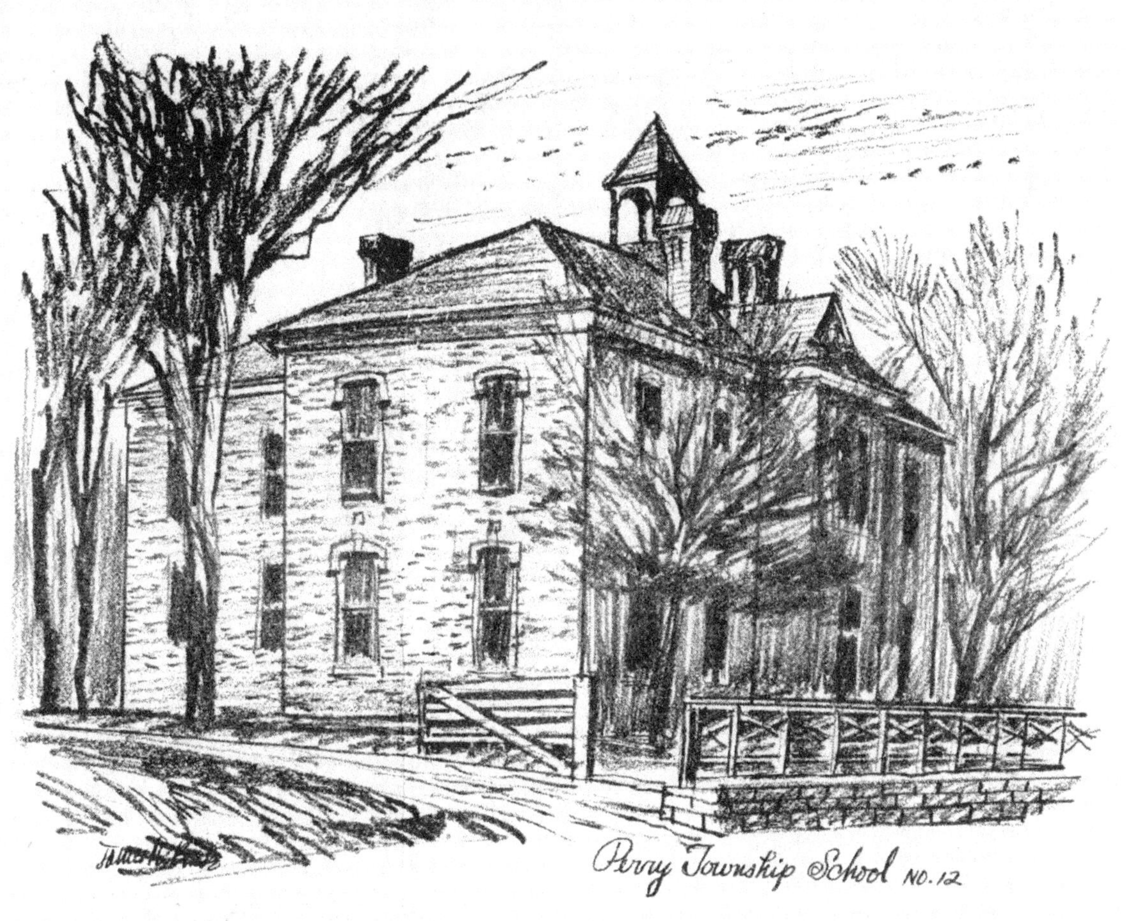

Perry Township's First High School. The first Southport High School, pictured here, was a two-story brick building constructed after a tornado destroyed the original school located on Jacob Smock's land in 1883. Following this original structure, a new school was constructed at a cost of $35,000. It was dedicated in March 1912. The lower level contained a gymnasium with a basketball court. (Perry Township/Southport Historical Society.)

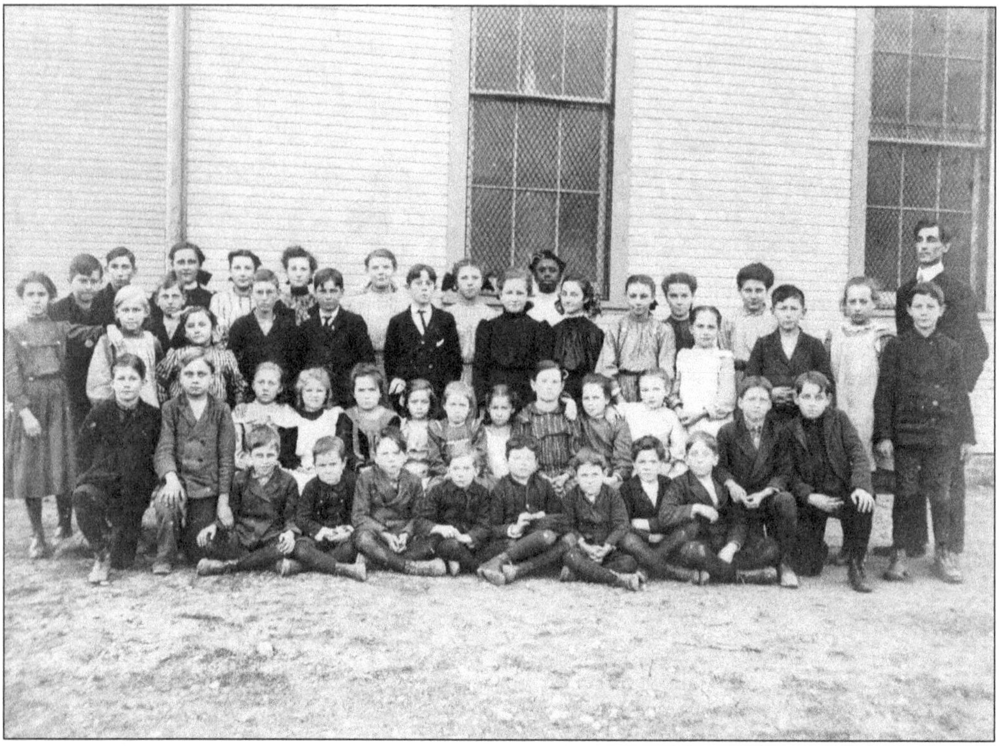

EARLY PERRY TOWNSHIP STUDENTS. Pictured here are students at the Silver Nook School—an early Perry Township school—on Carson Avenue between Thompson and Hanna Avenues. Glenns Valley, however, was one of the first Perry Township communities to get a school building. The school got its name from Archibald Glenn, the township's original settler who located there in 1822. After opening its first school in 1826, Glenns Valley would get a permanent brick school building by 1908 that was later replaced in 1962. Today, it is the oldest continuous elementary school at the same site in the Perry Township system. (Perry Township/Southport Historical Society.)

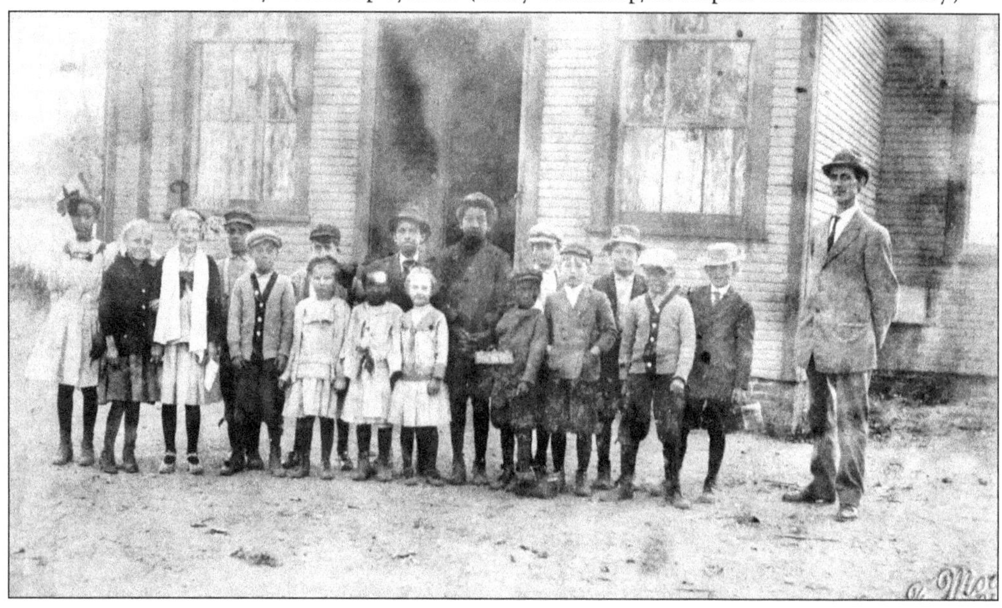

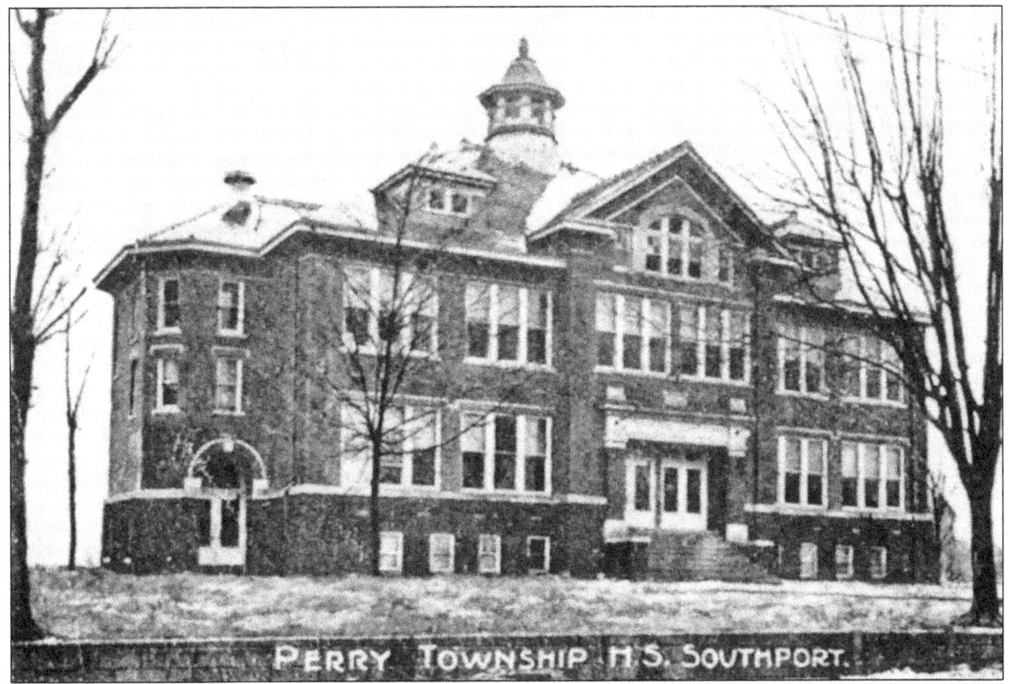

The Second Southport High School. In the fall of 1912, the second building to be known as Southport High School (SHS) opened its doors. In 1913, notable change came to the to SHS curriculum. Courses offered now included agriculture, manual training, and domestic science. In 1915, Latin was no longer a required subject. The Bible was still to be read at least once a week as an opening exercise. (Perry Township/Southport Historical Society.)

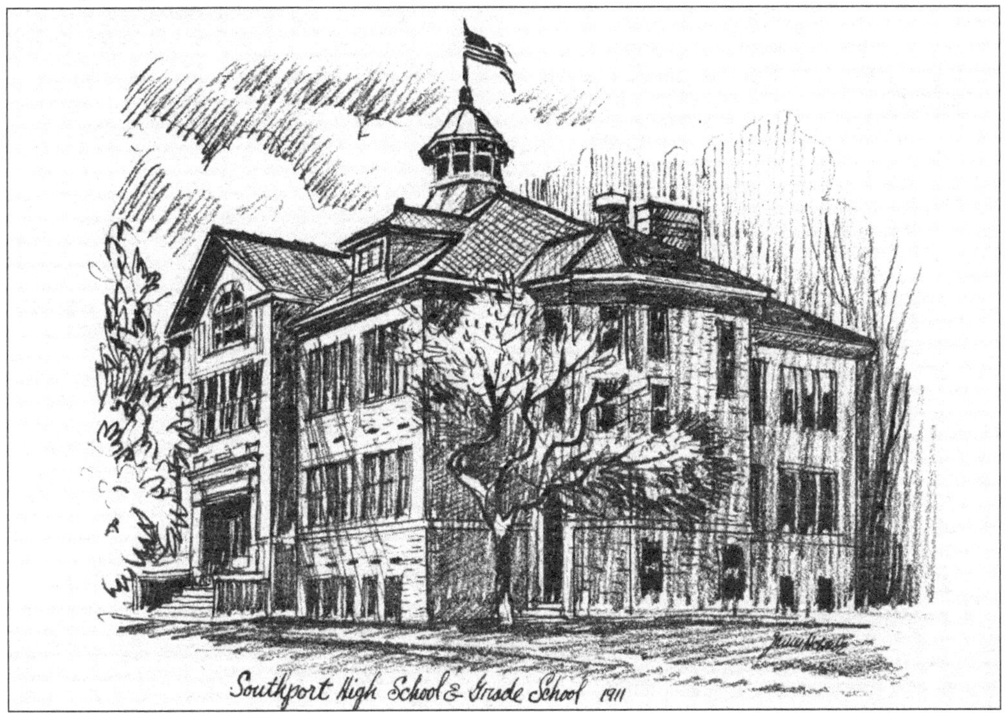

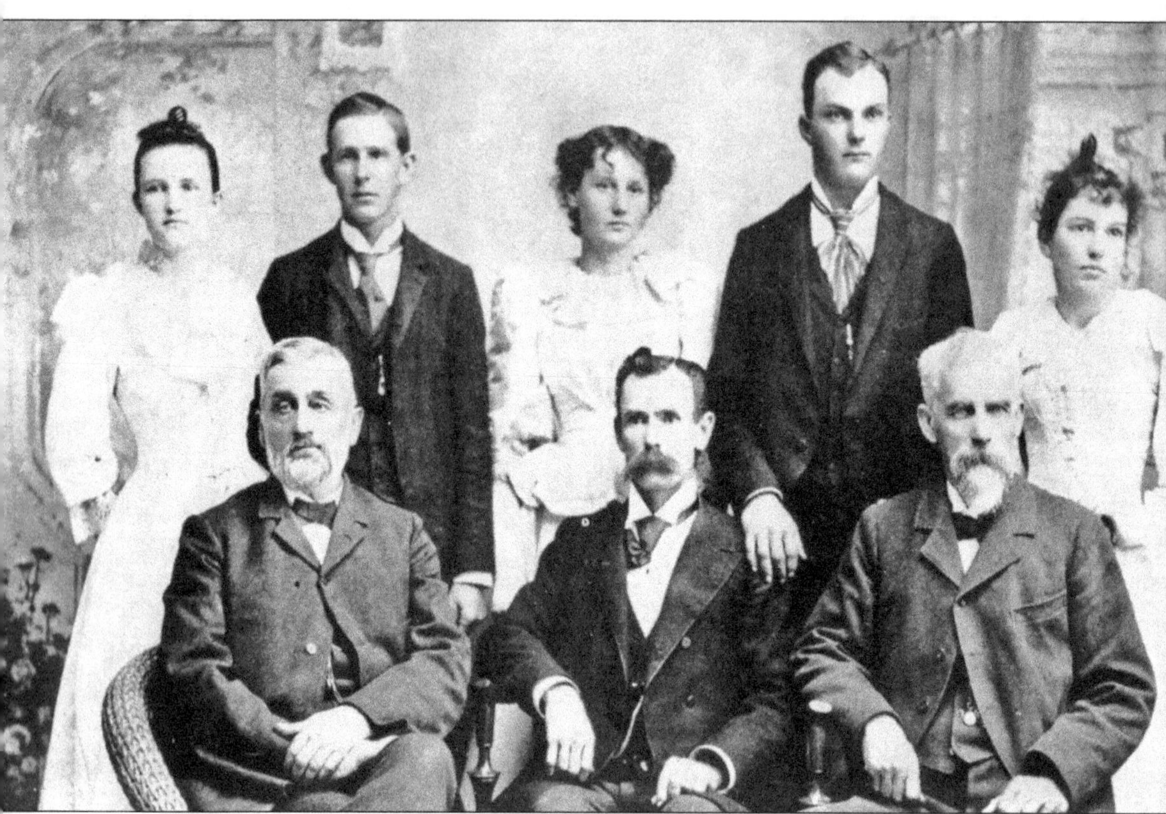

First Graduating Class. Members of Southport High School's first graduating class pose for this photograph in 1894. From left to right are (first row) Chris Grube, trustee; Josiah Puett, principal; and Henry Flick, Marion County superintendent; (second row) Minnie Clifford, John Hendricks, Jean Reno, William List, and Alice Todd. (Perry Township/Southport Historical Society.)

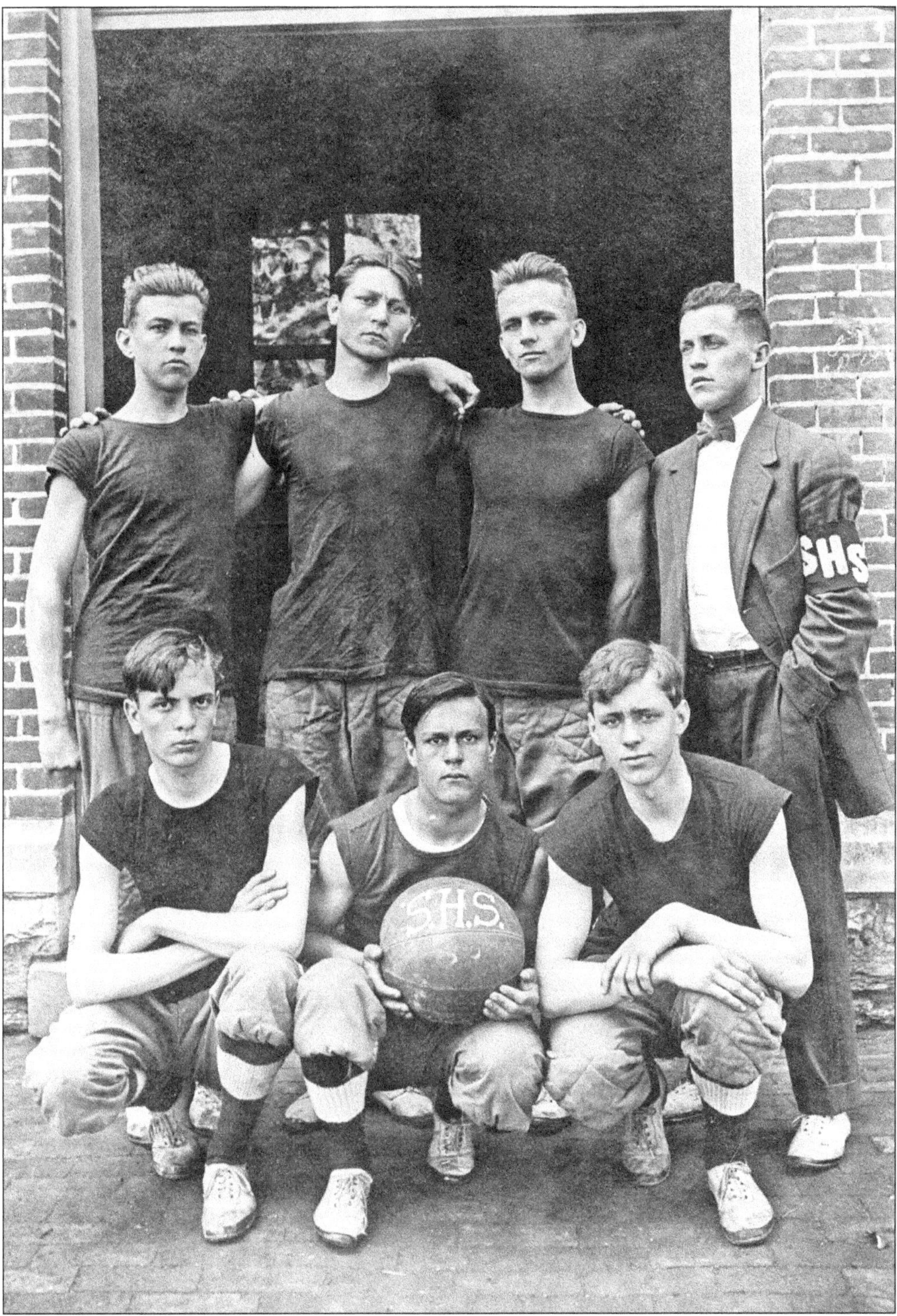

SHS Basketball Team. Members of the 1910 basketball team pose outside of the first Southport High School building. Because the building did not have its own gymnasium inside, students played their games outdoors. (Perry Township/Southport Historical Society.)

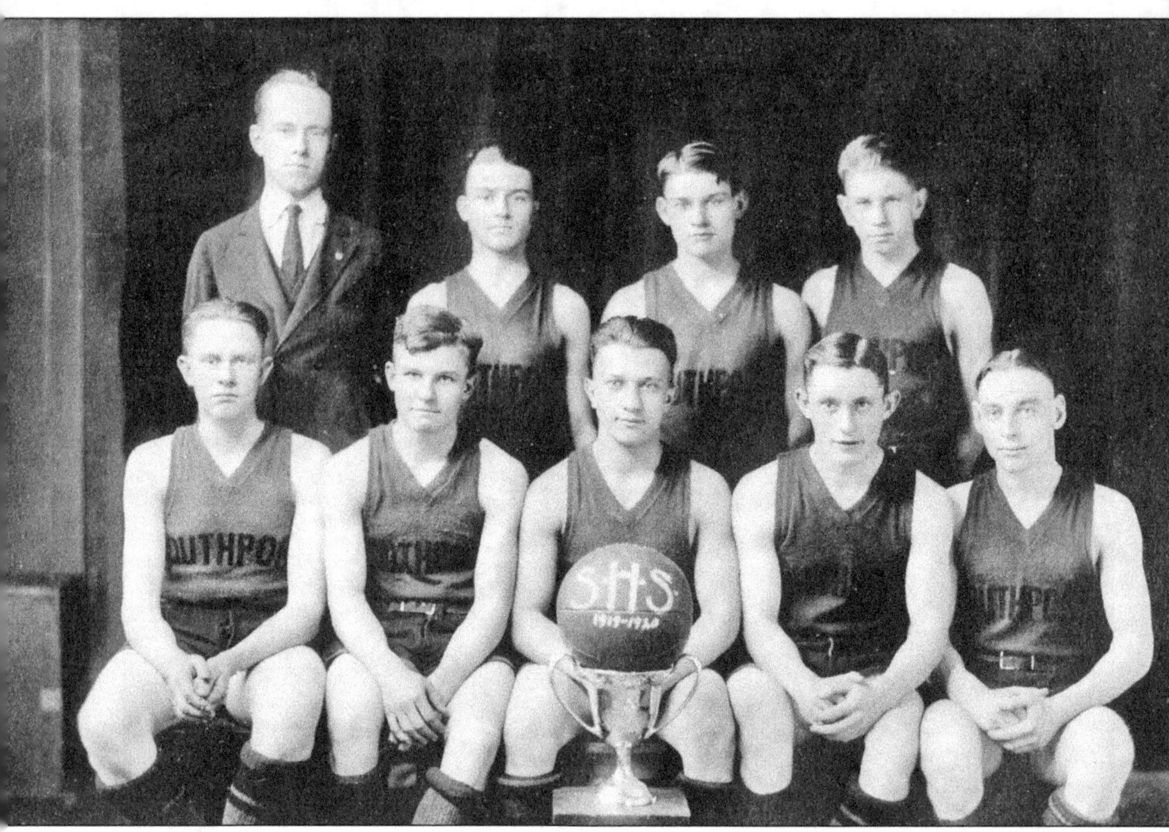

First Tournament Win. Southport quickly found success in athletics, especially once the new school building was in place and students could use the gymnasium inside. Members of the 1919–1920 boys' basketball team are pictured here with coach Browning after winning the first ever Marion County Tournament. Cardinal teams have since won 17 more county titles. (Perry Township/Southport Historical Society.)

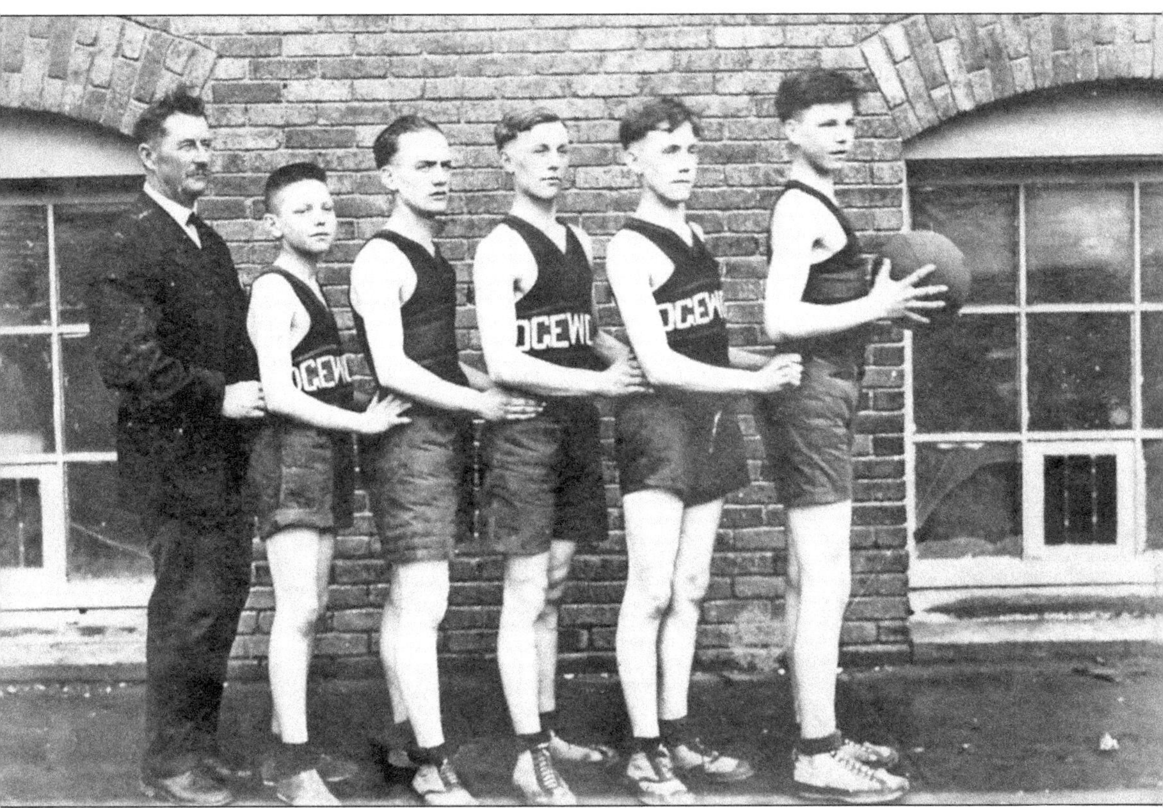

EDGEWOOD BASKETBALL TEAM. Pictured here is the first Edgewood Basketball Team in 1927. The Edgewood basketball scene became popular both for the school team and for the basketball courts accessible outside the school. Basketball tournaments were common, and they would be well attended by members of the community. (Perry Township/Southport Historical Society.)

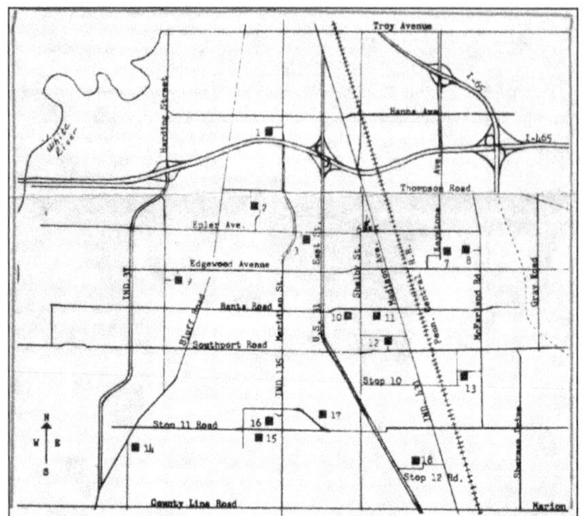

Map of Perry Township. By the early 1970s, Perry Township and its schools was look much different than it did several decades earlier. This map of Perry Township schools includes Southport High School in its fourth and current location at box No. 10 on the southwest corner of Banta Road and Shekby Street. The earlier Southport High School building is located just north of there at box No. 11. (Perry Township/Southport Historical Society.)

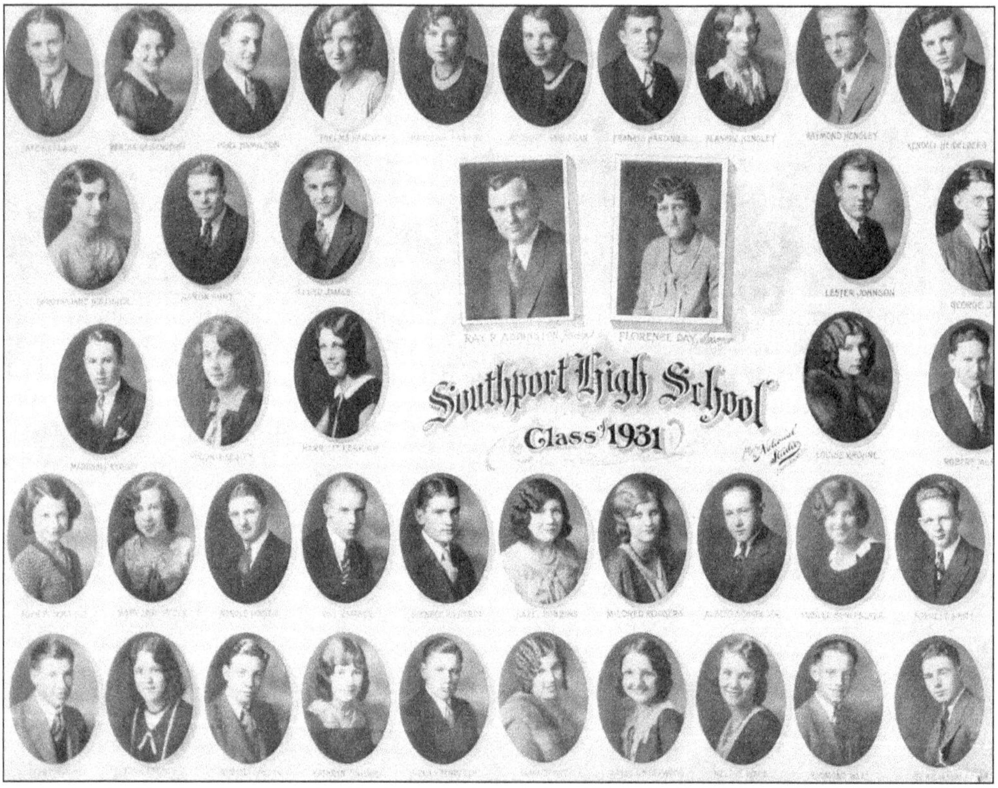

SHS Graduating Class, 1931. While Southport's athletic teams continued to grow, the community did too, and the need for yet a larger high school building were realized. On March 1, 1929, excavation began for the new facility located at the corner or Orinoco Avenue and Banta Road. The new school was located outside of the Southport town boundaries for the first time and now resided within the boundaries of a new Perry Township community called Homecroft, a residential development first laid out in 1923. The property for the new school had been sold to the township by former Southport principal Josiah Puett—the land was part of his farm. Pictured here is the first graduating class from Southport High School's new building in 1931. (Perry Township/Southport Historical Society.)

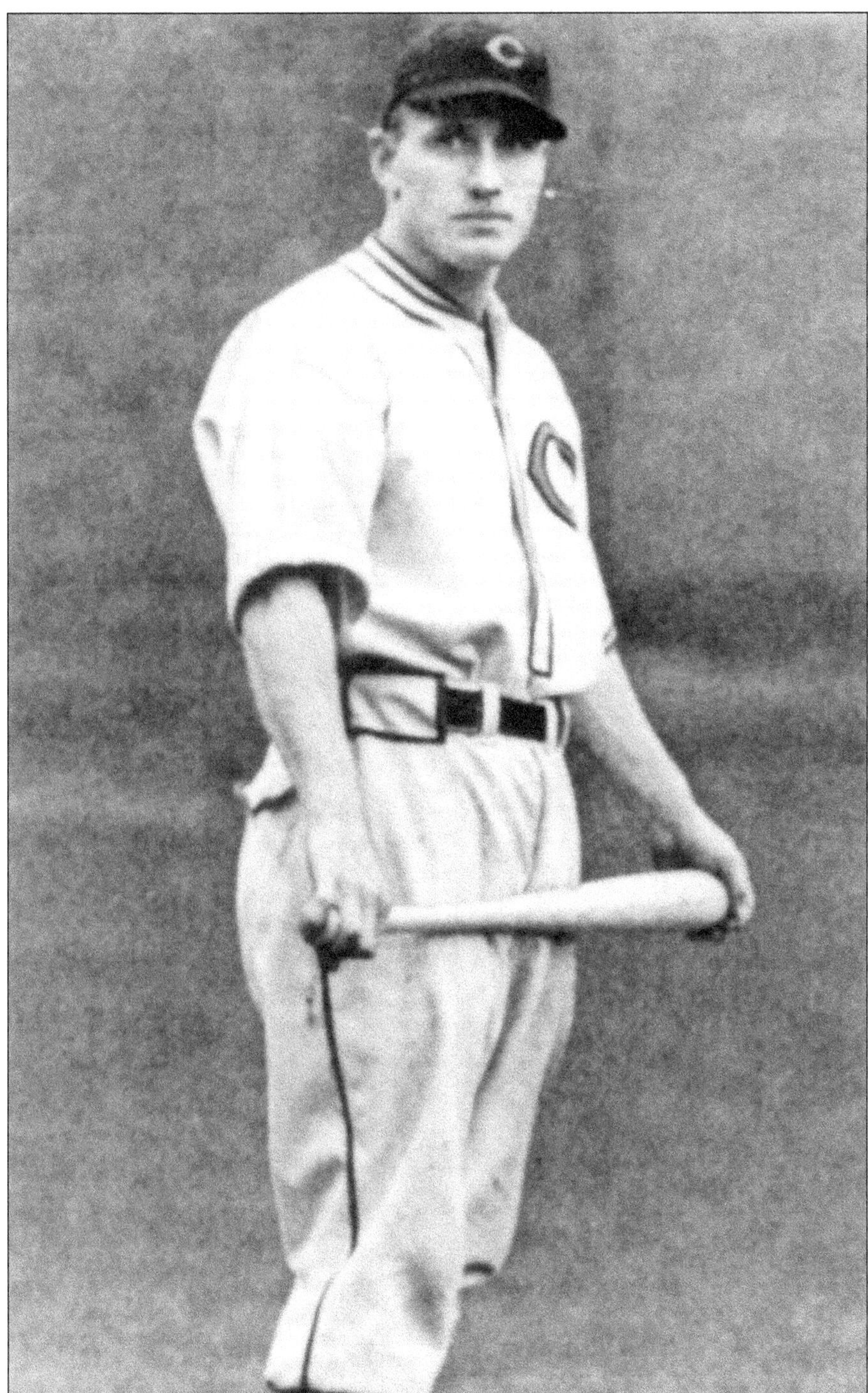

THE "HOOSIER HAMMER." Known as the "Hoosier Hammer," Herbert C. "Chuck" Klein was a 1921 Southport grad whose prowess in baseball took him to the major leagues and ultimately to the Hall of Fame in Cooperstown, New York. Klein, who had a batting average of .320, played Major League Baseball from 1928 through 1944 with the Philadelphia Phillies, the Chicago Cubs, and the Pittsburgh Pirates. (Perry Township/Southport Historical Society.)

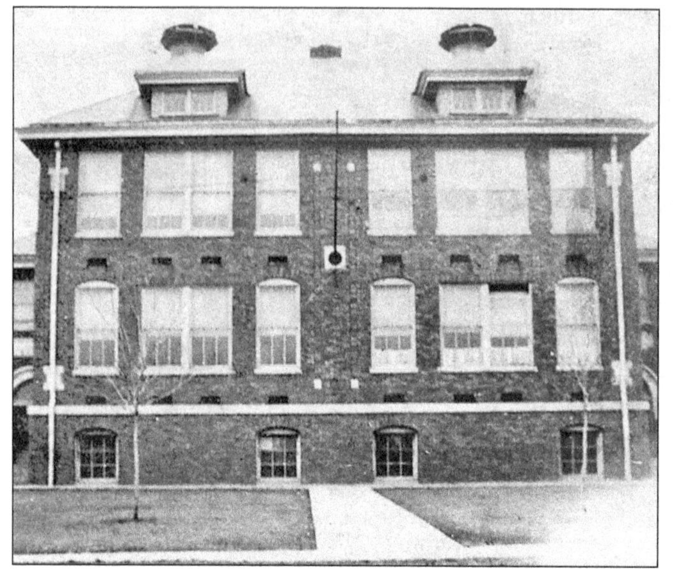

EDGEWOOD GRADE SCHOOL. This photograph was taken facing the south side corner of the Edgewood School building. The doors behind the students would lead down a series of steps to the cafeteria. The James Whitcomb Riley building was constructed on the same property and became the school for first- and second-graders in the area starting in the fall of 1948. After this time, third through eighth graders attended school in the old Edgewood building. (Perry Township/Southport Historical Society.)

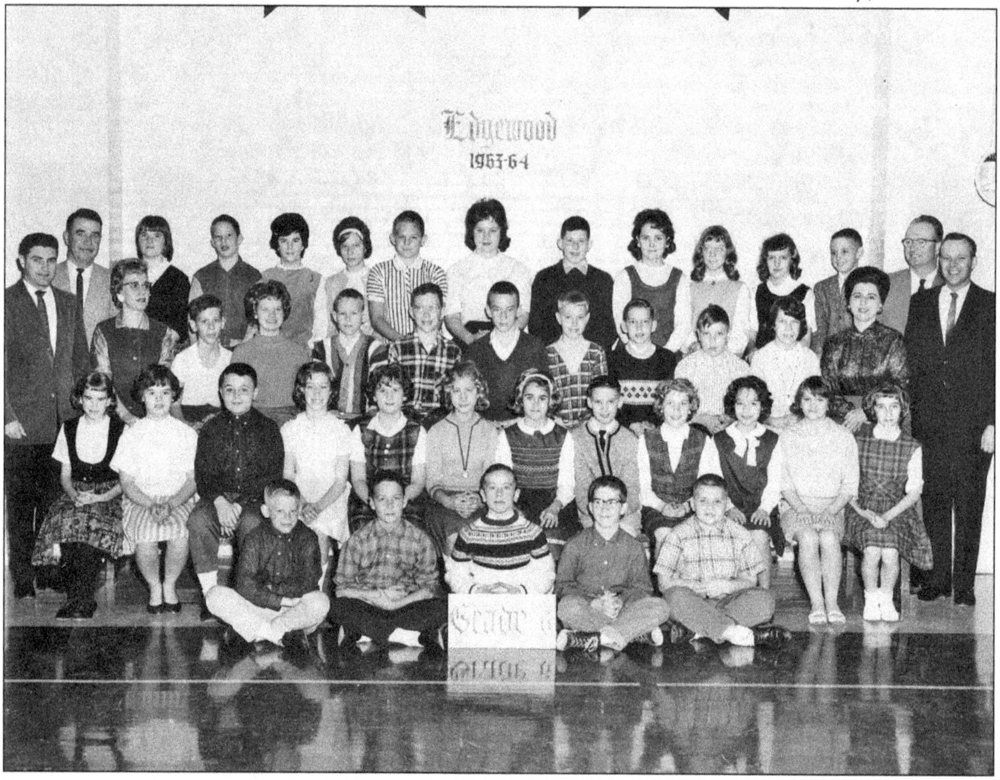

STUDENTS AT EDGEWOOD. The Edgewood School served students in grades first through ninth from 1914 until 1948. The school, located just west of the intersection of Madison and Epler Avenues in the Edgewood neighborhood, graduated thousands of students in the southeast portion of Perry Township over the years until 1980. The school stood next to a popular playground with numerous outdoor basketball courts. It was demolished in 1980 due to old age and inadequate space for growing classroom sizes. The Riley School building still stands today and houses Perry Township's Alternative School. (Photograph courtesy of Mary Edith Geiger.)

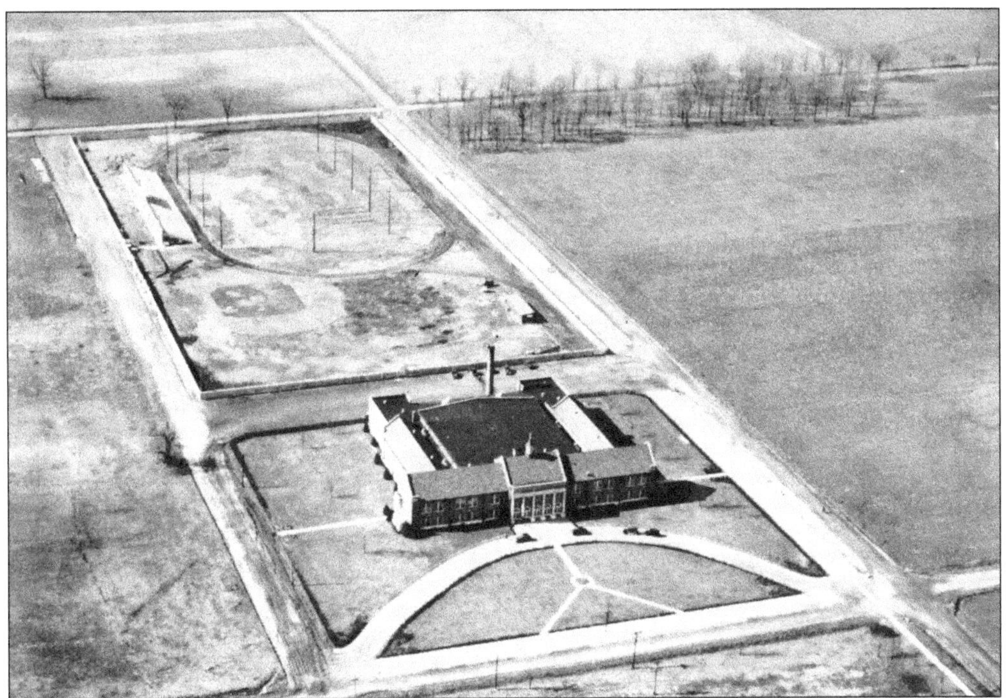

ARIEL SOUTHPORT HIGH SCHOOL. In 1936, this aerial photograph, looking west down Banta Road, was taken to show the sprawling Southport High School and stadium complex. Twenty years after this photograph was taken, houses would line all of the streets while the top of the picture would be occupied by the current high school building. (Perry Township/Southport Historical Society.)

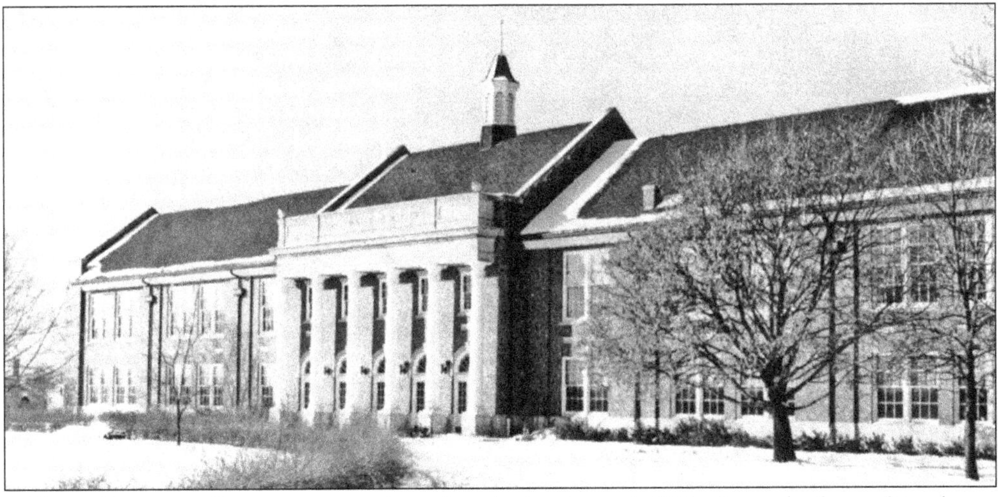

A THIRD BUILDING. This wintertime shot taken during the early 1930s shows the front of Southport High School at Orinoco Avenue and Banta Road. Southport's third high school building was modeled after the Wren Building at the College of William & Mary in Williamsburg, Virginia. Now serving as the Perry Township Education Center, it features a two-story, U-shaped, Colonial Revival style steel frame and concrete building sheathed in redbrick with limestone detailing. The building is also now home to the township's administrative headquarters and preschool. (Perry Township/Southport Historical Society.)

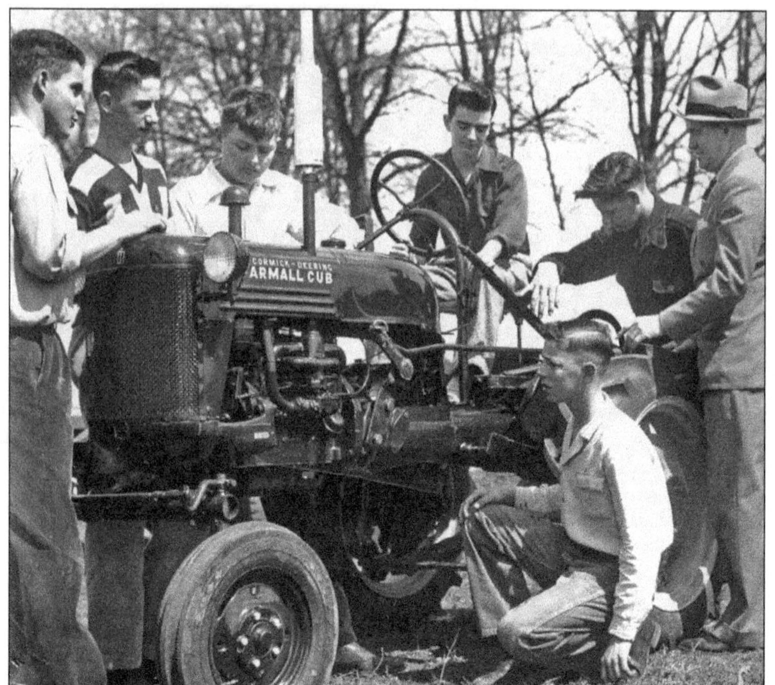

Future Farmers. Members of the Southport High School Future Farmers of America chapter gather to inspect a tractor in this 1949 photograph. Other active clubs around this time included Senior-ority, Hi-Y Booster Club, traffic club, student council, National Honor Society, and Quill and Scroll. (Perry Township/ Southport Historical Society.)

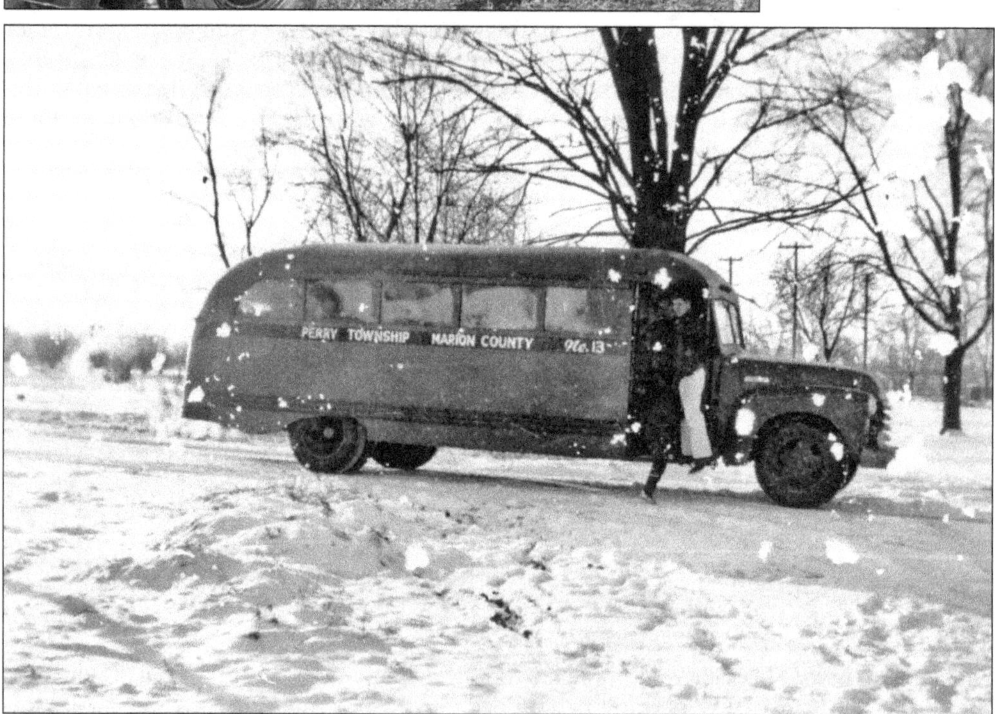

Perry Township Buses. Prior to 1916, virtually all students had either walked to school or traveled by horse or some sort of other horse-drawn vehicle. In 1916, horse-drawn school buses manufactured by Hamilton Wagon Works in Daleville, Indiana, were first used to transport Southport students. School bus transportation would change dramatically, however, with the introduction of motorized buses in 1922. (Perry Township/Southport Historical Society.)

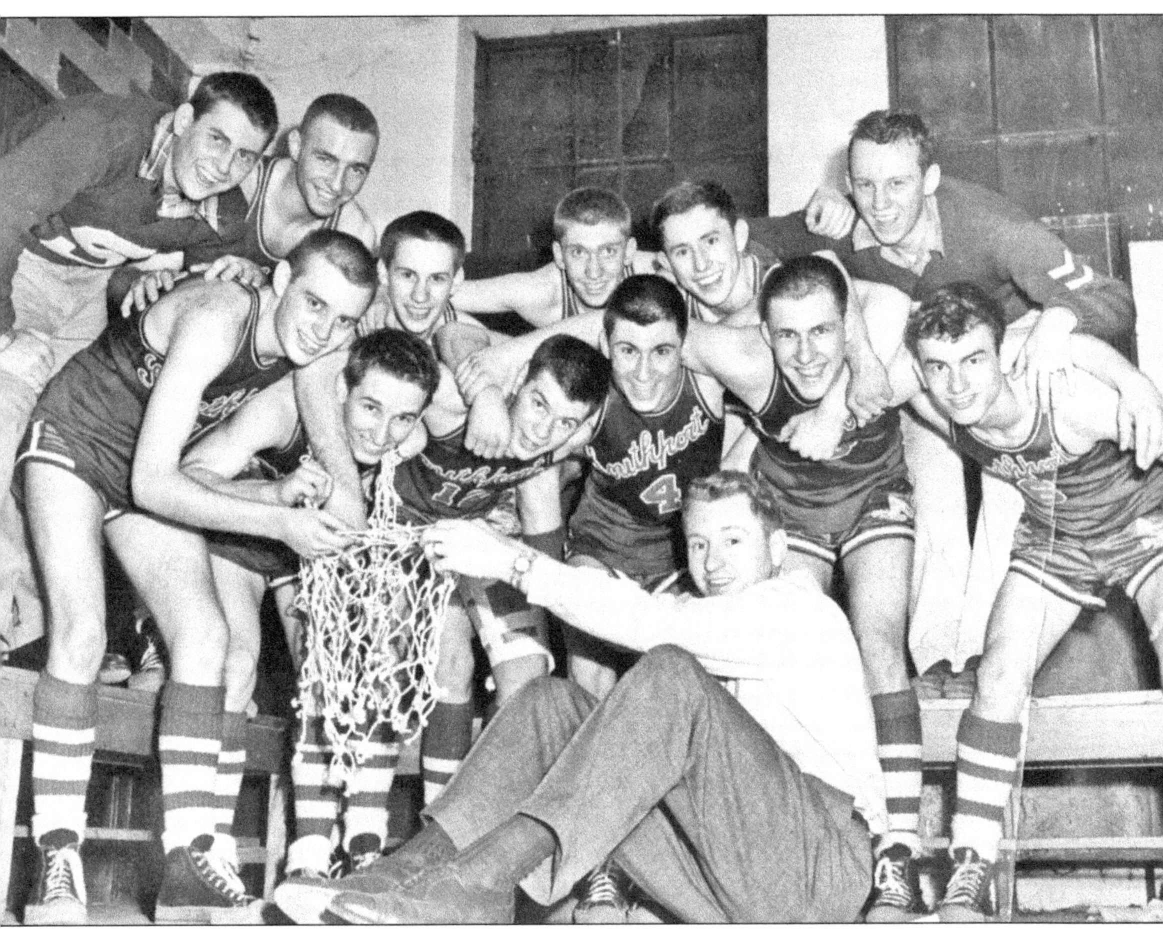

Sectional Champs. Members of the Southport High School basketball team celebrate the 1947 sectional championship. The team was coached by Jewell Young, pictured in the bottom center. This win at sectional championships was Southport's first since 1939. (Perry Township/Southport Historical Society.)

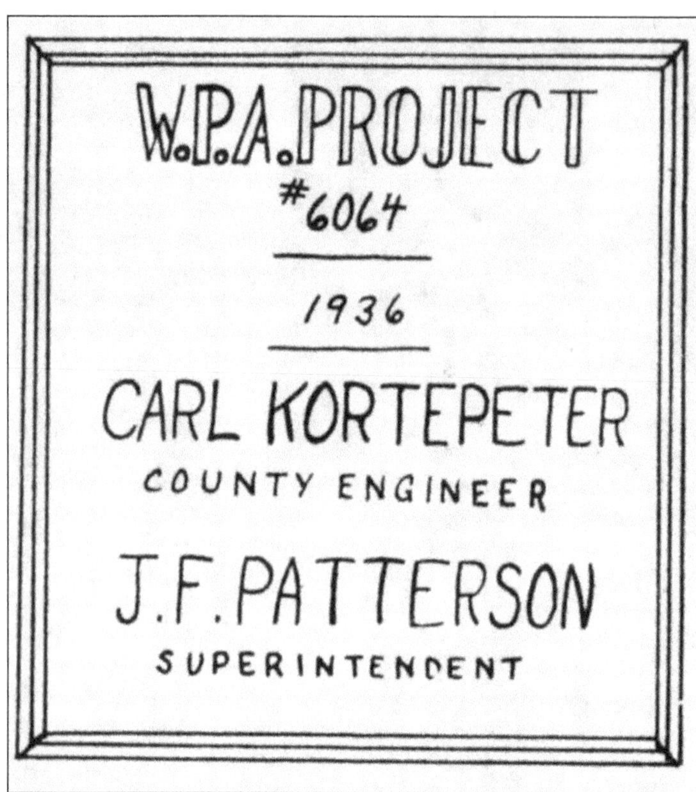

Roosevelt Stadium. Roosevelt Stadium, since known as Perry Stadium, and now Cardinal Stadium, was built in 1936 as a Works Progress Administration project. Its namesake comes from Franklin Roosevelt, who was president at this time. Those who built the stadium were Works Progress Administration (WPA) workers. The WPA was a relief program established in 1935 in response to the Great Depression. It offered work to the unemployed to construct and repair buildings and infrastructure. Cardinal Stadium was one of its projects. (Perry Township/Southport Historical Society.)

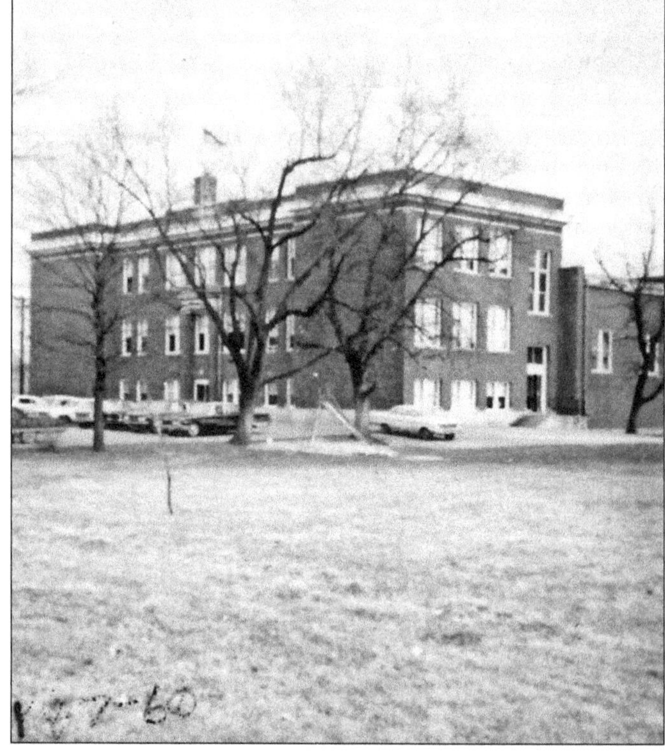

Bluff School. Bluff Elementary School, pictured here, was located at the southeast corner of Bluff Road and Hanna Avenue. Since the mid-1800s, the nearby area along Bluff Road has been prominent for many of Indiana's German immigrants and their families, as well as German greenhouses and truck gardens. In the first half of the 20th century, the area even had one of the largest concentrations of winter tomato and lettuce production under glass in the United States. In January 1968, Frank Hunter, then superintendent of Perry Township Schools, announced the school was closing. The area is now Bluff Park. (Perry Township/Southport Historical Society.)

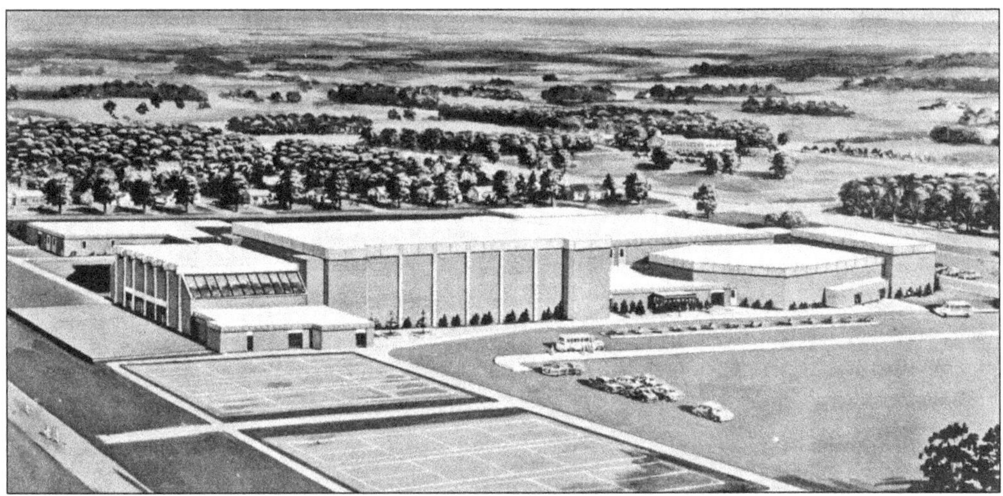

Plans for a Second High School. This architect's drawing illustrates Perry Meridian High School, a second high school proposed in the Perry Township district in the early 1960s. The drawing depicts what completed school would look like in August 1963 at Stop 11 Road and Rahke Road, adjacent to Perry Meridian Middle School. (Perry Township/Southport Historical Society.)

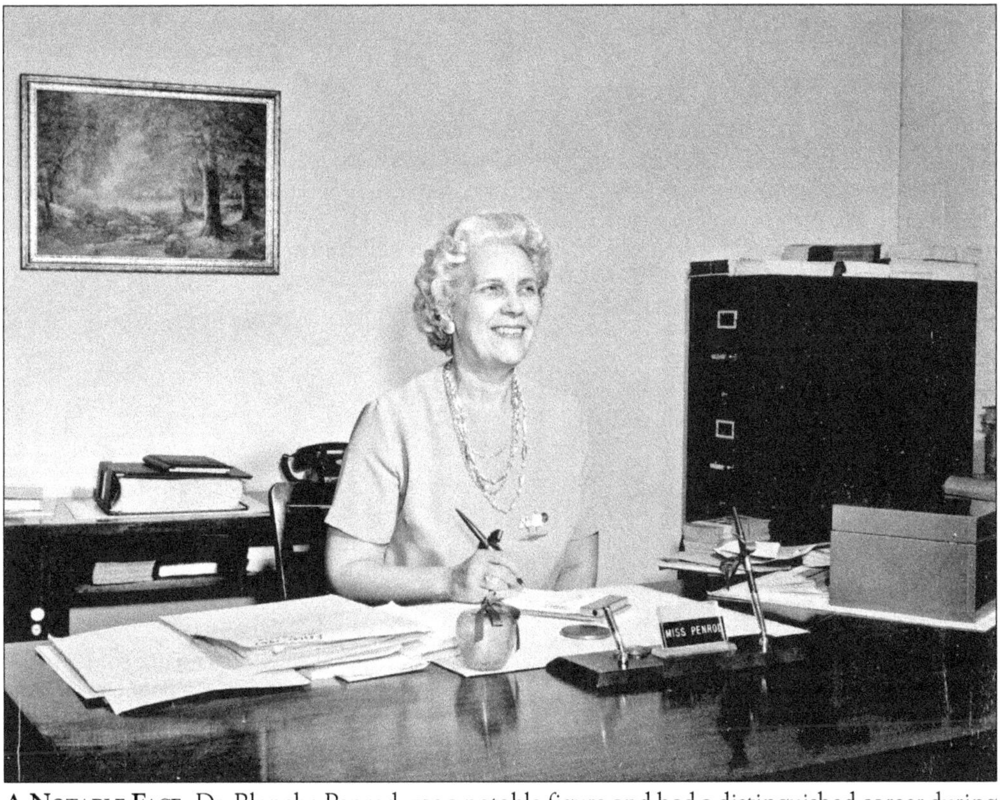

A Notable Face. Dr. Blanche Penrod was a notable figure and had a distinguished career during her time spent working in Perry Township. A 1922 Southport High School graduate, she began teaching biology at Southport in 1926. After that, from 1941 to 1969, she served as dean of girls at SHS before retiring. (Perry Township/Southport Historical Society.)

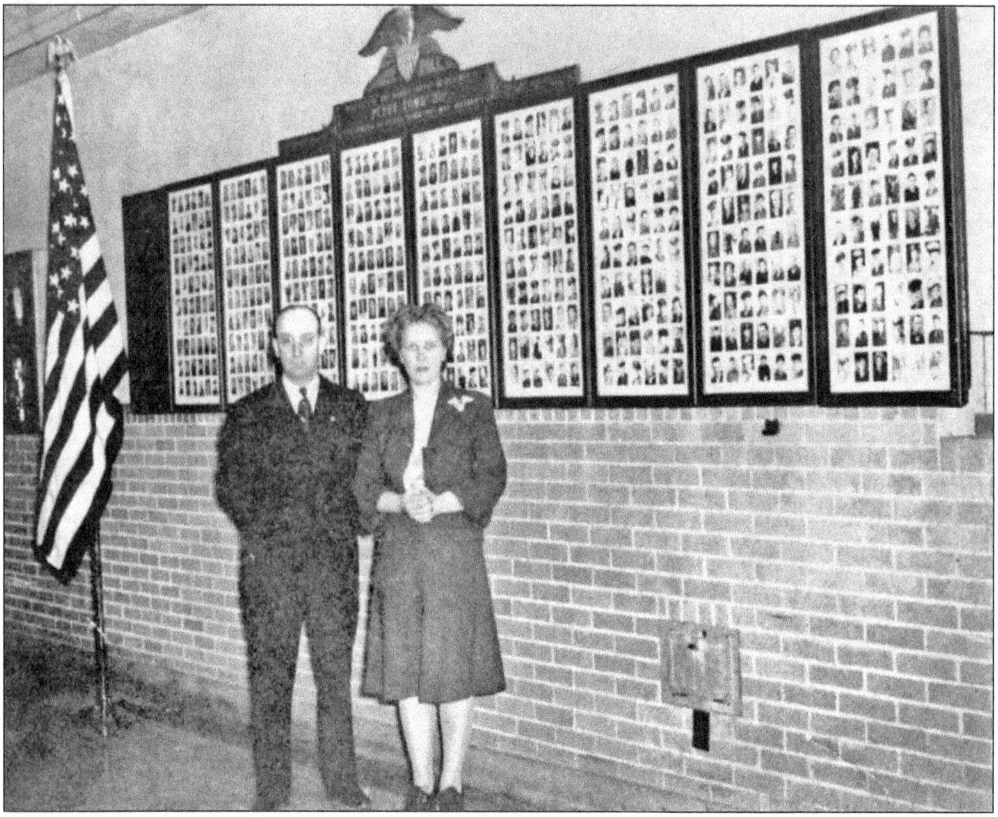

WALL OF HONOR. Southport High School principal Calvin Leedy and Dean of Girls Blanch Penrod stand before the plaque that commemorated the SHS graduates and former students who were involved in the military during World War II. More than 500 Southport High School graduates and former students took part in World War II, including 34 who made the ultimate sacrifice. (Perry Township/Southport Historical Society.)

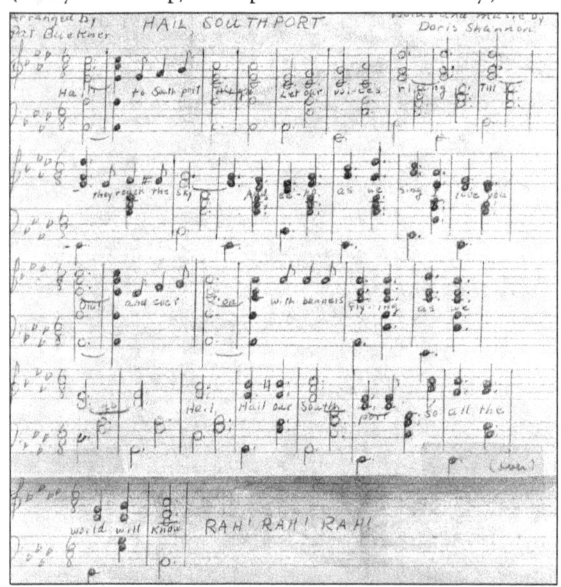

SOUTHPORT'S SCHOOL SONG. During the summer of 1932, incoming Southport High School senior Doris Shannon wrote the words and music for the school's fight song, "Hail to Southport High." In an era when most schools borrowed popular fight songs of major American universities and then lent their own lyrics to the tunes, the new song gave Southport a unique status. Shown here is Shannon's original score for the song. (Perry Township/Southport Historical Society.)

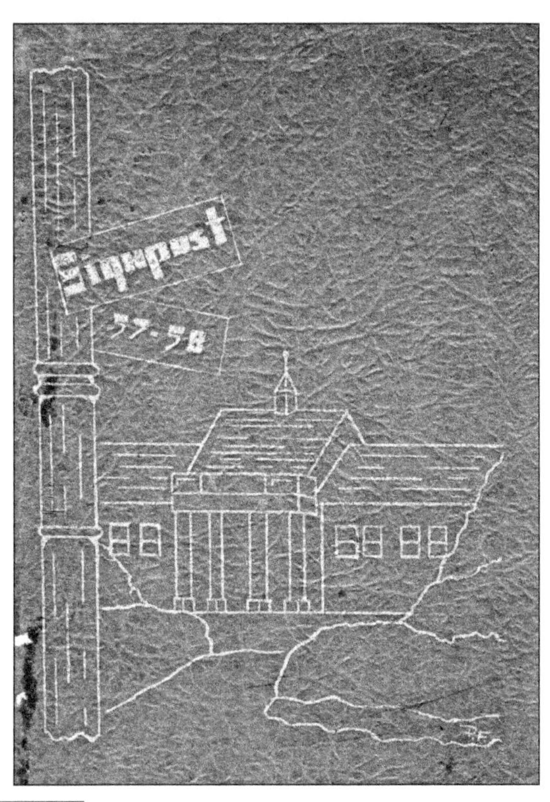

School Signposts. These Southport High School signposts were given to students in their first days of classes in the 1950s. By this time, preparations were being made for another new schooling facility. Due to growth in the number of students in the township, ground was broken in September 1951 for a new building that would be located at 971 East Banta Road. Although originally opening in fall of 1953 as Perry Township Junior High, the larger building was soon the new home for Southport High School in the fall of 1957. The township's junior high school was transferred back down the street to Orinoco site. (Janet Isaac.)

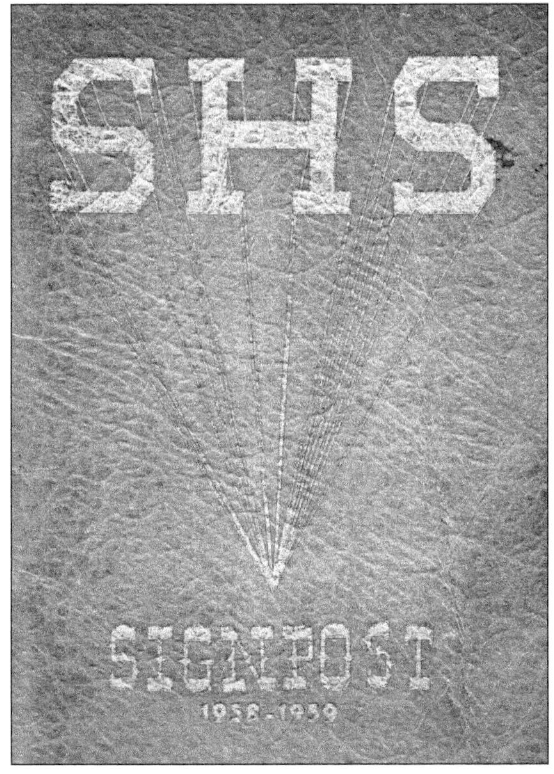

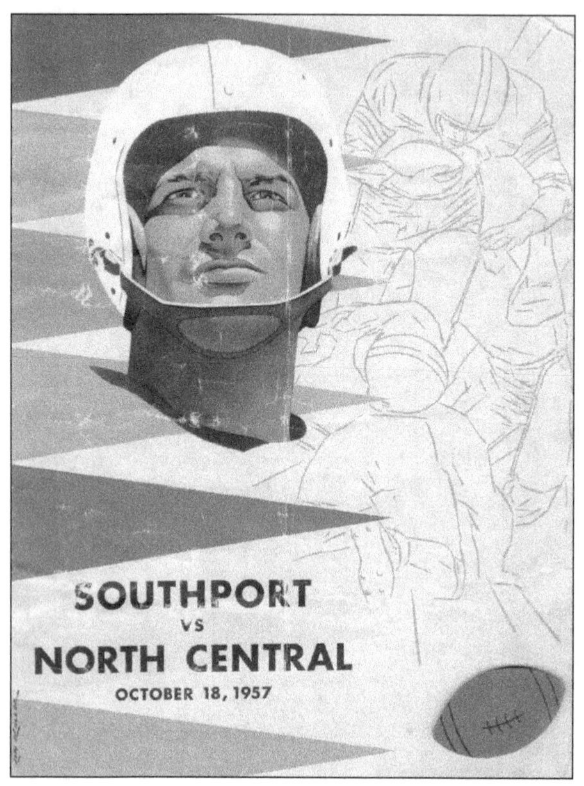

SHS FOOTBALL. At every home football game Southport High School hosted at Roosevelt Stadium (which was later renamed to Perry Stadium), programs like the one pictured here were distributed to fans attending the game. A new concession stand and lighted parking lot were added to the stadium in 1947, Today, football games are still played on the field, although AstroTurf has replaced the grass. (Janet Isaac.)

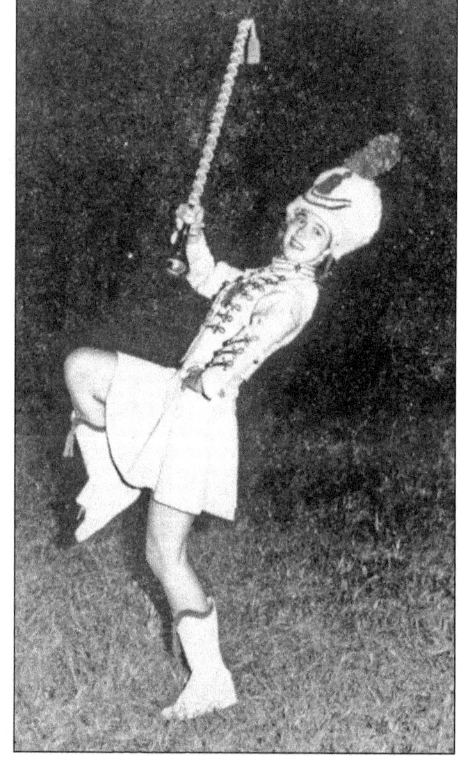

MARCHING BAND. Pattie Tuttle, pictured here, was Southport High School's drum majorette in 1950. Her older sisters, Shirley and Margie, had also been SHS majorettes before, when the Southport marching band frequently performed at football games and during parades. They also competed annually at the Indiana State Fair Marching Band Competition. (Perry Township/Southport Historical Society.)

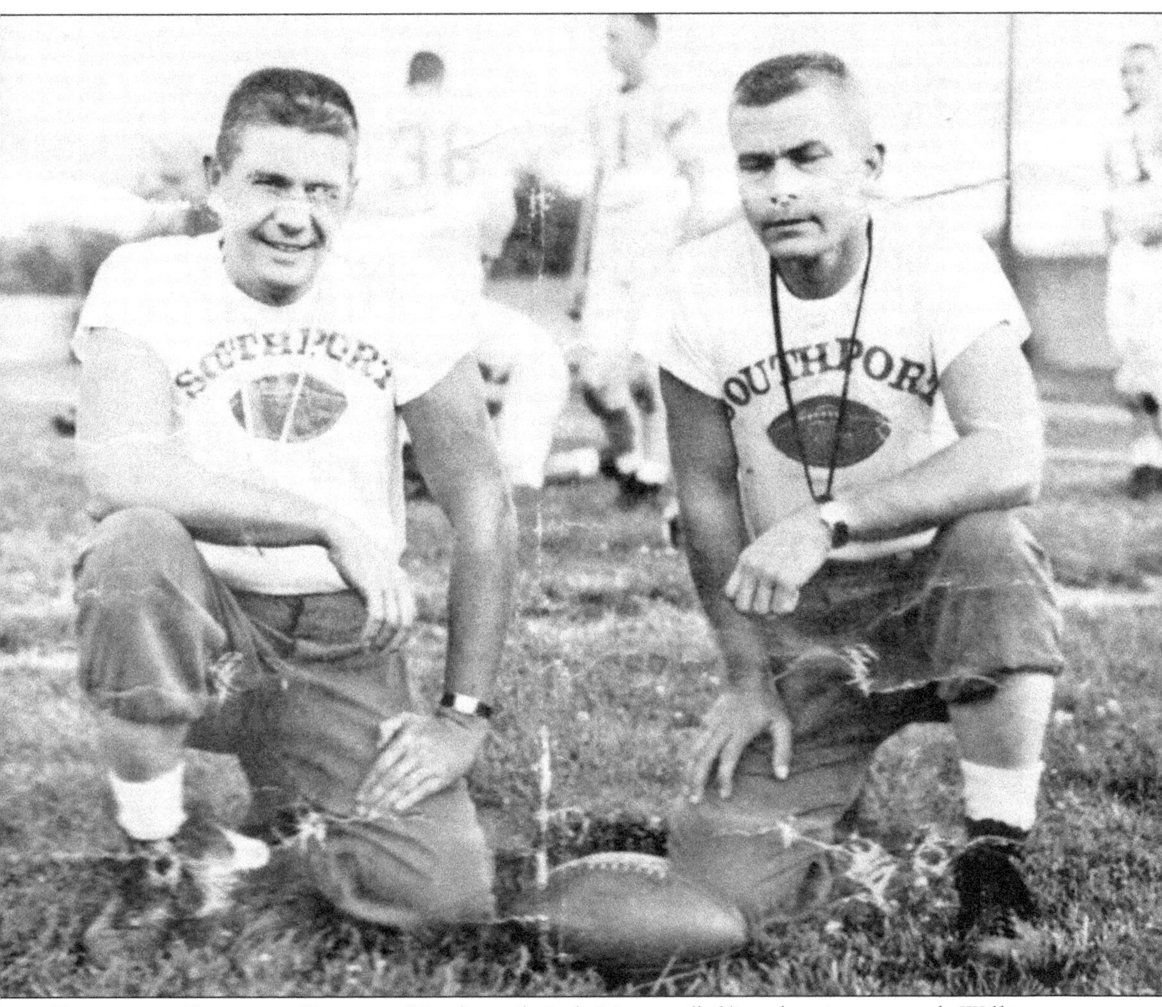

Southport Football Coaches. Head coach Jack Morgan (left) and assistant coach William Fredenberger lead the coaching staff for Southport High School's football team in the 1950s. Morgan was appointed head football coach in August 1951 after leading the freshmen team through and undefeated season the year before. Fredenberger, who served with the Army Air Force from 1943 to 1945, had previously been captain of the Indiana Central football team his senior year at Indiana Central College and was all-state quarterback on the 1947 Indiana Collegiate Conference team. He passed away in his Epler Avenue apartment in November 1958. (Perry Township/Southport Historical Society.)

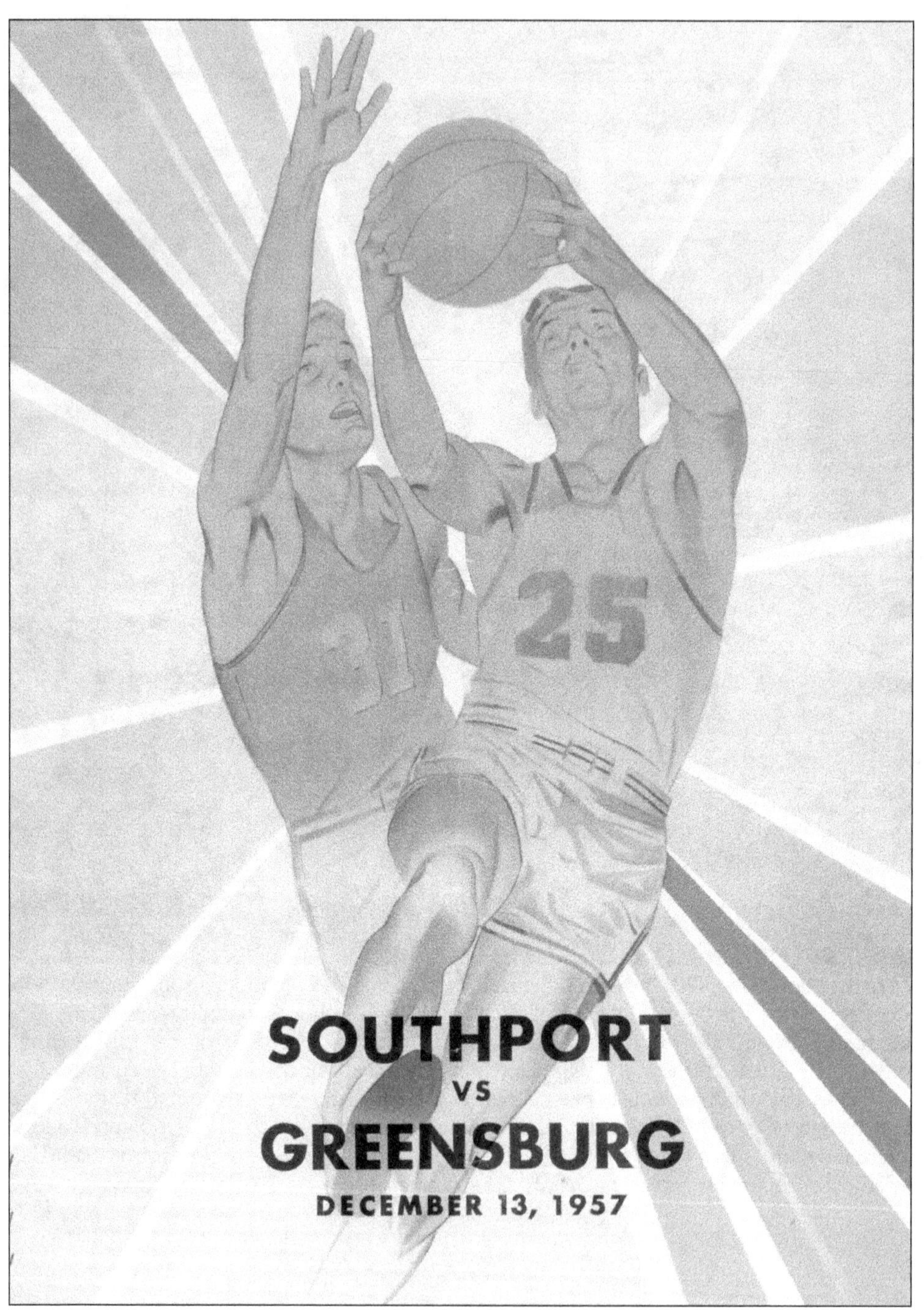

Southport Basketball. During the 1950s, the Southport boys' basketball team underwent some coaching changes. Carl "Blackie" Braden replaced Jewell Young as head coach and opened on a winning note by leading the Cardinals to the school's first sectional championship since 1947. The 1957 team did even better, with the Cardinals capturing the county tourney, a sectional and the school's first regional title. Southport went all the way to the final game of the Indianapolis Semi-State at Butler Fieldhouse, losing to Crispus Attucks, who then lost in the state final to South Bend Central. (Janet Isaac.)

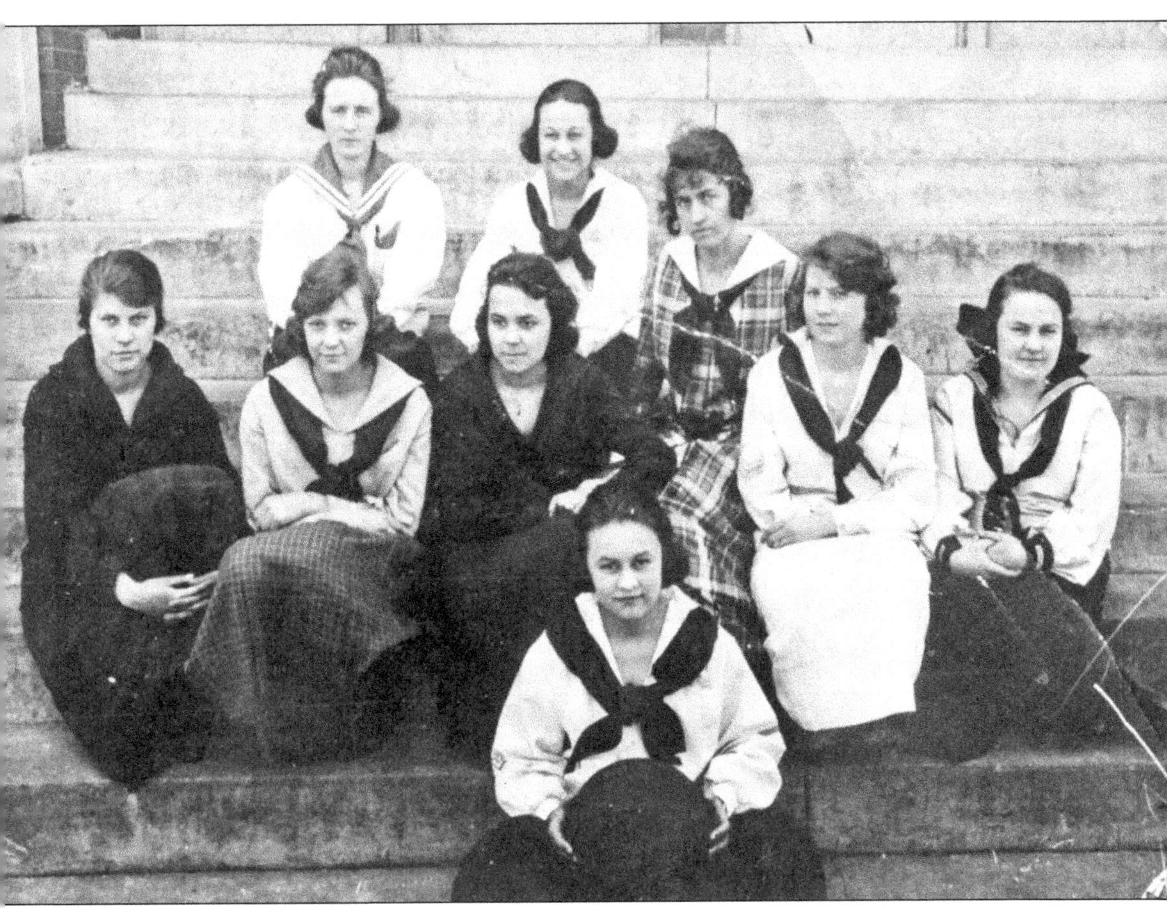

SHS Women's Basketball Team. Long before the Indiana High School Athletic Association sanctioned athletic teams for girls, Southport had a girls' basketball team. The 1919–1920 girls' team is pictured here and included Ruth Derbyshire, Olive Derbyshire, Blanch Smith, Charlotte McLaughlin, Wilnetta Brewer, Eleanor Ross, Kathryn Fishback, Cecil Toon, and coach Marjorie Presti. (Perry Township/Southport Historical Society.)

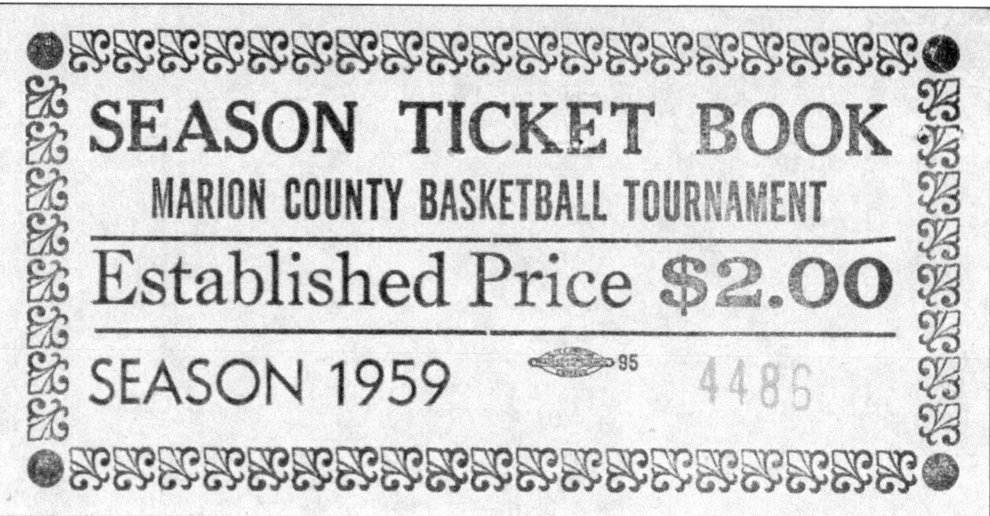

SEASON TICKET BOOK

MARION COUNTY BASKETBALL TOURNAMENT

Established Price $2.00

SEASON 1959 95 4486

County Basketball Tournament. Attending basketball games was a given for most students at Southport High School. Season ticket books, like the one above, could be purchased for $2 in 1959. At the games, boys and girls both had their own cheer blocks to encourage their peers on the court. The boy's cheer block garnered notoriety for their cheer-block nickname, "Braden's Raiders," coined for a notable teacher at the time. (Janet Isaac.)

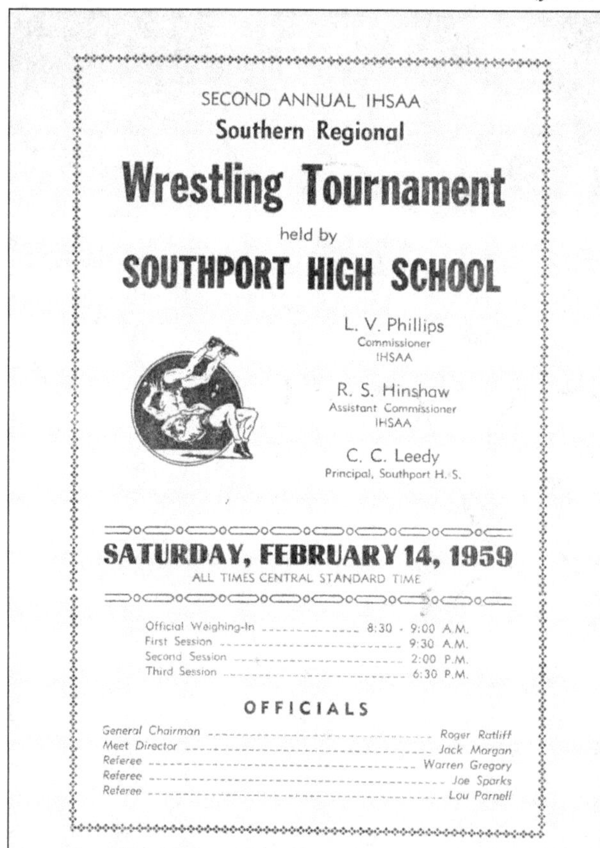

SECOND ANNUAL IHSAA

Southern Regional

Wrestling Tournament

held by

SOUTHPORT HIGH SCHOOL

L. V. Phillips
Commissioner
IHSAA

R. S. Hinshaw
Assistant Commissioner
IHSAA

C. C. Leedy
Principal, Southport H. S.

SATURDAY, FEBRUARY 14, 1959

ALL TIMES CENTRAL STANDARD TIME

Official Weighing-In .... 8:30 - 9:00 A.M.
First Session .... 9:30 A.M.
Second Session .... 2:00 P.M.
Third Session .... 6:30 P.M.

OFFICIALS

General Chairman .... Roger Ratliff
Meet Director .... Jack Morgan
Referee .... Warren Gregory
Referee .... Joe Sparks
Referee .... Lou Parnell

Southport Wrestling. Southport's wrestling program became a statewide power in the 1950s. Coached by Chauncey McDaniel, the Cardinal grapplers captured the team state championship in 1951, 1954 and 1955. Bill Edwards, Don Hinds, Harry Rasdall, and Harry Beck were all individual weight champions in 1954, while Bob Herzog and Fred Redeker won state titles in their respective weight classes in 1955. (Janet Isaac.)

INSTRUCTIONAL
CULTURAL AND
COMMUNITY
RESOURCE CENTER

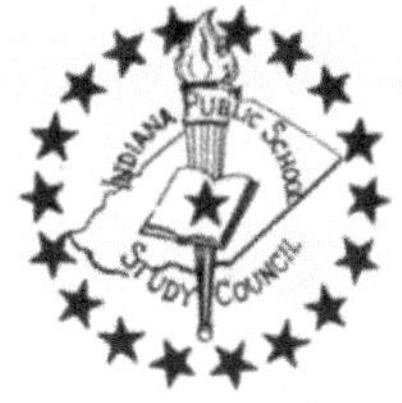

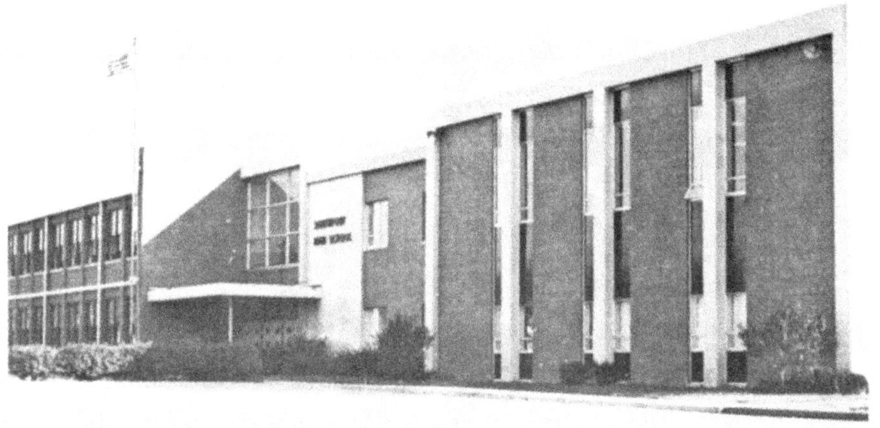

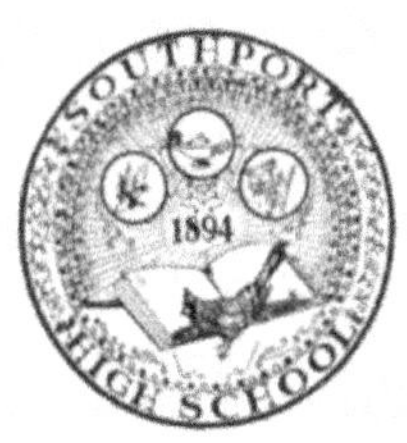

M.S.D. of Perry Township
Southport High School

971 East Banta` Road
Marion County

THE SOUTHPORT INSTRUCTIONAL, CULTURAL AND COMMUNITY RESOURCE CENTER. Continued growth in enrollment resulted in another construction project to expand Southport High School. In 1966, a significant addition included several new classrooms for band and choir, home economics, industrial arts, art and science, a new cafeteria, an auditorium, the library, and expansion of the administrative and guidance departments. The library would then be known as the ICCRC, which stood for the Instructional Cultural and Community Resource Center. (Perry Township/Southport Historical Society.)

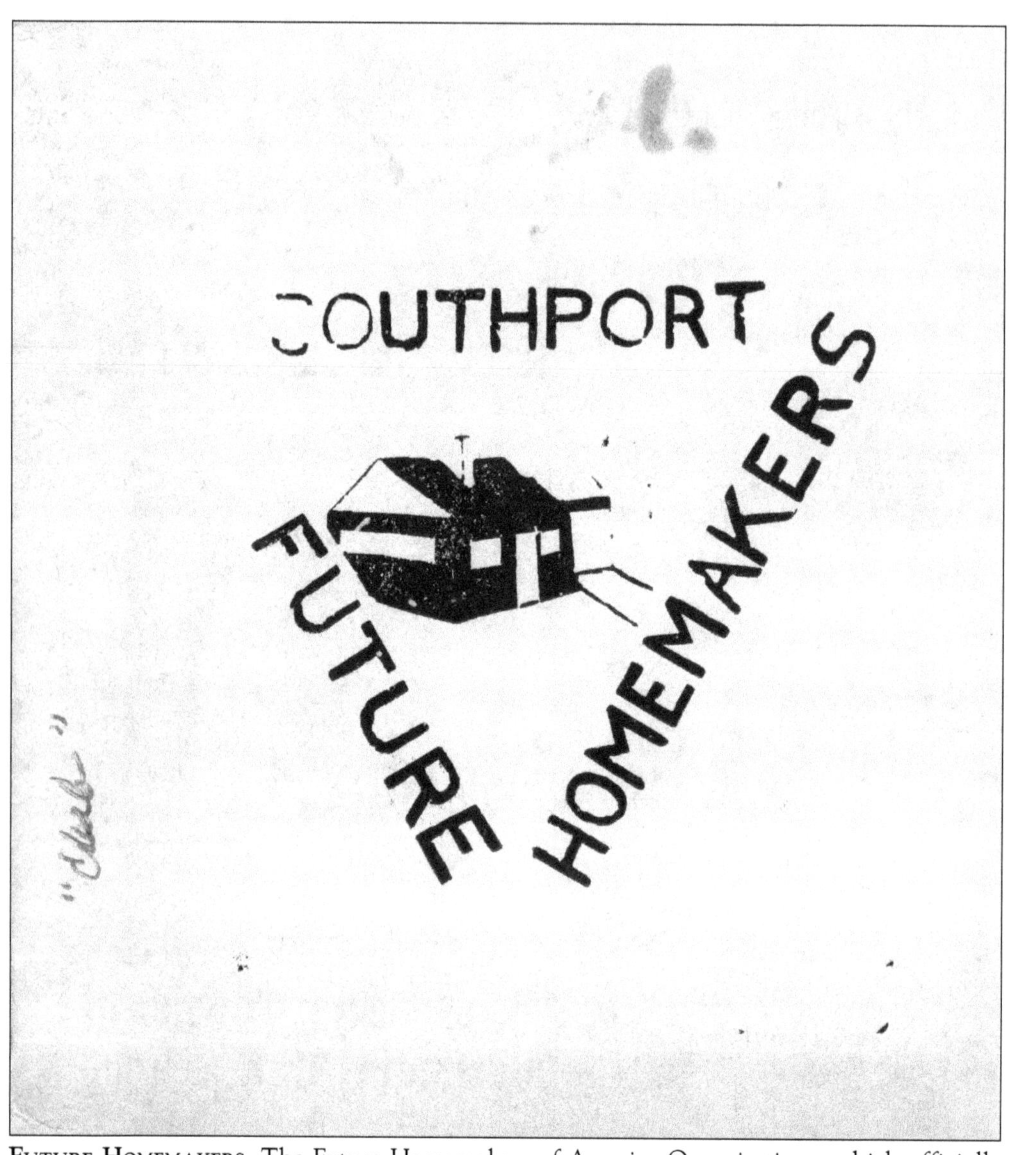

Future Homemakers. The Future Homemakers of America Organization—which officially began nationally in 1945 to unify home economic clubs and classes in high schools across the United States—distributed small booklets (like the one pictured here) to students several times a year. At Southport, students in home economics classes and clubs received the pamphlets, which discussed topics like staying in school, personal values, way to focus on family and action for citizenship. (Janet Isaac.)

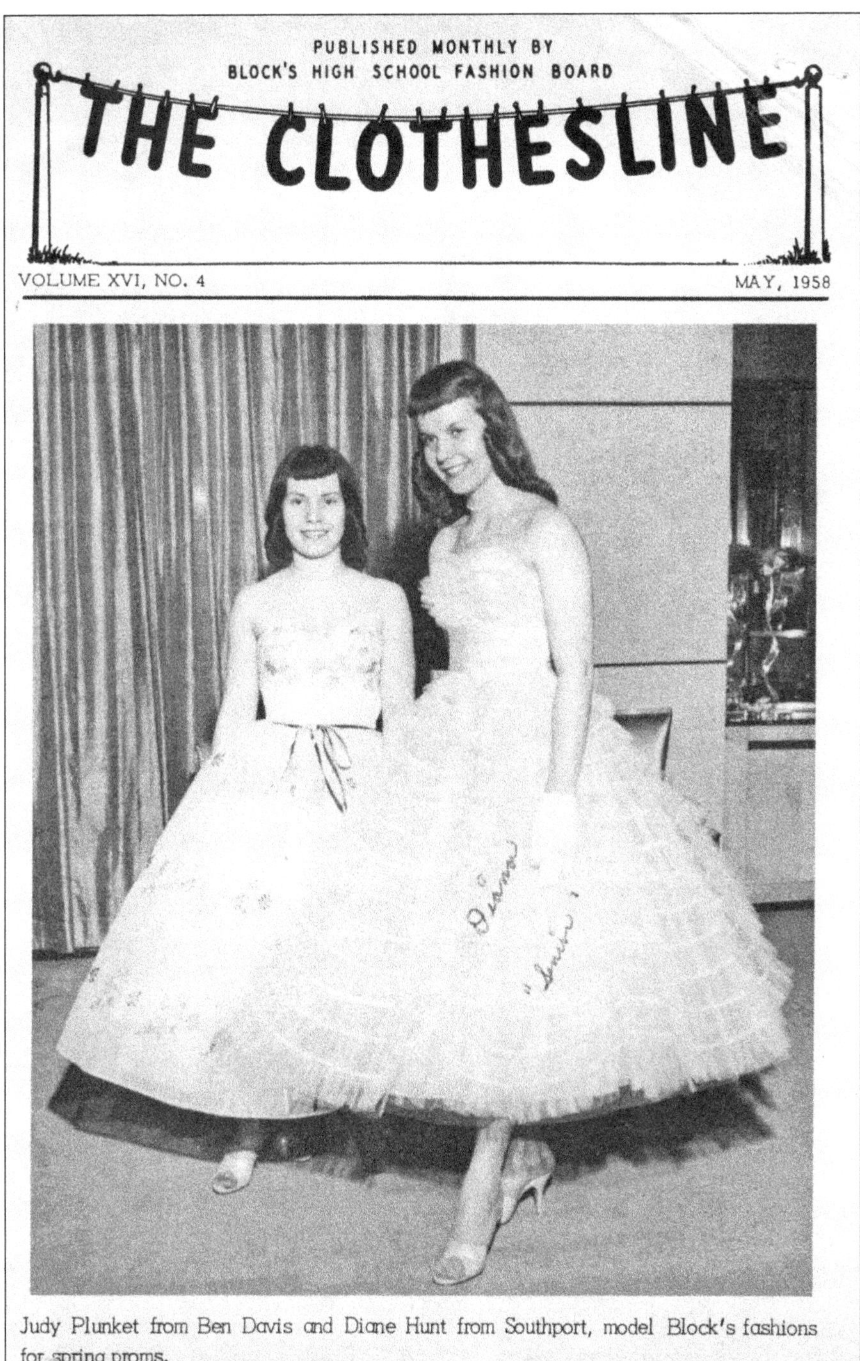

PUBLISHED MONTHLY BY
BLOCK'S HIGH SCHOOL FASHION BOARD

THE CLOTHESLINE

VOLUME XVI, NO. 4 MAY, 1958

Judy Plunket from Ben Davis and Diane Hunt from Southport, model Block's fashions for spring proms.

The Clothesline. Published several times locally throughout the year, *The Clothesline* was published by the Block's High School Fashion Board of the William H. Block Company department store chain in Indianapolis. The small magazine featured students at high schools around the area. On this cover, Southport High School student Diane Hunt (right) is pictured. Hunt, a member of the 1958 graduating class, was crowned the 500 festival queen for the year's Indianapolis 500. She remains the only Southport alumna to do so. (Janet Isaac.)

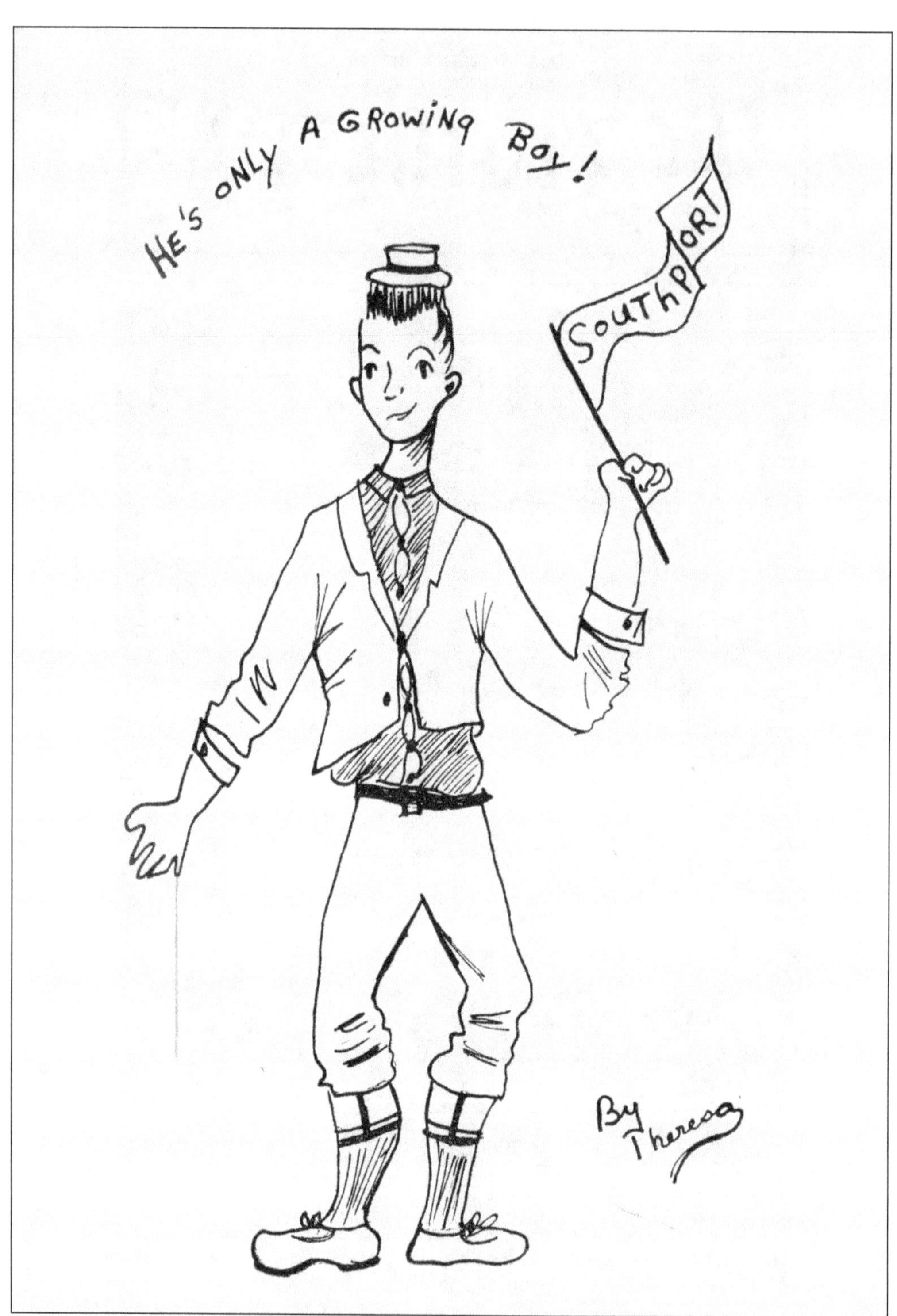

Southport Pride. This drawing comes from a 1958 Southport High School signpost. School pride shined beyond athletic events, and as enrollment continued to increase at Southport throughout the 1950s and 1960s, student enthusiasm and involvement increased as well. (Janet Isaac.)

PERSONNEL

Pat Shay	President
Marilyn Kottkamp	Vice-President
Sondra Turner	Sec.-Treas.
Dave Wegehoft	Sarg. at Arms
Edward Tenholder	Librarian
Sandra Mitchell	Ass't. Librarian

SOPRANO

ishop, Judy
lankenship, J.
rown, Florence
arpenter, T.
lrod, Judy
erking, C.
all, Delores
ottkamp, M.
ong, Jowana
cGinnis, E.
itchell, Sandra
ichols, Kathy
ark, Connie
ich, Melva
iegel, Sandra
oberts, Nancy
uscher, C.
hay, Pat
aylor, Rhonda
out, Judy
ygrett, Susan
an Winkle, Judy
illiams, Linda

ALTO

Bush, Beverly
Church, Marilyn
Cowden, Peggy
Eder, Judy
Fulford, Sandy
Graham, Sue
Hoss, Anita
Jackson, D.
Jackson, D.
Jackson, Linda
Jann, Sharon
King, Mozelle
Lane, Cherl
Lavengood, L.
McClure, Judy
Planker, J.
Turner, Sondra
Webb, Carolyn

TENOR

Boswell, Wm.
Burch, Joseph
Caywood, Ross
Gunn, Burton
Lee, Donald
Leser, Larry
Tenholder, Ed
Williams, Thos.

BASS

Benedict, Chas.
Clairborne, D.
Perry, Allan
Reed, Gary
Sparks, Edwin
Tracy, Wm.
Unversaw, J.
Wegehoft, D.

PIANO & ORGAN

Darnell, Judy

THE SOUTHPORT HIGH SCHOOL

CHOIR

Presents

THE CRUCIFIXION

by

John Stainer

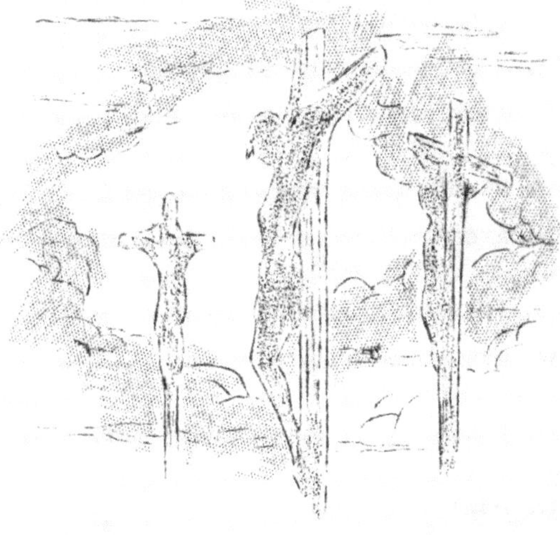

9:30 A. M. 7:45 P. M.

March 28, 1958

SHS Easter Service. For many years, Southport High School's choir would host special Easter performances. In 1958, this program was handed out to service attendees. Choir students performed a number of hymns, like "Jesus, the Crucified," and a total of 18 pieces were included in the program. (Janet Isaac.)

THE SOUTHPORT JOURNAL

VOLUME XXX NO. 1 SOUTHPORT, HIGH SCHOOL, INDIANAPOLIS, IND. OCTOBER 1, 1958

THE JOURNAL. Before it came to be known as the *Journal*, Southport High School's student newspaper was called the *Perry News*. The student publication first began publication in 1922. The *Journal*'s masthead, seen here, was first published under that name in the fall of 1958. This is the first edition of the paper under the new *Southport Journal* name. (Perry Township/Southport Historical Society.)

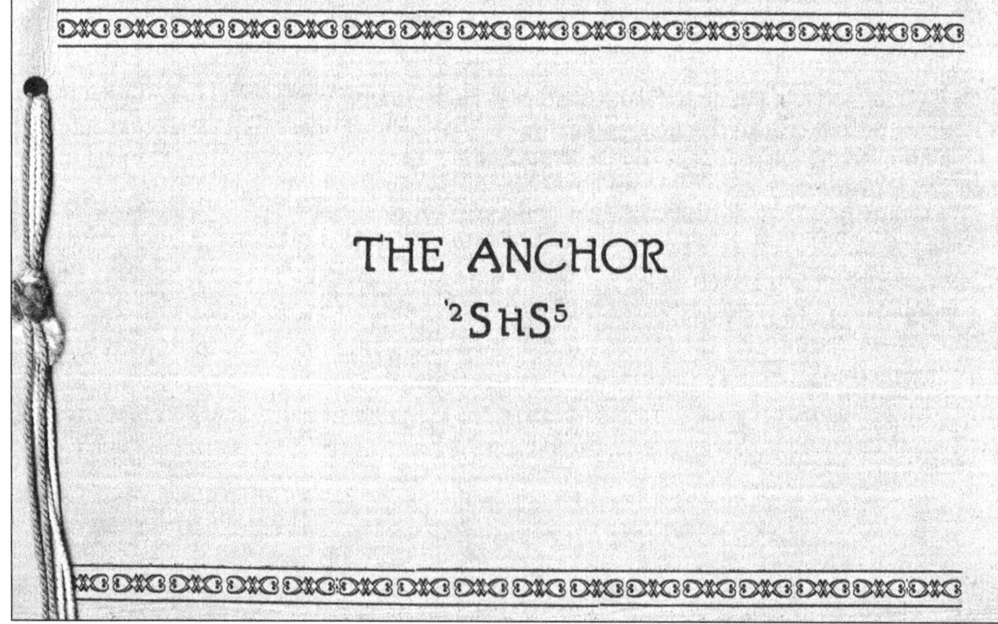

THE ANCHOR. Southport High School's yearbook, *The Anchor*, was first published for the 1924–1925 school year. The simple cover evolved and changed from year to year, and the publication continues to be produced by students at SHS today. (Perry Township/Southport Historical Society.)

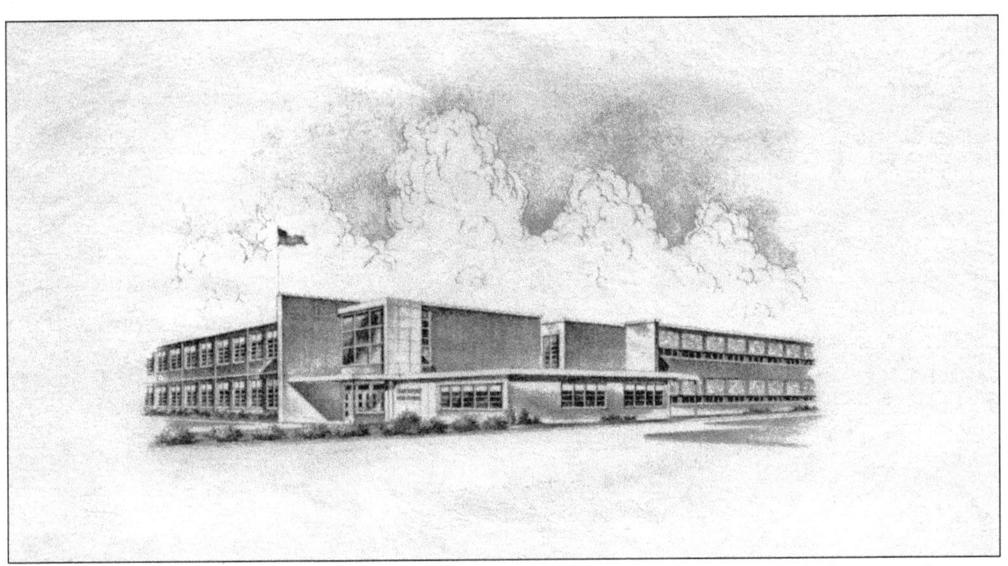

SOUTHPORT FACADE. This image of Southport High School was included on graduation announcements in the late 1950s and early 1960s. The school had recently been remodeled, and this image depicts the front entrance to the building after the construction changes were completed. (Perry Township/Southport Historical Society.)

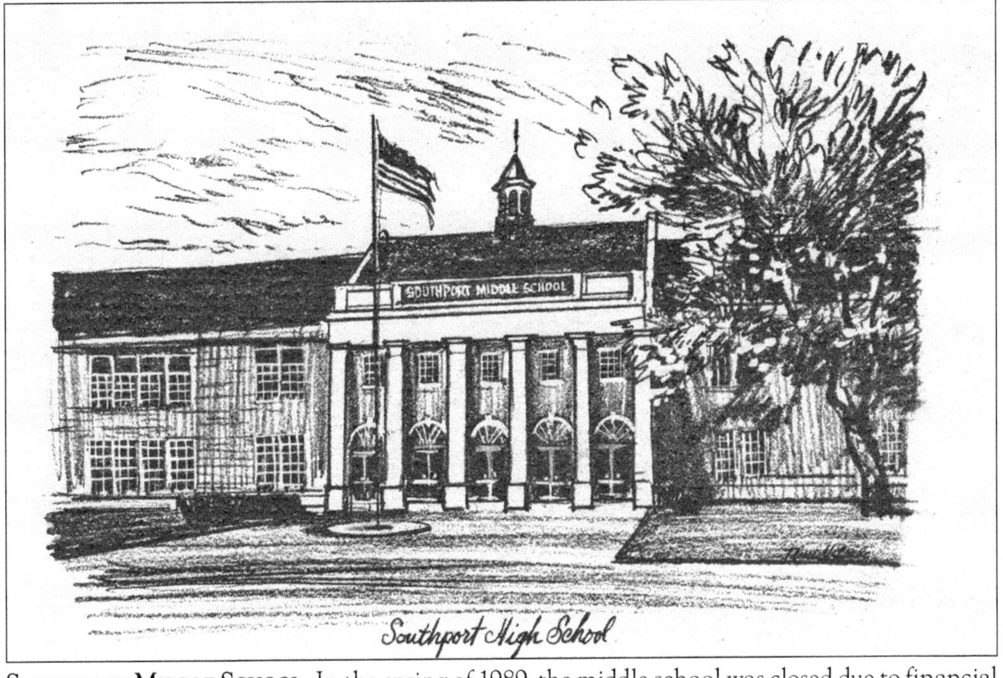

SOUTHPORT MIDDLE SCHOOL. In the spring of 1989, the middle school was closed due to financial problems and needs for repairs. Students in the Southport High School attendance area were redirected to Keystone Middle School on Keystone Avenue, which was later rename Southport Middle School. In 2001, the township school office moved from its longtime Epler Avenue location to this Orinoco location. During this process, the building underwent a number of changes, including demolition of the northwest wing that had been added in the early 1960s. (Perry Township/Southport Historical Society.)

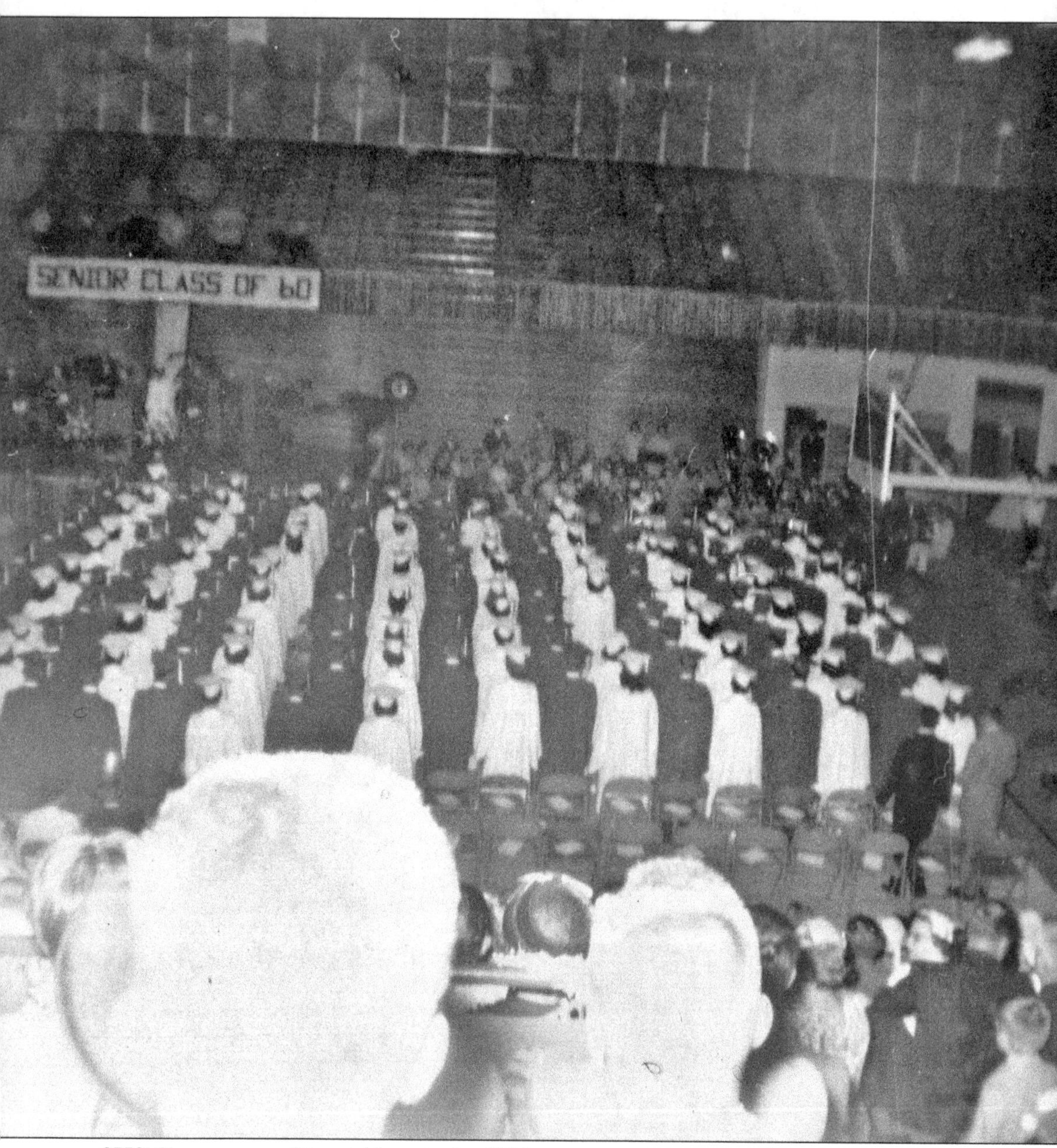

SHS GRADUATION. Pictured here is the 1960 commencement proceedings for Southport High School students. The 1960 class was only the second to have their graduation ceremonies in the newly constructed Southport Fieldhouse. Having started construction in 1957, the 7,290-seat field house was opened for the first time during the 1958–1959 school year. (Janet Isaac.)

Graduation Ceremony. Taking place in the field house, the 1960 graduating class was also the second class to graduate from the newest Southport High School building. The commencement program took place over the course of two days—June 5 and 6, with a special church service taking place on Sunday, June 5—and included music from the high school orchestra, a performance of "Ave Maria" by the school choir, a sermon by the reverend at Center Methodist Church, scripture reading, diploma presentations, and singing of the school song. (Janet Isaac.)

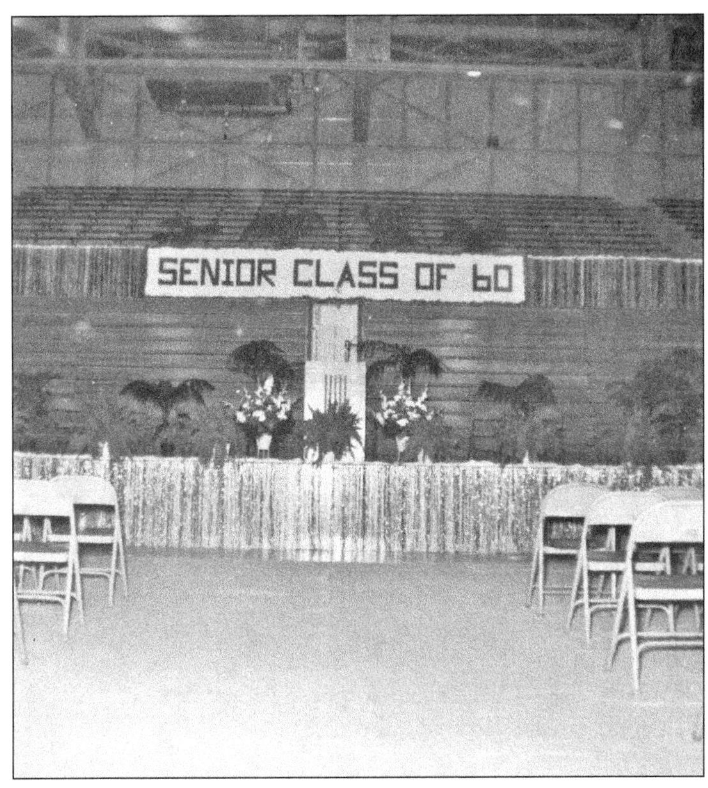

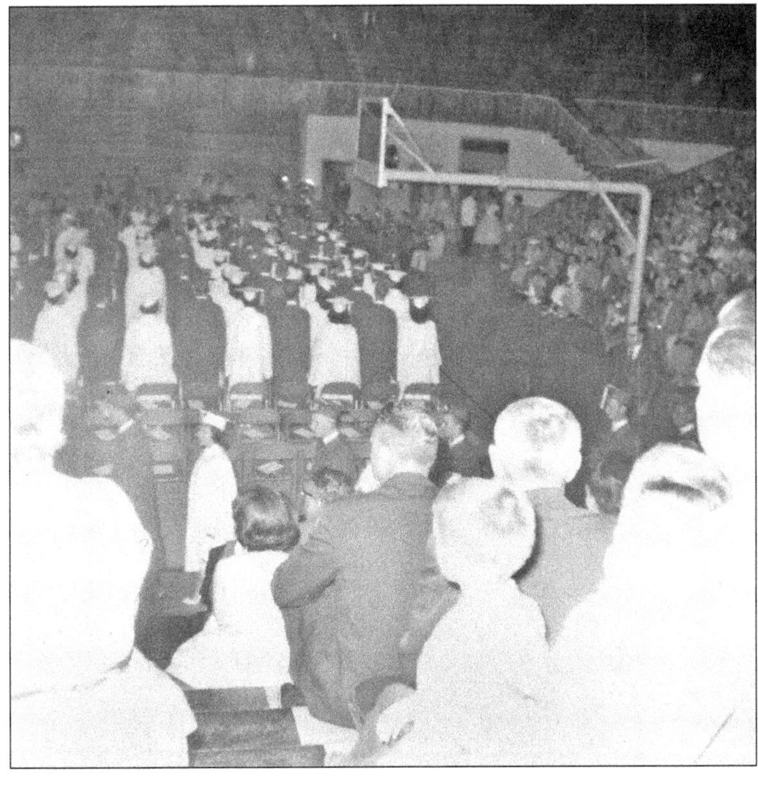

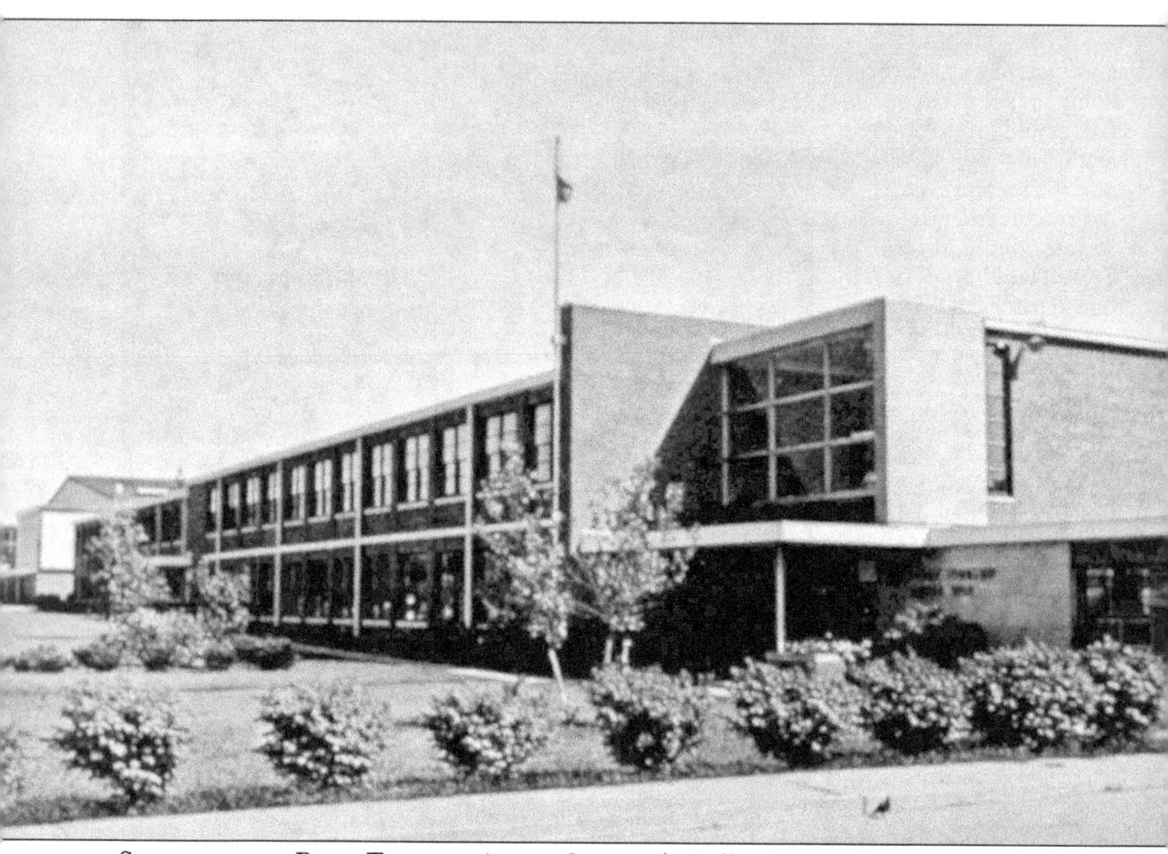

SOUTHPORT AND PERRY TOWNSHIP ADJUST. Increased enrollment, new construction projects and changes to curriculum took place at Southport and across Perry Township throughout the 1960s and 1970s. In 1973, the township opened a second high school, allowing more students to be educated in a suitable environment. For the 1981 school year, federally mandated court-ordered busing also began, and students and faculty in the township welcomed primarily African American students from north of the township. (Perry Township/Southport Historical Society.)

CONTRACT OF SALE

November 9 19 61

To HILL VALLEY DEVELOPMENT CORP.

We hereby agree to purchase from the owner through you as his agent the following described real estate

(See attached "Exhibit A" for description)

located in Marion County, Indiana. The purchase price of said real estate to be the sum of

--------Eighty Thousand --------- No/100 ----------- ($ 80,000.) Dollars

payable upon the following terms, viz ----Eighty Thousand ---No/100 --- ($ 80,000.) Dollars

which to be paid upon delivery of a General Warranty deed, the

Subject to the approval of an additional appropriation by the State Board of Tax Commissioners of Indiana for purchase of the above described property.

Subject to the approval of the Indiana State Superintendent of Public Instruction.

Subject to Seller installing city water to the property line of Purchaser, said water connection being that of the Indianapolis City Water Company, as shown on attached "Exhibit B".

Subject to Seller installing of adequate sewer to the Purchaser's property line, said sewer to be the part of the operation of a sanitation plant serving Seller's subdivisions, as shown on attached "Exhibit B".

Complete possession to be given on delivery of General Warranty Deed.

Rents and premiums of insurance to be prorated to

(we) will assume the taxes for the year 1962 payable in May, 1963, and/thereafter, and all assessments for municipal improvements completed after this date. Also

That (we are) to be furnished free of charge an original and complete merchantable abstract of title to date, said abstract to show a merchantable or insurable title to said real estate in the name of the grantors who will sign the deed conveying said real estate, free and clear of all liens and encumbrances except as stated herein. This transaction is to be closed within 30 days after a merchantable abstract showing good title or policy of title insurance is delivered and the Additional Appropriation has been approved by the State Board of Tax Commissioner of Indiana 18th day of Nov. , 19 61

It is also agreed that this purchase includes electrical, gas and water fixtures, window shades, linoleum, screens, awnings and shutters, together with all other appurtenances belonging to the above property that are on the premises or elsewhere.

It is expressly agreed that all terms and conditions are included herein and that no verbal agreements of any kind shall be binding or recognized.

(we) deposit herewith One Dollar ($ 1.00) as earnest money to apply upon the cash payment

PERRY MERIDIAN LAND AGREEMENT, 1962. In 1961, the Perry Township School Board decided to build a second high school in Perry Township. A combination of baby-boomer births and suburban migration made Southport High School unable to accommodate their burgeoning enrollment. The new high school would be named Perry Meridian High School (PMHS), located at 401 West Meridian School Road, and the attendance boundaries for this new school would cover the western part of Perry Township. Before building began, the township purchased the land for which to build the school for $80,000. (The Perry Meridian Alumni Association.)

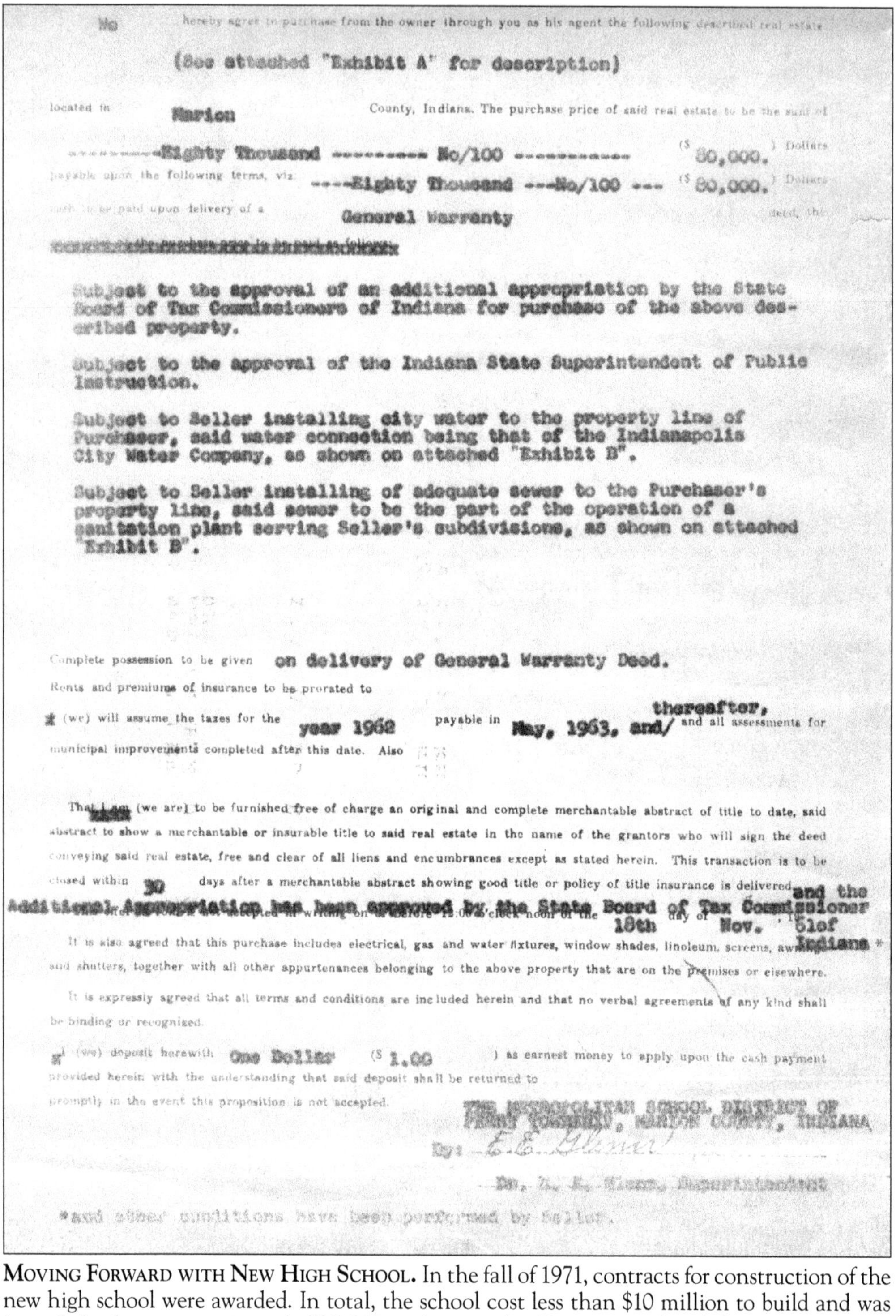

We hereby agree to purchase from the owner through you as his agent the following described real estate

(See attached "Exhibit A" for description)

located in Marion County, Indiana. The purchase price of said real estate to be the sum of

--------Eighty Thousand --------- No/100 ----------- ($ 80,000.) Dollars

payable upon the following terms, viz: ----Eighty Thousand ---No/100 --- ($ 80,000.) Dollars

cash to be paid upon delivery of a General Warranty deed, the

~~balance of the purchase price to be paid as follows:~~

Subject to the approval of an additional appropriation by the State Board of Tax Commissioners of Indiana for purchase of the above described property.

Subject to the approval of the Indiana State Superintendent of Public Instruction.

Subject to Seller installing city water to the property line of Purchaser, said water connection being that of the Indianapolis City Water Company, as shown on attached "Exhibit B".

Subject to Seller installing of adequate sewer to the Purchaser's property line, said sewer to be the part of the operation of a sanitation plant serving Seller's subdivisions, as shown on attached "Exhibit B".

Complete possession to be given on delivery of General Warranty Deed.

Rents and premiums of insurance to be prorated to

~~I~~ (we) will assume the taxes for the year 1962 payable in May, 1963, and/thereafter, and all assessments for municipal improvements completed after this date. Also

That ~~I am~~ (we are) to be furnished free of charge an original and complete merchantable abstract of title to date, said abstract to show a merchantable or insurable title to said real estate in the name of the grantors who will sign the deed conveying said real estate, free and clear of all liens and encumbrances except as stated herein. This transaction is to be closed within 30 days after a merchantable abstract showing good title or policy of title insurance is delivered and the Additional Appropriation has been approved by the State Board of Tax Commissioner of Indiana * ~~This offer to be accepted in writing on or before 12:00 o'clock noon of the~~ 18th day of Nov., 1961

It is also agreed that this purchase includes electrical, gas and water fixtures, window shades, linoleum, screens, awnings and shutters, together with all other appurtenances belonging to the above property that are on the premises or elsewhere.

It is expressly agreed that all terms and conditions are included herein and that no verbal agreements of any kind shall be binding or recognized.

~~I~~ (we) deposit herewith One Dollar ($ 1.00) as earnest money to apply upon the cash payment provided herein with the understanding that said deposit shall be returned to promptly in the event this proposition is not accepted.

THE METROPOLITAN SCHOOL DISTRICT OF PERRY TOWNSHIP, MARION COUNTY, INDIANA

By: E. E. Glenn

Dr. [illegible], Superintendent

*and other conditions have been performed by Seller.

Moving Forward with New High School. In the fall of 1971, contracts for construction of the new high school were awarded. In total, the school cost less than $10 million to build and was intended to have a capacity to hold 3,000 students in the 60-acre complex. (The Perry Meridian Alumni Association.)

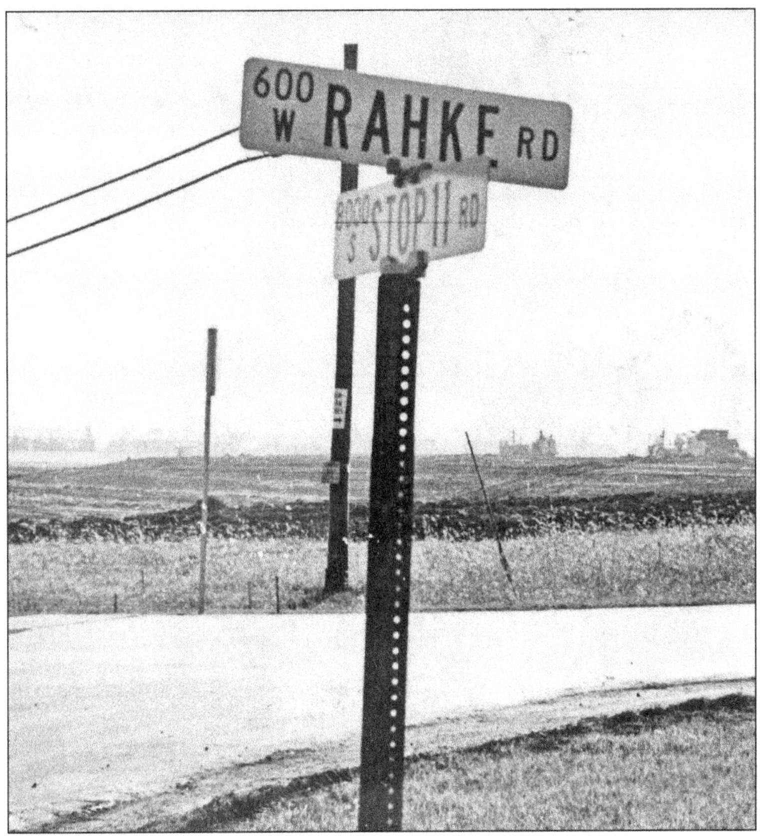

Before Perry Meridian. Before PMHS construction began, the area was undeveloped and consisted only of one old farm road—Rahke Road, seen here. As construction continued for the school (Perry Meridian Middle School would follow several years later across the street), Rahke Road remained and soon served as an area for homes to be built. (The Perry Meridian Alumni Association.)

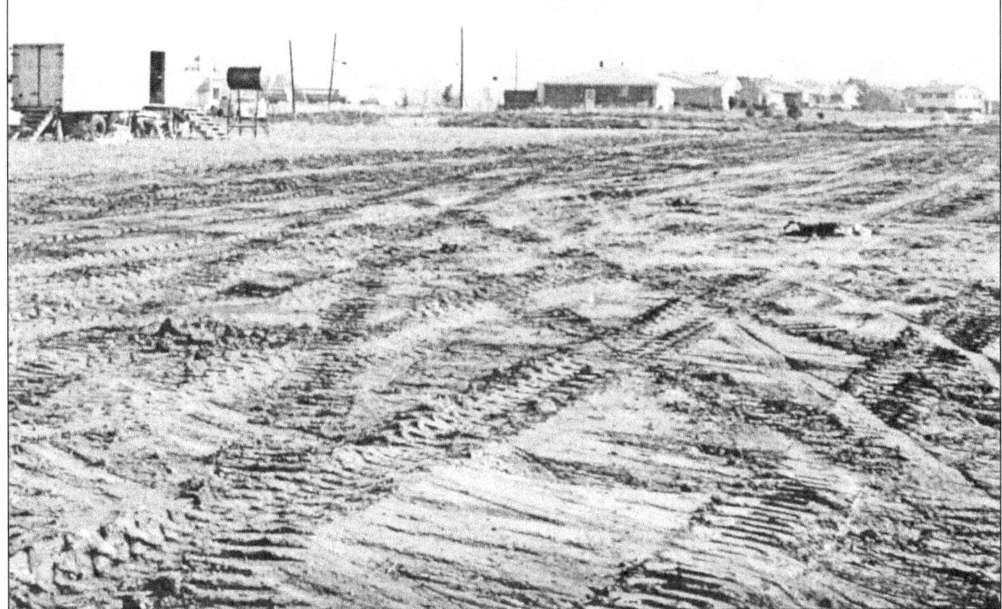

Building Perry Meridian. Ground preparation for the Perry Meridian High School can be seen in this image. PMHS was built on the site of a former field, and a construction trailer and houses are visible in the background. (The Perry Meridian Alumni Association.)

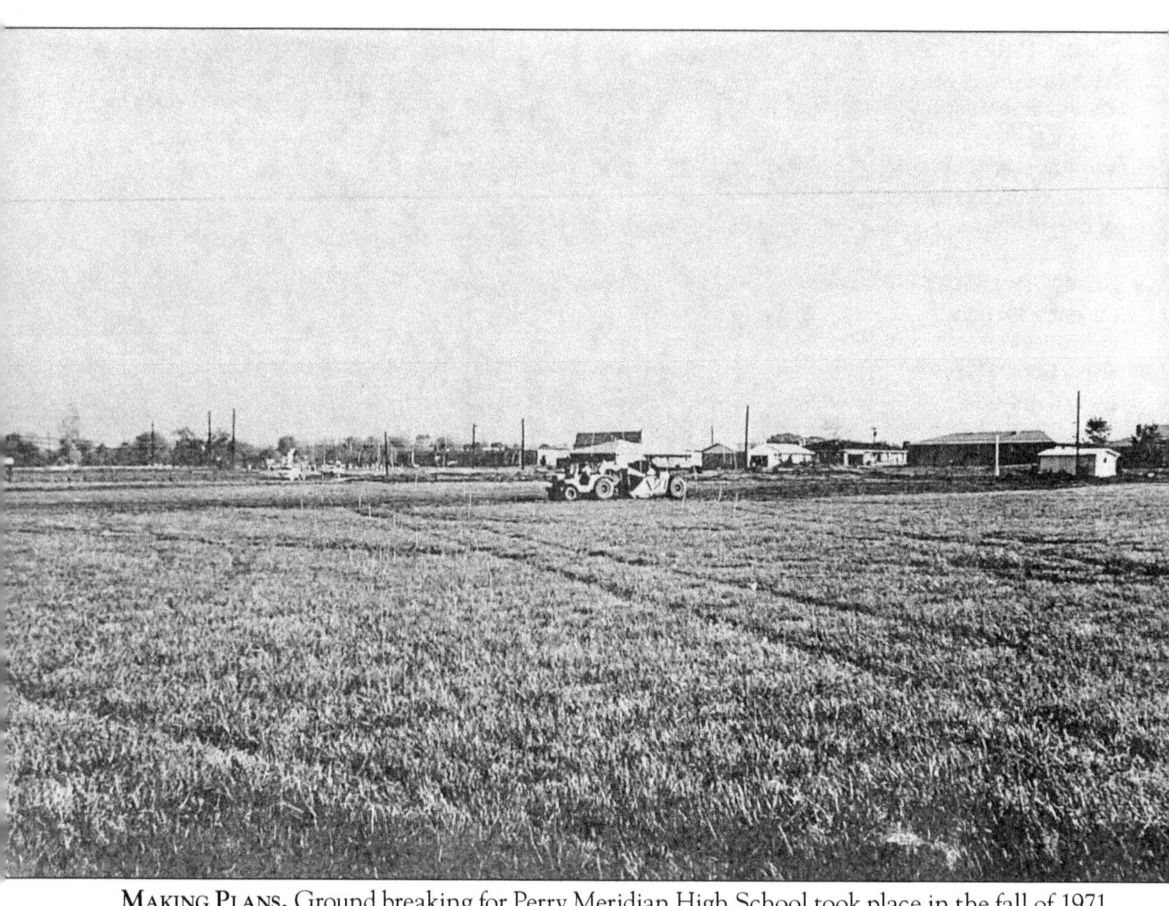

Making Plans. Ground breaking for Perry Meridian High School took place in the fall of 1971. The building plans included a 4,000-seat gymnasium, a swimming pool, and an auditorium. When Perry Meridian officially opened, students and teachers came from Southport High School, which had previously been the only high school in Perry Township. However, Perry Meridian only enrolled grades nine through eleven during its first year. (The Perry Meridian Alumni Association.)

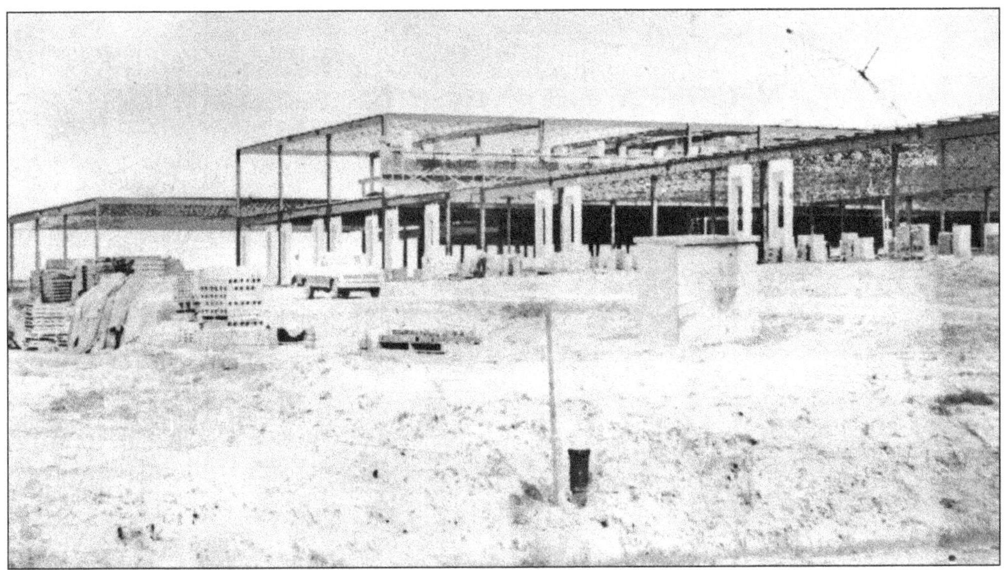

Construction Continues. PMHS construction continued into August 1973 when classes began. Although plans to build a skating rink at the school were discussed, it was not constructed at PMHS. Several years later, however, Perry Township and the Department of Parks and Recreation worked together to plan, build and open Perry Park, a few blocks down the street from the high school. (The Perry Meridian Alumni Association.)

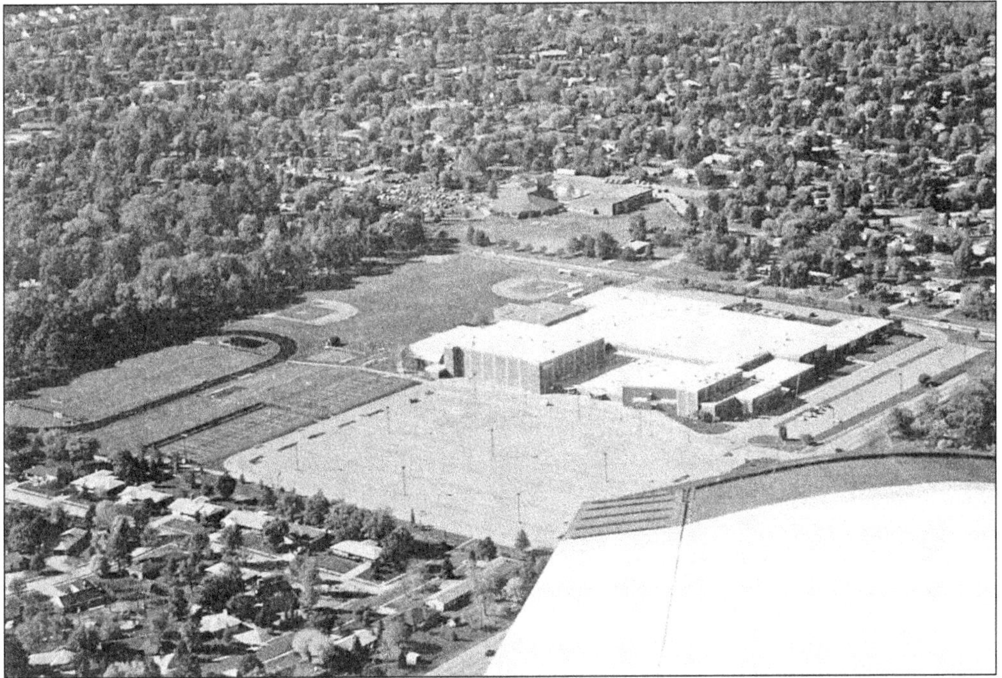

Perry Meridian Complete. This photograph depicts the newly built Perry Meridian High School in 1973. This image shows the northeast side of the school. In addition to the building complete, new teachers, faculty, and athletic staff. Sports teams, including football, basketball, baseball, tennis, golf, and gymnastics were available to students entering PMHS that fall. (The Perry Meridian Alumni Association.)

First newspaper 1973

PM opening day spells adjustment

Perry Meridian High School opened for the first time Monday, August 27. The new building is practically finished with approximately 2000 students attending.

Despite the problems of being a first year school, PM students and faculty show a remarkable ability to adjust, and now most things seem to be running very smoothly.

When asked about the difference between P M and other county schools, Mr. James Head, principal, replied, "We have more of a built-in flexibility because of the portable dividers in the English, math, and social studies areas. Because of this we should be able to have a program of cooperative study and team teaching."

The student body consists of approximately 600 juniors, 720 sophomores, and 710 freshmen. There are 88 teachers.

Mr. Robert Dunn, assistant principal, said the balancing and equalization of classes is completed.

The Guidance department is developing a program involving all students. The two counselors for each grade make sure each student works up to his potential and has the required credits for graduation.

Summing up faculty comments, Miss Patricia Maloof, counselor, said, "School spirit is coming right along. The faculty has been very enthusiastic and cooperative."

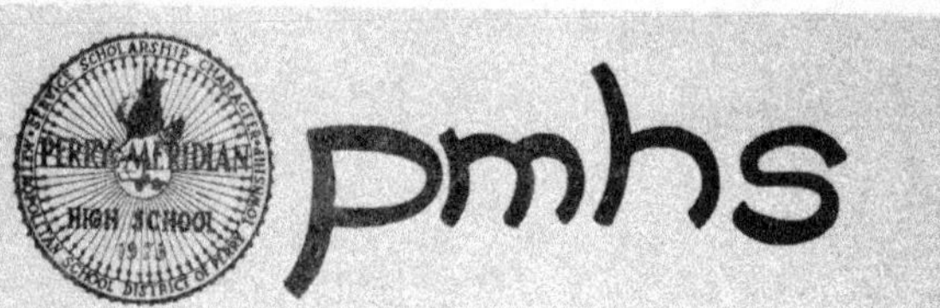

Community Crier

BY

MR. HAL COLE, ASSISTANT PRINCIPAL

We are in a unique position in being the group of people helping to start a new high school in Perry Township. This column's purpose is to provide information of developments and programs to parents of Perry Meridian HighSchool (PMHS) students.

School opened as scheduled and the whole facility with the exception of the gymnasium, auditorium, and planetarium is being used.

Sponsors are organizing and students selecting clubs that interest them. The first student council is being formed starting with the selection of homeroom representatives. Nominees for various council offices have been conducting their campaigns.

The Instructional Materials Center is open and has approximately 14,000 volumes and audio-visual materials. The IMC staff is aided by PTA mothers who donate three hours per week in the center from 9-12 p.m. or 12-3 p.m. Any interested mother may call Mrs. Penoff at 786-5932.

In future columns, we will concentrate on specific areas. In this way you will learn more about PM's total program. This is an exciting time in working with the first class at PMHS.

Nameless newspaper needs PM lobster lover

Picture you and a friend dining by candlelight at Pete Steffey's. . . a lobster dinner for two can be yours by winning Perry Meridian's "Name the Newspaper Contest".

The entire student body is eligible for the contest sponsored by the newspaper staff. A student may submit as many entries as he wishes.

To enter, fill out the accompanying coupon and take it to room 208. Hurry, as the contest ends September 21.

A screening committee of Mr. James Head, principal, Mrs. Frances Huff, English department chairman, and Miss Linda Wright, newspaper advisor, will select approximately 20 entries.

The newspaper staff will determine the winner, to be announced by Mr. Head during homeroom Wednesday, September 26.

STUDENT NAME ____________________

HOMEROOM ____________ CLASS __________

NEWSPAPER ENTRY ____________________

THE FIRST DAY. The Perry Township School Board opened Perry Meridian High School on August 27, 1973. James Head, then the assistant principal at Southport, was named principal of the new Perry Meridian. Southport students were allowed to pick the school colors (navy blue, powder blue and silver) and mascot (the falcon) for Perry during the 1972–1973 school year before PMHS opened its doors. When the school first opened, only freshman, sophomore, and juniors were enrolled. (The Perry Meridian Alumni Association.)

PERRY MERIDIAN'S FIRST COMMENCEMENT. The first PMHS commencement took place in the spring of 1975. More than 300 students were conferred degrees, and the ceremony took place in the school's new gymnasium. (The Perry Meridian Alumni Association.)

COMMENCEMENT

of

PERRY MERIDIAN
HIGH SCHOOL

MSD PERRY TOWNSHIP

INDIANAPOLIS, IN

HIGH SCHOOL GYMNASIUM

Saturday, May Twenty-Fourth
Nineteen Hundred Seventy-Five

Eight O'Clock

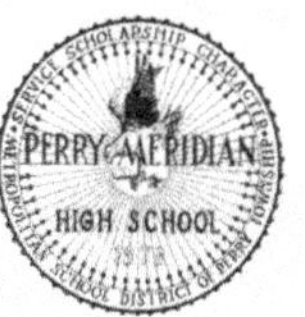

BOARD OF EDUCATION

Robert L. Bush, President
James R. Stainbrook, Vice-President
Roy R. Carpenter, Secretary
Kenneth G. Wheeler, Member
James L. Davis, Member

DR. FRANK W. HUNTER
SUPERINTENDENT

MR. JAMES E. HEAD
PRINCIPAL

THE COMMENCEMENT PROGRAM. The ceremony included music from the school's symphonic band and the reading of Psalm 67. (The Perry Meridian Alumni Association.)

COMMENCEMENT
PROGRAM

Processional - "Pomp and Circumstance"........................Edward Elgar
Symphonic Band
(Directed by MR. ROY GEESA)

Flag Salute - Senior Class - Lead by ANN E. HETTLE, *Class Secretary*
(Audience Remain Standing)

"Star-Spangled Banner" (Sung by All Present).............Francis Scott Key
Symphonic Band

Invocation....................................THE REVEREND ALDA I. CARTER
Edgewood United Methodist Church

Introductions................................MR. JAMES E. HEAD, *Principal*

Welcome................................ROBERT W. WILLSEY, *Class President*

"Psalm 67"..John Ness Beck
A Capella Choir
(Directed by MR.GUY H. RUMSEY)

"Battle Hymn of the Republic"...............................James Ployhar
Symphonic Band

"We've Only Just Begun"................................arr. Harry Simeone
Senior Choir

"A First Rate Something".................MARK E.LEWIS, *Class Valedictorian*

Presentation of Scholarships, Awards..........MR. JAMES E. HEAD, *Principal*

Presentation of Diplomas..................DR. FRANK HUNTER, *Superintendent*
(Assisted by DAVID ALAN HAGER, *Class Vice-President*,
and ROBERT L. BUSH, *School Board President*)

Changing of Tassel......................ROBERT W. WILLSEY, *Class President*

Benediction...................................THE REVEREND ALDA I. CARTER
Edgewood United Methodist Church

Recessional - "Pomp and Circumstance".........................Edward Elgar
Symphonic Band
(Audience Remain Seated)

Gold Tassels worn by top ten percent of Senior Class

Departmental Awards

Art
William F. Stumpf

Business
Sharon D. Daniels

English
Karen McKeehan

Language
Linda K.Johnson

Physical Education
Robin L. Nicoloff

Home Economics
Jill A. Hueber

Mathematics
Manfred P. Mueller

Science
Joseph H. Yeager, Jr.

Industrial Arts
John Alan Corbin

Music
Debra Ruth Humes

Social Studies
Joseph H. Yeager, Jr.

Scholarships and Financial Aids

Butler University
Brenda Brethauer

DePauw University
Jane Ann Judkins
Honor Scholarship
William W. Mills

Indiana Central College
James Romack

Indiana Vocational Technical College
Marilee Clifford

Lincoln Technical Institute
Thomas B. Kraeszig

Miami University of Ohio
Linda K. Johnson

Millikin University
Michael K. Tomey

Purdue University
Jerry D. Andrews
Cynthia L. Mason
Sara Ann Orme
Mark L. Shunk
David C. Best
R.O.T.C. Navy Scholarship

United States Air Force Academy
James A. Flickinger

University of Evansville
Nancy Ann Croker
Presidential Scholarship

Wabash College
Joseph M. Overhage
Lilly Award
Norman Clay Robbins
Lilly Award

Wake Forest University
Karen McKeehan

West Point Academy
David L. Feeney

Special Scholarships and Awards

Betty Crocker State Contest
Nancy Jean Johnson
Honorable Mention

Indianapolis News Scholarship
Norman Clay Robbins

Central Newspaper Foundation Scholarship
Jane Ann Judkins

Ryan Homes Scholarship
Michael W. Schuessler

Junior Achievement Awards
Donna Lee Jennings
Data Processing
Cheryl J. Rayback
Chamber of Commerce

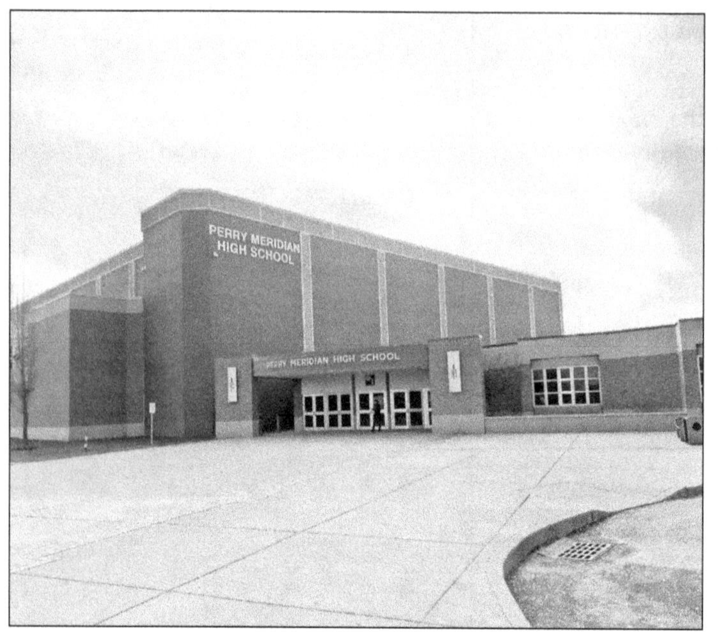

Perry Meridian Today. PMHS stands today at the same 401 West Meridian School Road location. Major additions and renovations were made to PMHS from 1999 to 2001 and again from 2011 to 2012. Across the street is Perry Meridian Middle School—formerly known as Meridian Middle School—which opened its doors in the fall of 1970. Today, the two schools now serve more than 2,500 students on the west side of Perry Township. (Photograph by Casey Smith.)

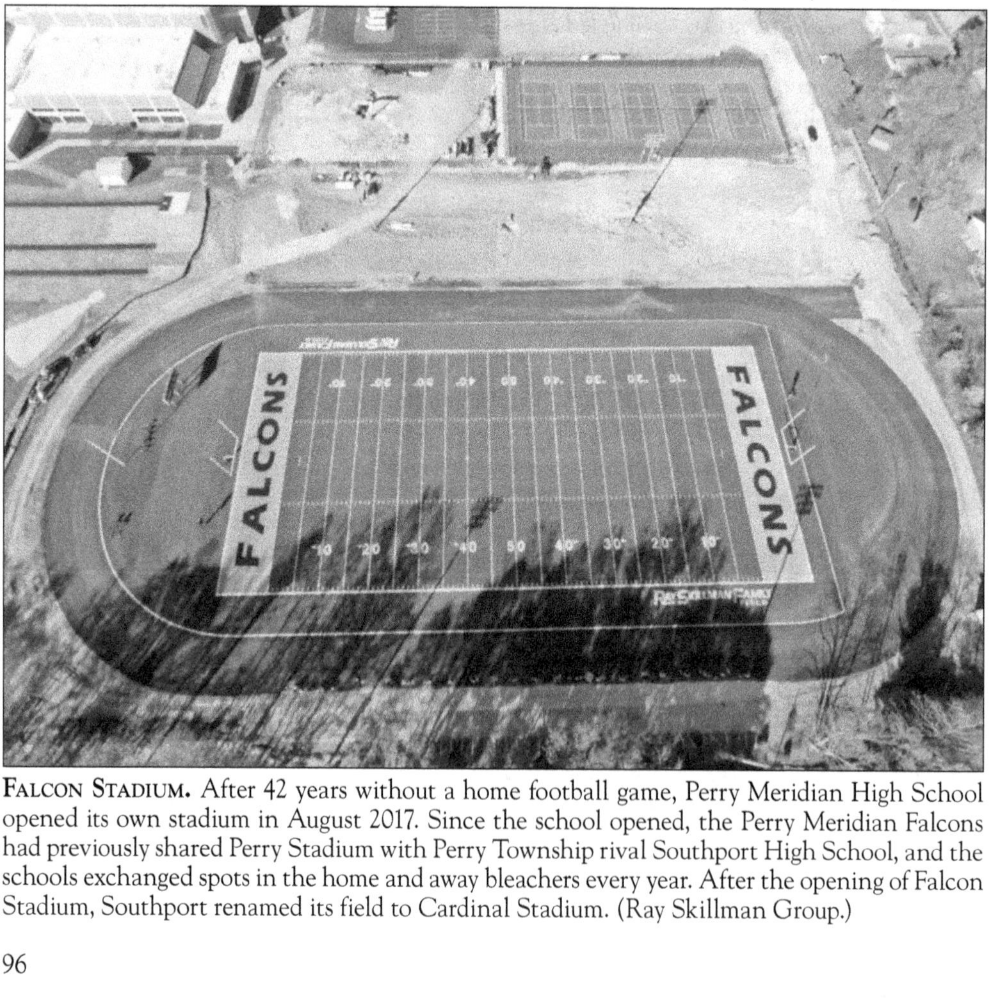

Falcon Stadium. After 42 years without a home football game, Perry Meridian High School opened its own stadium in August 2017. Since the school opened, the Perry Meridian Falcons had previously shared Perry Stadium with Perry Township rival Southport High School, and the schools exchanged spots in the home and away bleachers every year. After the opening of Falcon Stadium, Southport renamed its field to Cardinal Stadium. (Ray Skillman Group.)

Five

Life and Recreation

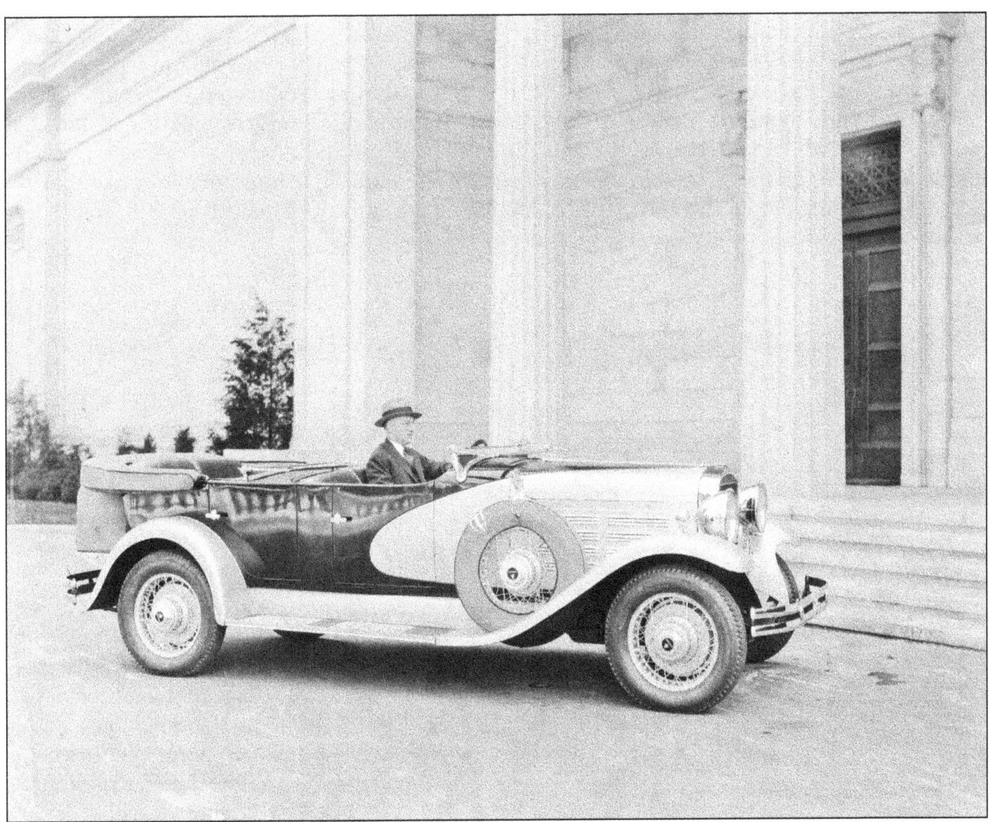

CRUISING AROUND. An unidentified man is captured in this photograph in Perry Township. (the car pictured is most likely a Jordan Speedboy.) Indianapolis's impressive Interurban Railways gave the city the name "the Interurban Capital of the World," and combined with the intersection of numerous locomotive railroads and interstate highways, it also became known as "the Crossroads of America." (Perry Township/Southport Historical Society.)

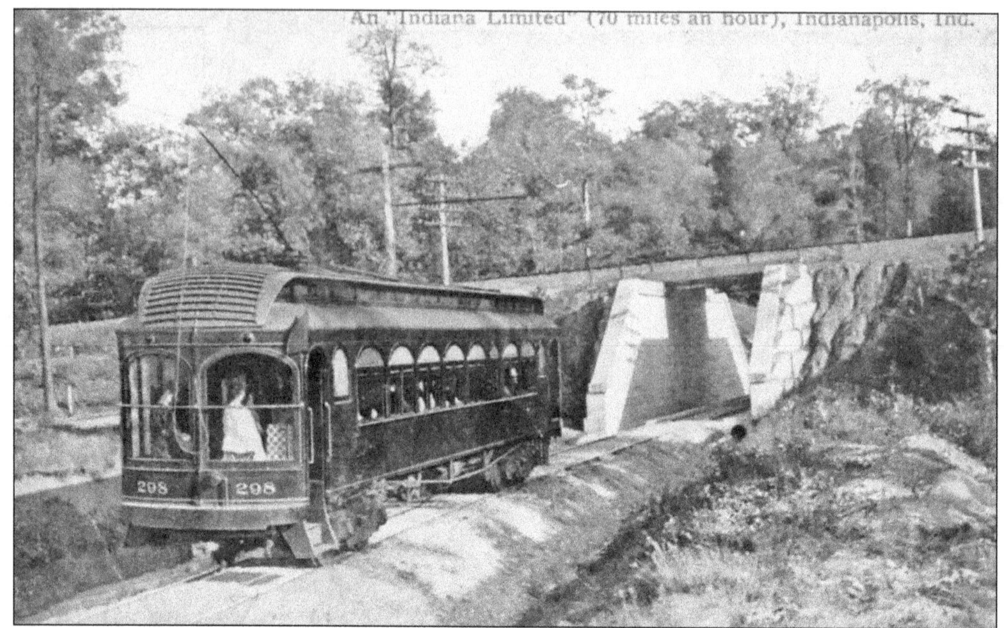

Downtown and Back. Interurbans were like city streetcars, but they traveled from city to city along dedicated tracks—single-car electric trains powered by electricity and tethered to power lines running just above the track. They first appeared around 1900 and grew rapidly. Indianapolis was the hub of all the interurban lines in the state, and the Indianapolis Terminal Traction station was the largest of its kind in the nation and in the world. The interurban car, like the one pictured here, frequented the Perry Township area in the early 20th century. (Perry Township/Southport Historical Society.)

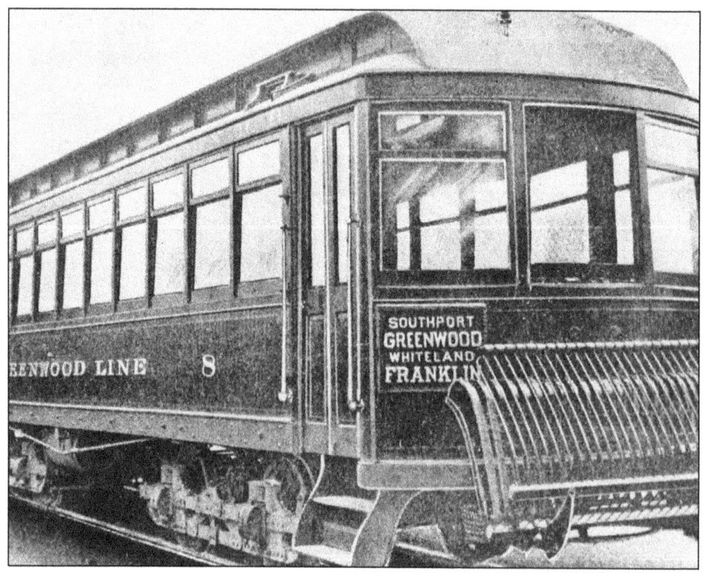

The Interurban. The Greenwood Line Interurban, pictured here, traveled between Southport and Franklin. Today, scattered remnants of the interurban system remain around Perry Township. Some of the stations still stand but have long since been repurposed. Street names like Stop 11 Road—which this car would stop at—were so named because they were interurban stops. (Perry Township/Southport Historical Society.)

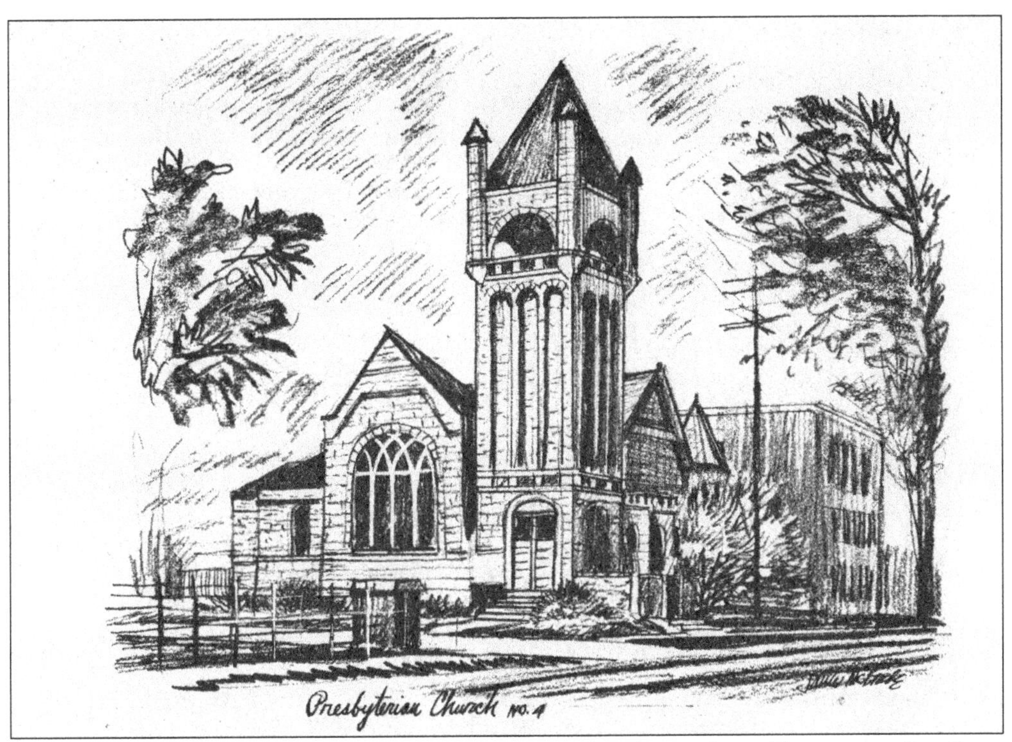

PRESBYTERIAN CHURCH. The Southport Presbyterian Church was planted by minister Rev. Isaac Reed in the log cabin of John B. Smock, located at what is now the intersection of Madison Avenue and County Line Road, where Greenwood Park Mall now sits. In this cabin, on December 31, 1825, Reverend Reed constituted the Greenfield Church, the first Presbyterian church to exist in the wilderness area south of Indianapolis. (In the early 1800s, the Greenwood area was known as Greenfield.) Nine persons made up the congregation. In 1831, the Presbytery divided the Greenfield church into two congregations—one to serve Southport, the other to serve the Greenwood area. In Southport, the church was located at the southwest corner of Southport Road and Church Street. The building was replaced in 1956 by a new one on Southview Drive, and in 1997 the church moved to its current location on McFarland Boulevard. (Perry Township/ Southport Historical Society.)

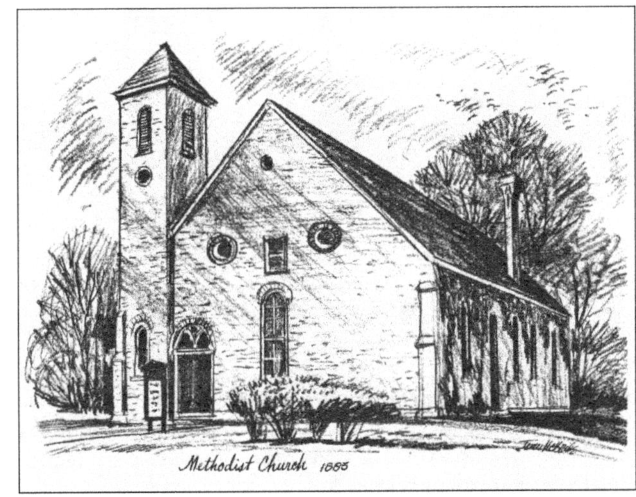

METHODIST CHURCH. The Southport Methodist Church, depicted here, was located on Union Street (now Southport Road) from 1883 to 1972. Today, the United Methodist Church of Southport sits in this location. Plans were also made here in 1965 to construct another Methodist church in Perry Township—now known as Christ United Methodist Church—on the southwest corner of US Route 31 South and Stop 12 Road. (Perry Township/ Southport Historical Society.)

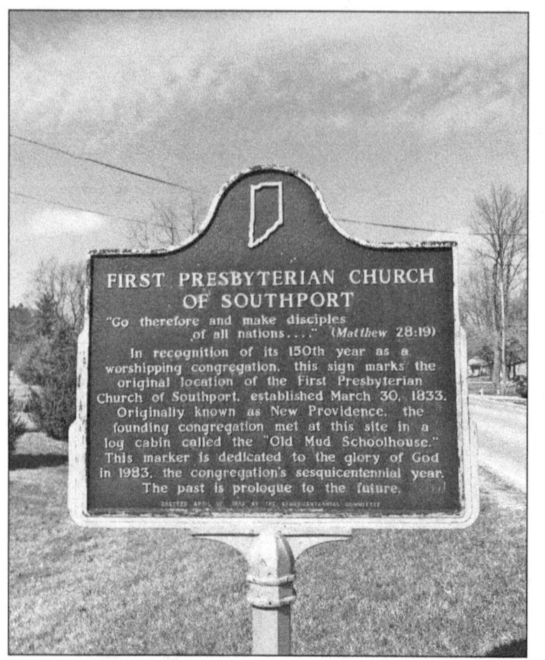

HEADED TO CHURCH. In 1833, the Southport Presbyterian Church congregation began worshiping in a school building, known as the "Old Mud Schoolhouse," which stood on the corner of Banta and McFarland Roads (near where this historical marker now stands). Later, the church relocated to a log building on the northeast corner of Madison Avenue and Union Street, which is now Southport Road. This sanctuary was succeeded by two on the south side of Union Street east of the railroad at the corner of Church Street. By 1956, the congregation had outgrown the facilities there and moved to a new church at 1427 Southview Drive in Homecroft. In 1997, the congregation began worshiping in the new church, in its present-day location, near the intersection of Stop 11 Road and McFarland Boulevard. (Southport Presbyterian Church.)

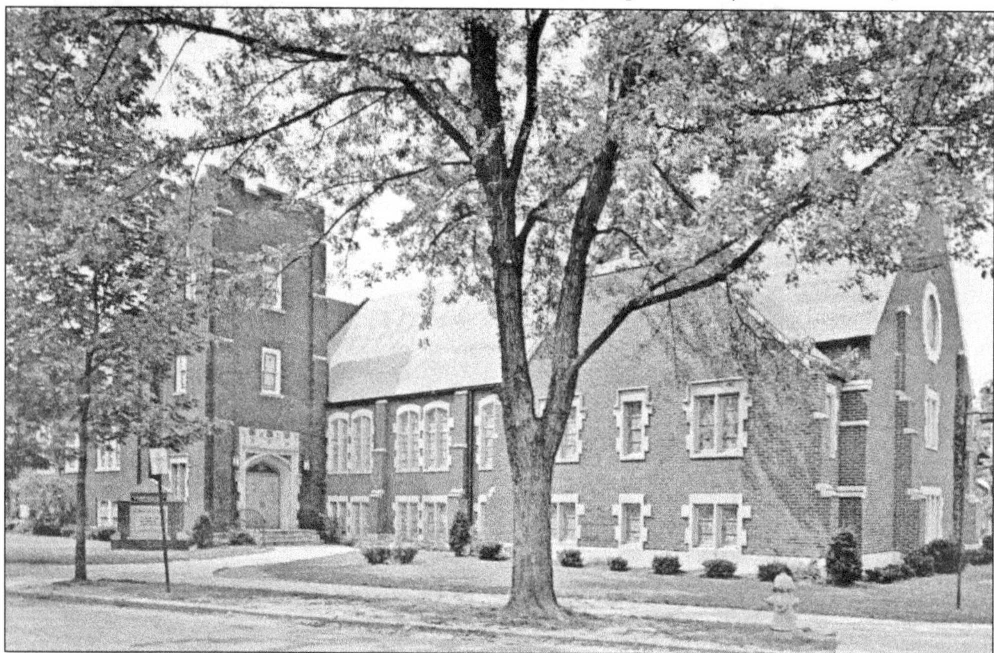

UNIVERSITY HEIGHTS. The University Heights neighborhood is surrounded by Hanna Avenue to the north, Lawrence Avenue to the south, Keystone Avenue to east, and Shelby Street to the west. The area first began as a business deal between the Church of the Brethren and Indianapolis realtor William Elder In 1902, Elder offered to donate eight acres for a church-affiliated university and to construct a campus building if church members would buy lots in his nearby Madison heights subdivision. The agreement came to fruition in 1904, and the first Indiana Central University building was constructed, now known as the University of Indianapolis. (Perry Township/ Southport Historical Society.)

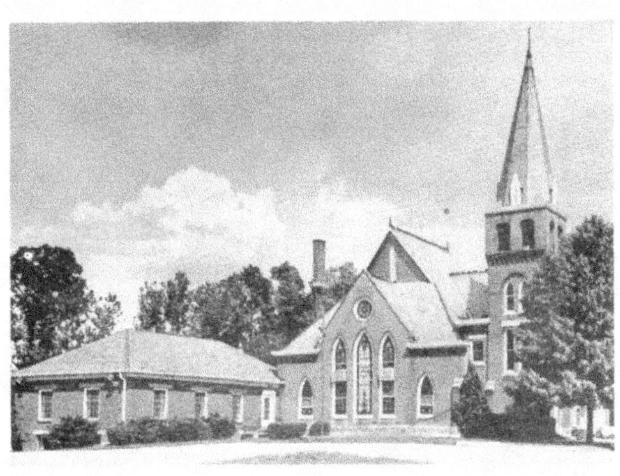

Southport Baptist Church

SOUTHPORT, INDIANA

REV. R. H. LINDSTROM, Pastor
MR. BILL SCHMALFELDT, Director of Music
MISS EVELYN CARPENTER, Organist

1929 - Anniversary Services - 1954

HONORING REV. and MRS. R. H. LINDSTROM
For 25 years of Fruitful Service
in the Pastorate of the Church

SUNDAY - OCTOBER 3, 1954

SOUTHPORT BAPTIST CHURCH. In 1822, a young pioneer from Kentucky named Jeremiah Featherston migrated to Indiana and moved close to the town of Southport, where he lived until he died. Upon moving to Southport, he bought 160 acres of land from the federal government, sold half of it, and with the remaining 80, he built a log cabin. He began having friends and neighbors over to hold small prayer services, and they eventually began to call it "Little Buck Creek Church." People from all over the area would attend the services. In May 1832, it was decided that the congregation had outgrown the setting, and they sought after a new home for their church. They eventually settled on 80 acres of land that belonged to Jacob Smock. There, they built a similar log cabin, but it was devoted entirely to the church. In 1858, the Little Buck Creek Church was officially renamed the Southport Baptist Church. By 1896, the church required another relocation to an even larger setting. A new church was built at the southwest corner of McFarland and Banta Roads and remained the official Southport Baptist Church until 1962, when the church that is still there today was erected and dedicated. (Perry Township/Southport Historical Society.)

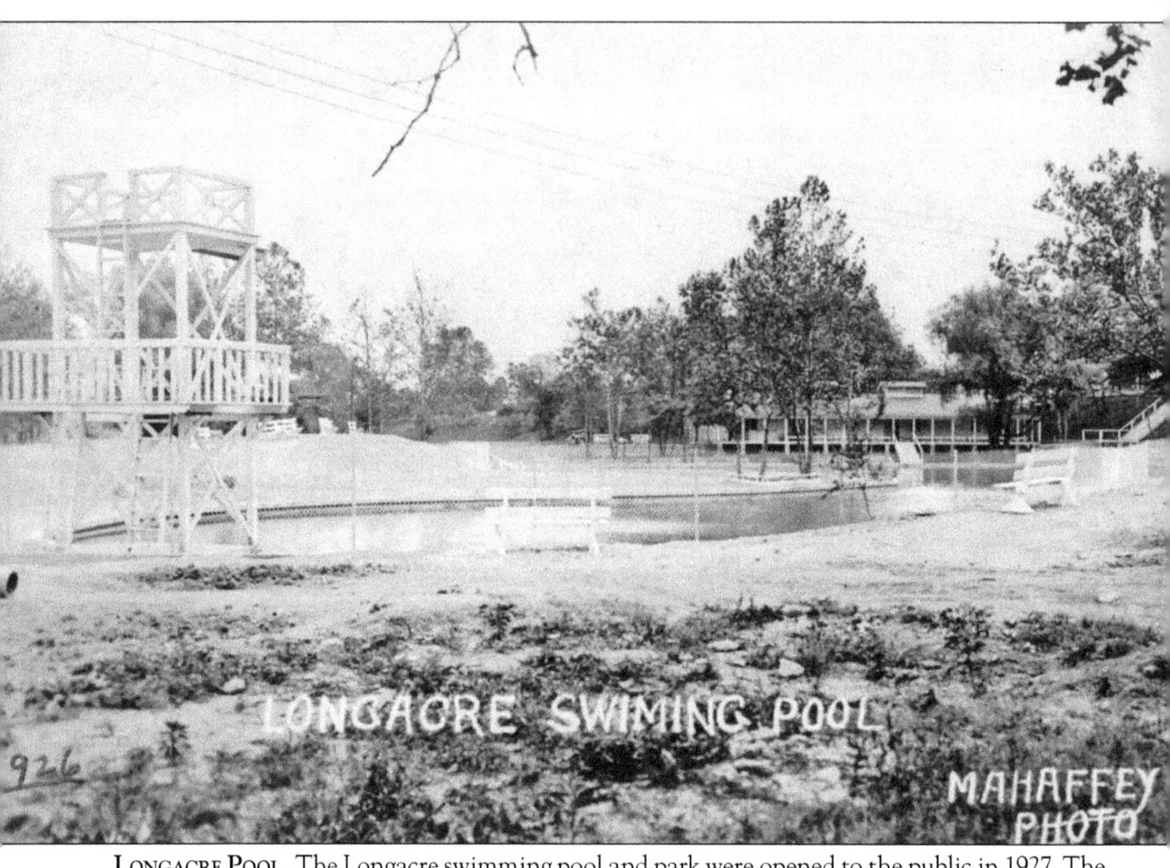

Longacre Pool. The Longacre swimming pool and park were opened to the public in 1927. The pool, which gained its name for being more than an acre in size, was built and owned by Perry Township resident and attorney Edwin Thompson after developing a nearby subdivision between the areas of University Heights and Edgewood east of Madison Avenue in 1913. (Perry Township/Southport Historical Society.)

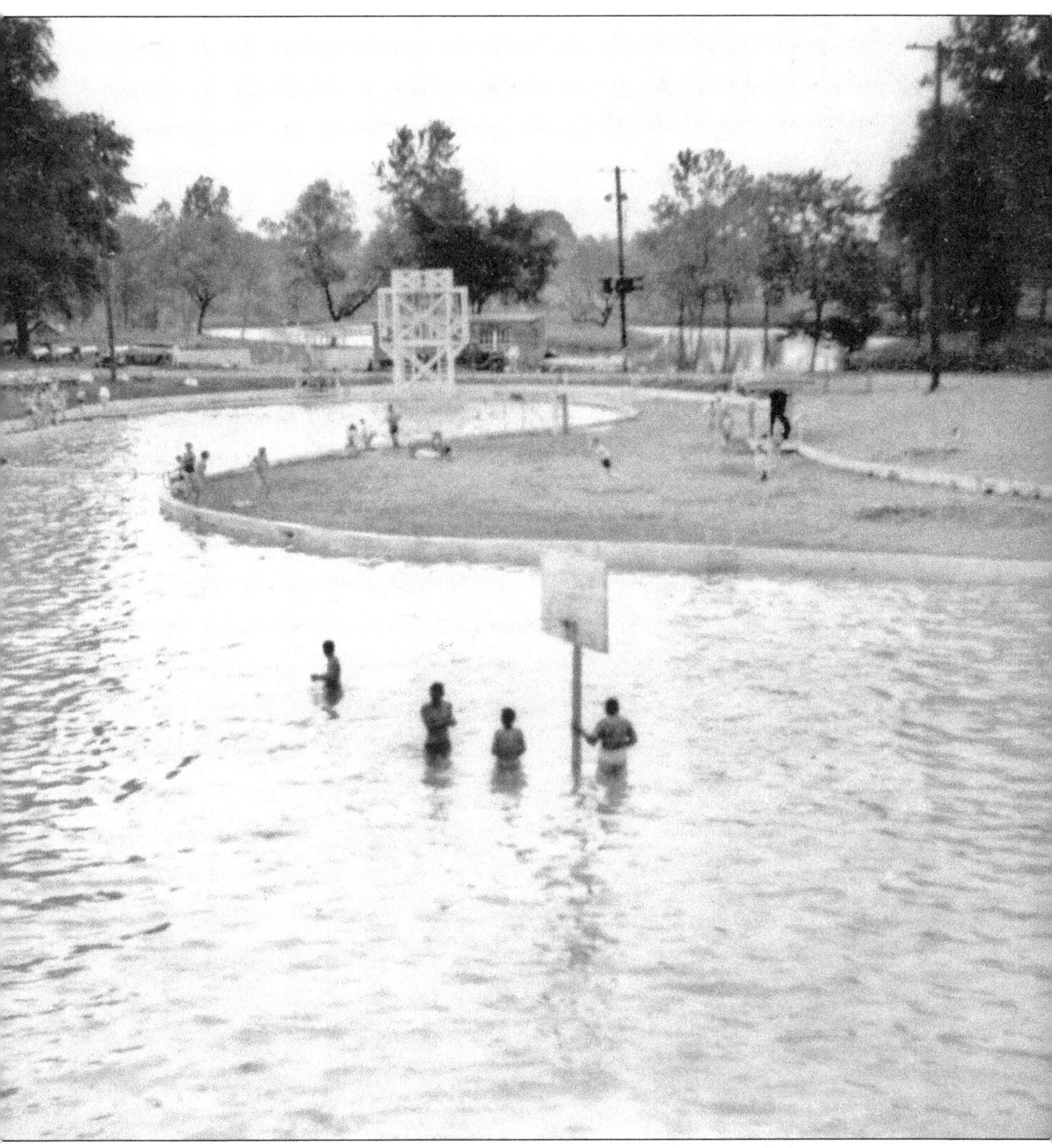

The Pool's Early Years. When Longacre first opened in 1927, the cost of admission was 10¢ to enter the grounds and 25¢ to enter the pool. Located just six miles south of Monument Circle in downtown Indianapolis, people from all around the city were noted to have visited the pool. Longacre pool boasted its size from the start; at approximately 400 feet long, 200 feet wide, and with depths ranging from 2 to 9 feet, the fresh, filtered water was unique to the south side. (Perry Township/Southport Historical Society.)

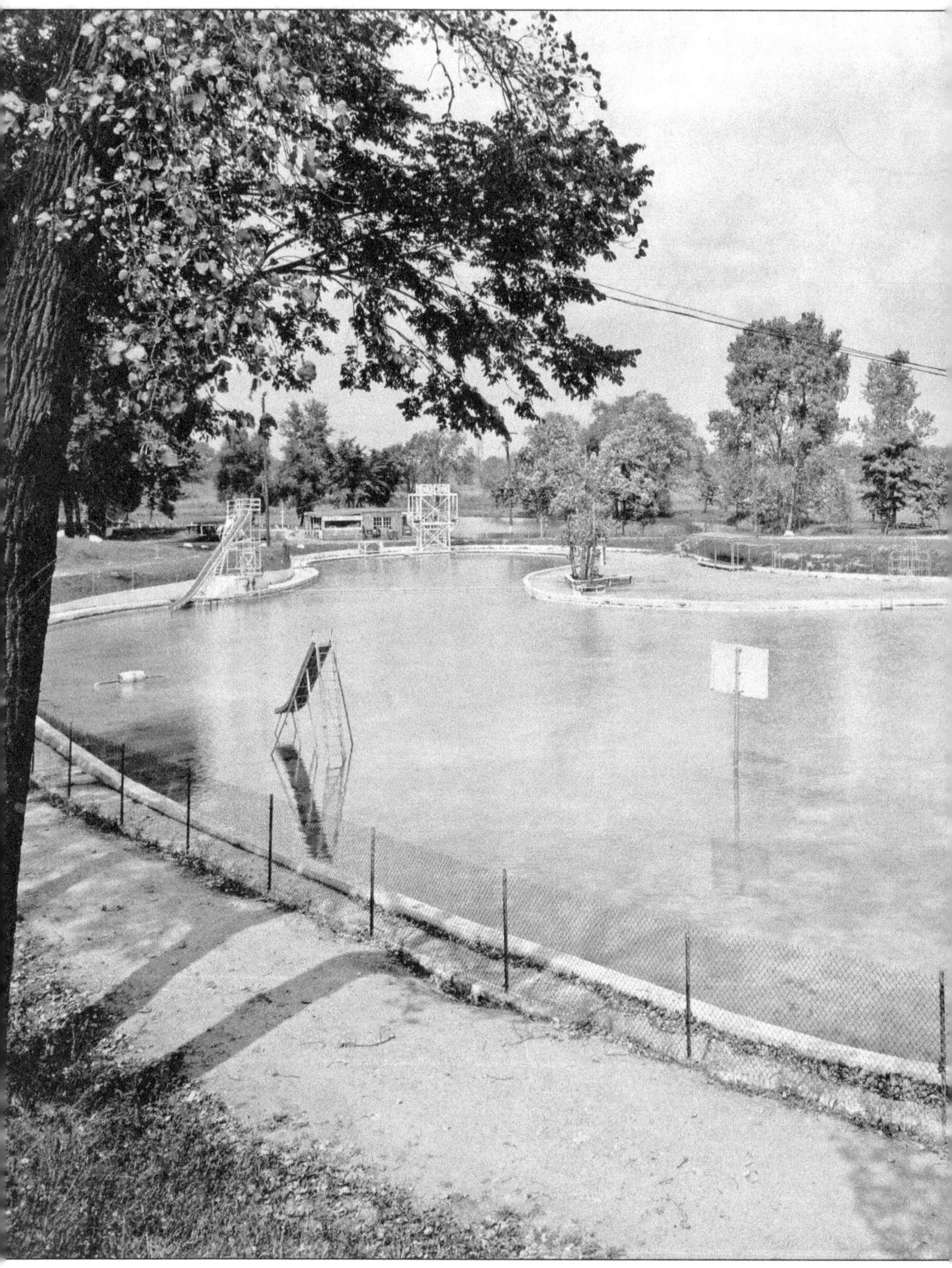

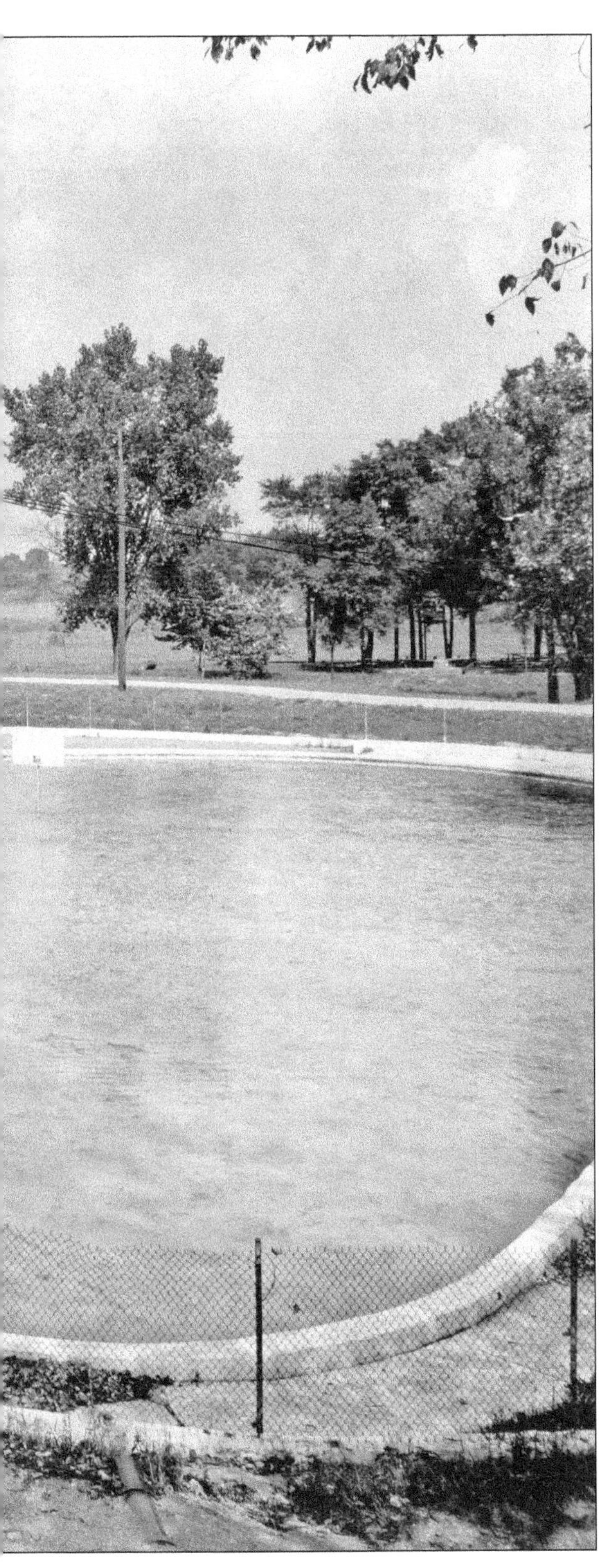

"THE BEAN." When this photograph was taken in 1936, only the sides of the pool were concrete. The bottom was all natural, and the bathhouse in the background had a dance hall on the second floor. In the 1950s, the pool was fully concreted. Thanks to its shape, the pool came to be known as "the bean" by many who visited. (Perry Township/Southport Historical Society.)

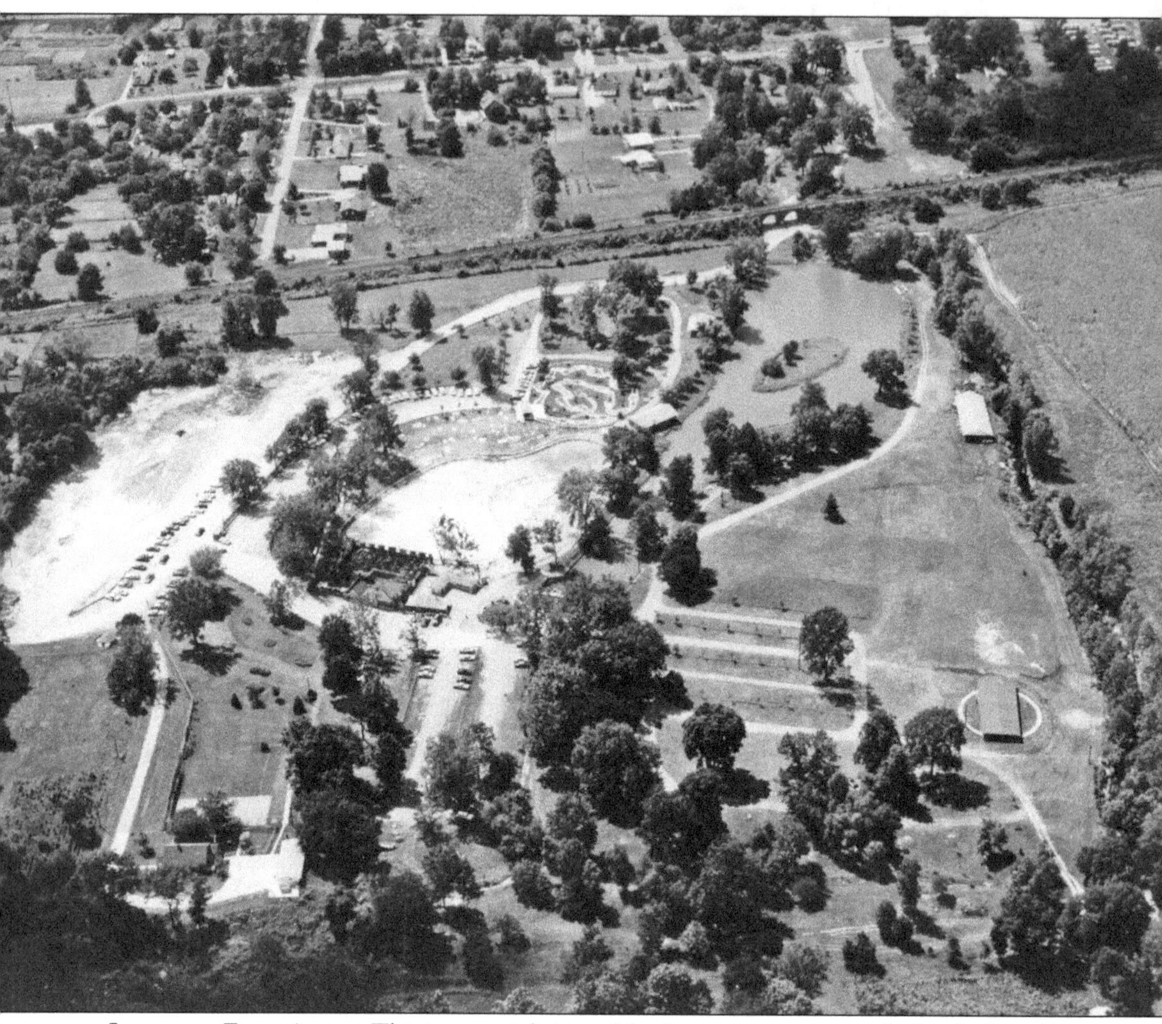

Longacre From Above. This is an aerial view of the Longacre swimming facility looking West. Visible in the photo, Longacre offered more than just a pool. Since it first opened, the grounds also featured a bathhouse, parking spaces for vehicles, picnic areas, and designated sand for sun bathing. Visitors could also make purchases at Longacre, including ice cream, sandwiches, coffee, and soda from the refreshments stand. Swimsuit rentals were also available. (Perry Township/Southport Historical Society.)

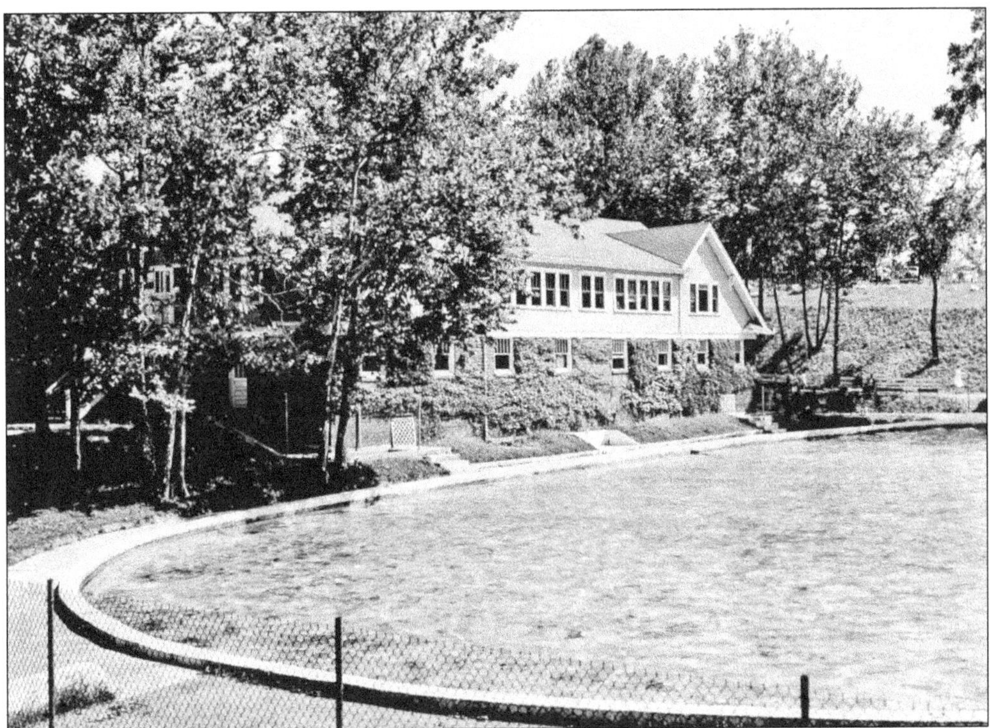

The Pool House. The bathhouse at Longacre sat on the southwest side of the pool facing north toward Edgewood Avenue. The large pool house was 100 feet long with porch on all sides. An original bathhouse existed before this one was built as a replacement in 1948, but it burned down in 1961. (Perry Township/Southport Historical Society.)

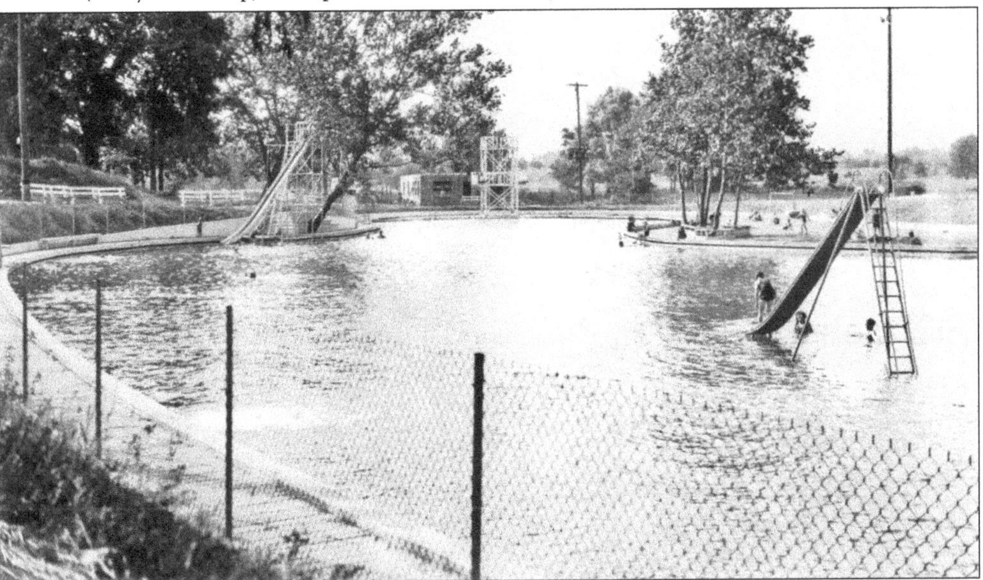

Endless Swimming. Throughout the summer months, thousands of swimmers were recorded coming from around Indianapolis to Longacre to swim. The pool was equipped with a powerful filtering apparatus that could pump 600 gallons of freshwater into the pool each minute. (Perry Township/Southport Historical Society.)

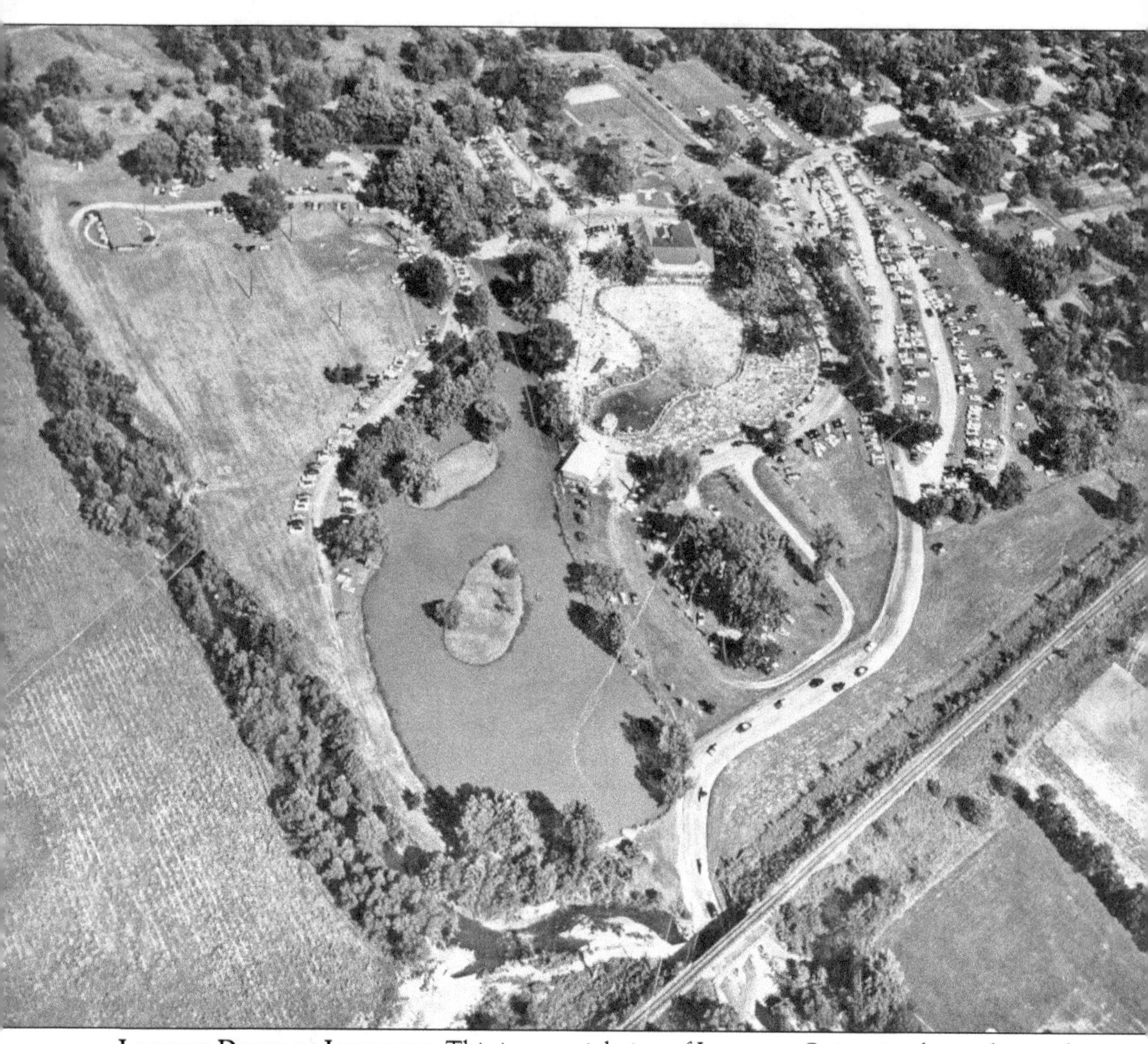

Looking Down at Longacre. This is an aerial view of Longacre. Swimming hours during the summer lasted from 9:00 a.m. to 9:30 p.m. every day. In extreme hot weather, the pool remained open until after midnight. (Perry Township/Southport Historical Society.)

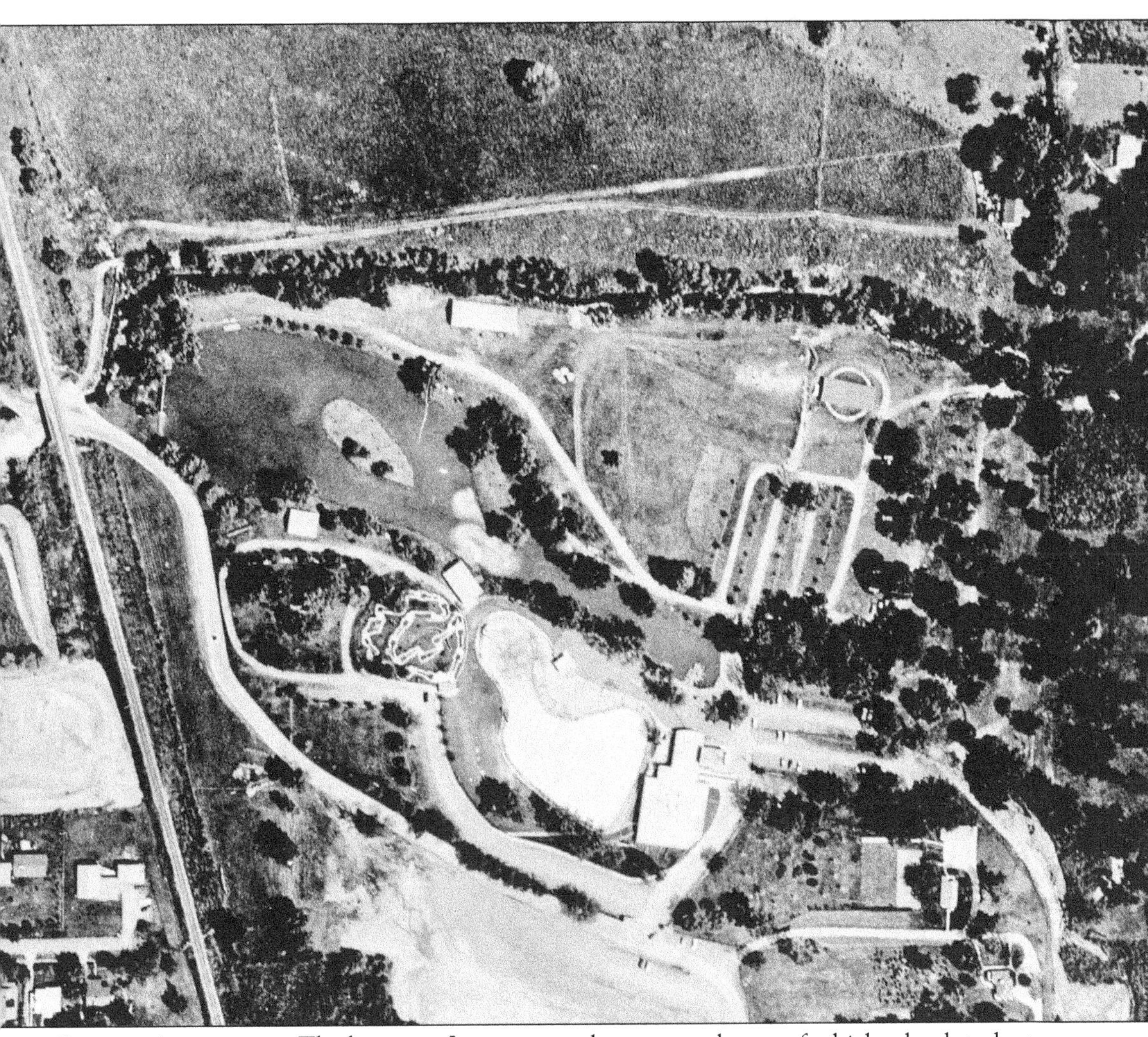

Summer Attraction. The lagoon at Longacre pool was a popular spot for high school students during the summer months. The man-made waterway, located in Edgewood along Edgewood Avenue and Bluff Road, served as an area for paddle boating and swimming. (Perry Township/ Southport Historical Society.)

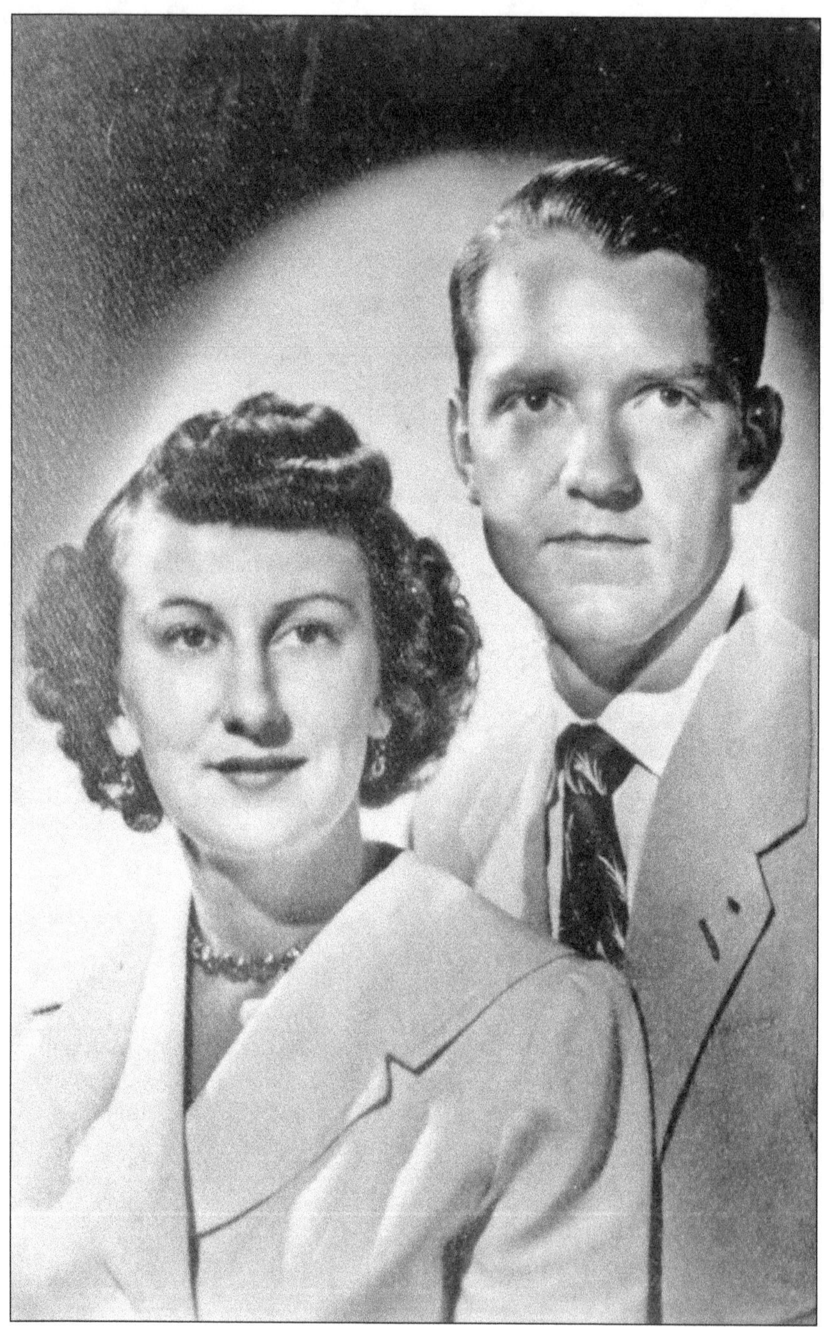

Managing Longacre. Thompson and his wife were the first developers of the Longacre park in the early 1920s, which developed as a byproduct of a subdivision. The subdivision was platted in lots 100 feet wide and 400 feet long, roughly an acre of land. On a trip to New York, Thompson made a phone call to a friend in a Longacre exchange, and he subsequently named his land Longacre. The park developed through the 1920s and 1930s, and eventually a concrete swimming pool was created. Thompson got tired of the operation, however, and wanted to spend more time with his law firm. He put the park up for sale for $100,000 at the end of World War II, and the Dodrills, pictured here, purchased the property. (Perry Township/Southport Historical Society.)

Diving Boards. A very early picture of Longacre Pool looking west toward the big diving board. In the late 1940s, two more diving boards were added to the pool, standing at more than 15-feet high. (Perry Township/Southport Historical Society.)

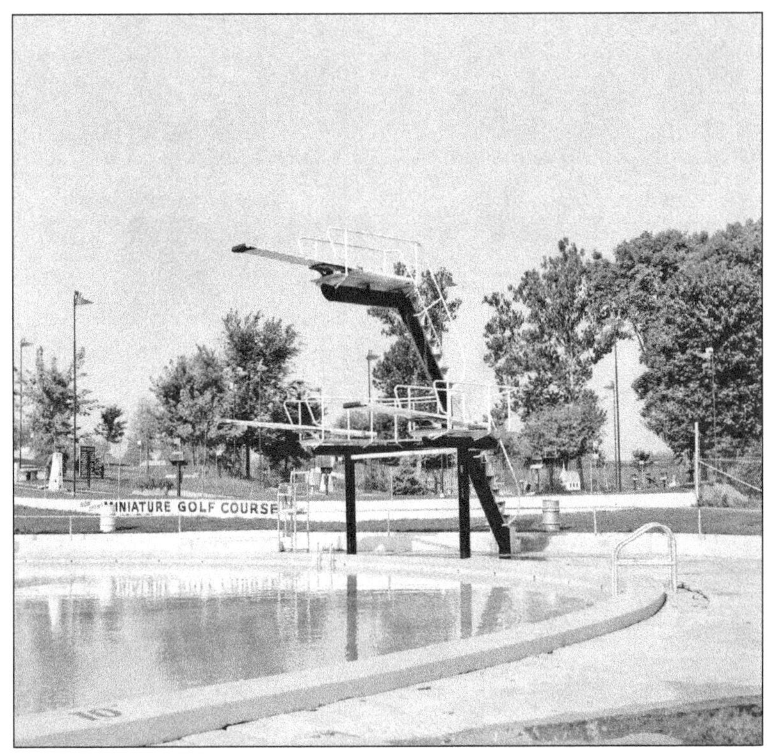

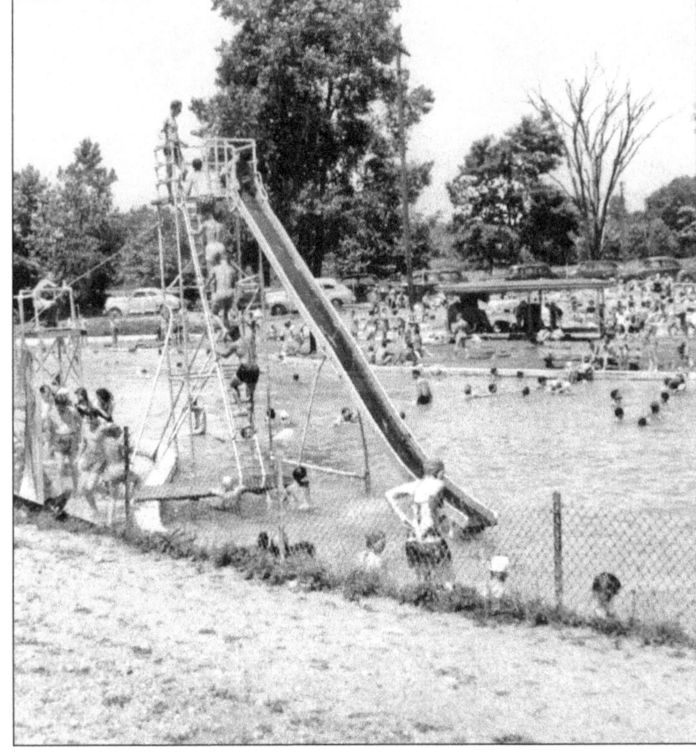

Crowds Grow. As more and more people visited Longacre each summer, improvements and additions were made to the pool and recreational areas. Longacre was sold in 1946 to Rufus Dodrill Jr., whose family operated it until 1972. Dodrill had survived the 1944 Normandy invasion during World War II. In a 1994 interview with the Indianapolis Star, his widow Violet said her husband poured his heart into the park because he could not stand what he had seen during the war, leading him to keep busy during all hours of the day so he would not think about it. (Perry Township/Southport Historical Society.)

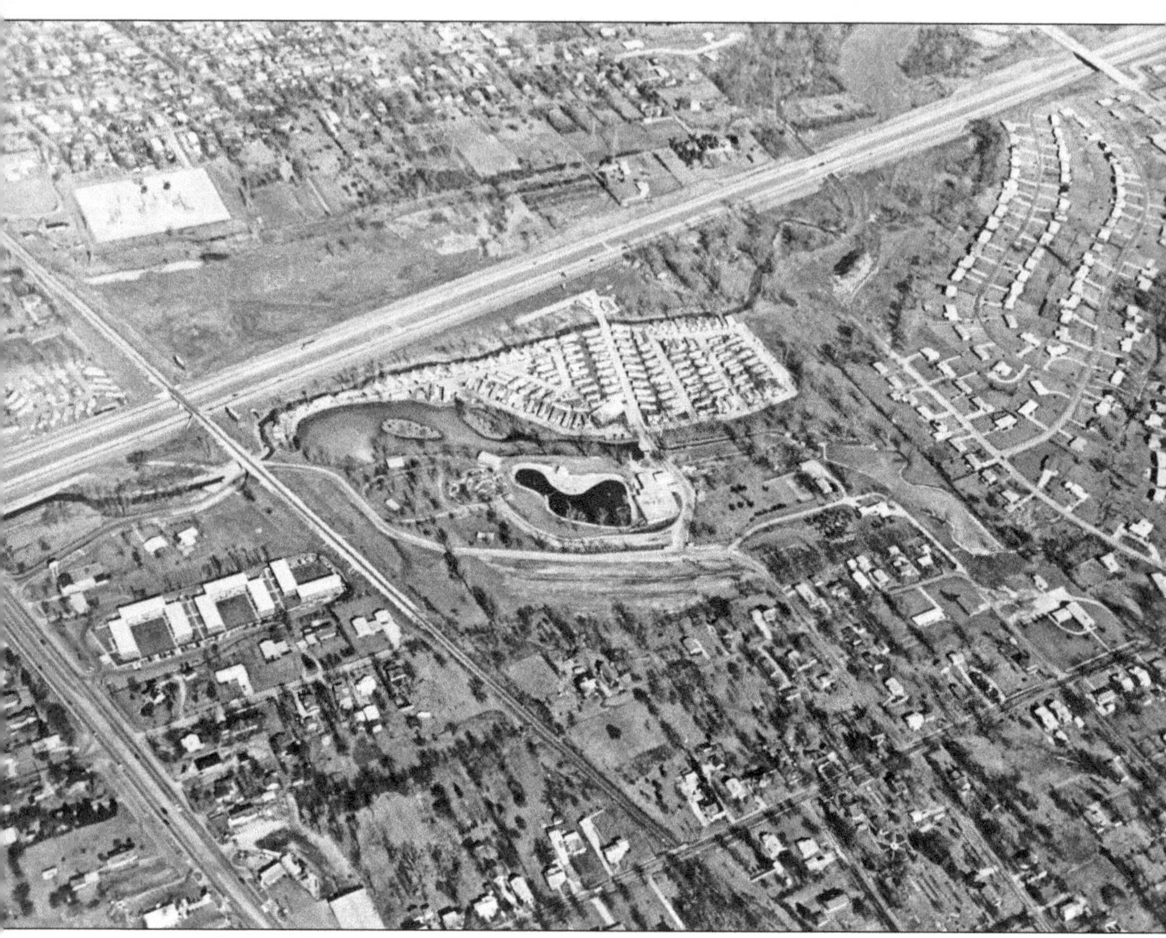

Mobile Homes Move In. In the 1960s, Dodrill developed the park into an early prototype of mobile home parks with well-spaced lots and paved and lighted streets. Visible in this photograph, mobile homes began making their way into the surrounding area shortly after. (Perry Township/Southport Historical Society.)

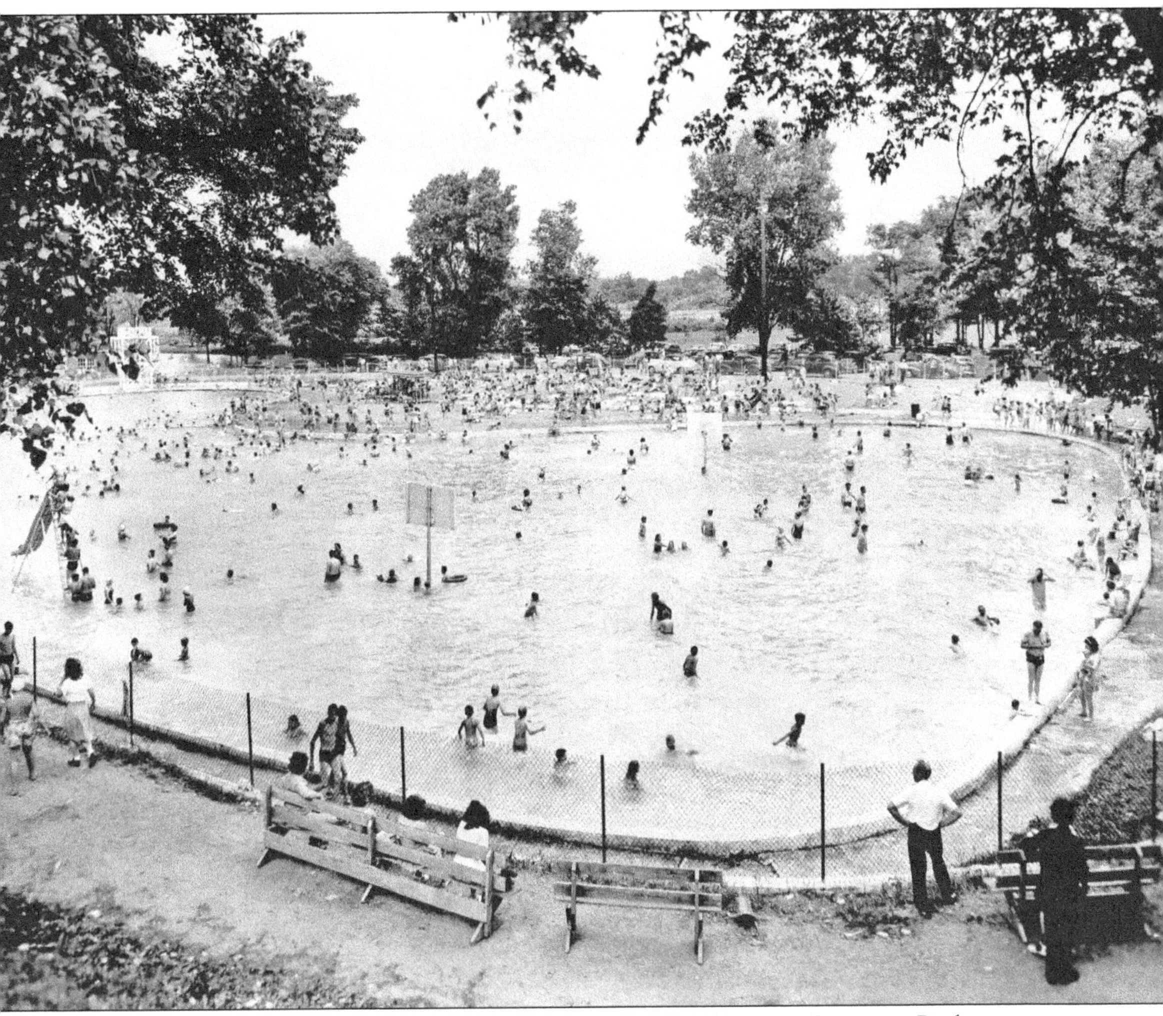

Fun for Everyone. A 20-foot diving platform was a popular feature at Longacre Pool, as were long slides. The 60-acre resort was equipped with a sand beach, bathhouse with a dance hall, playground, and picnic area. In 1930, a baby pool was added. A large lake was a favorite of boaters. (Perry Township/Southport Historical Society.)

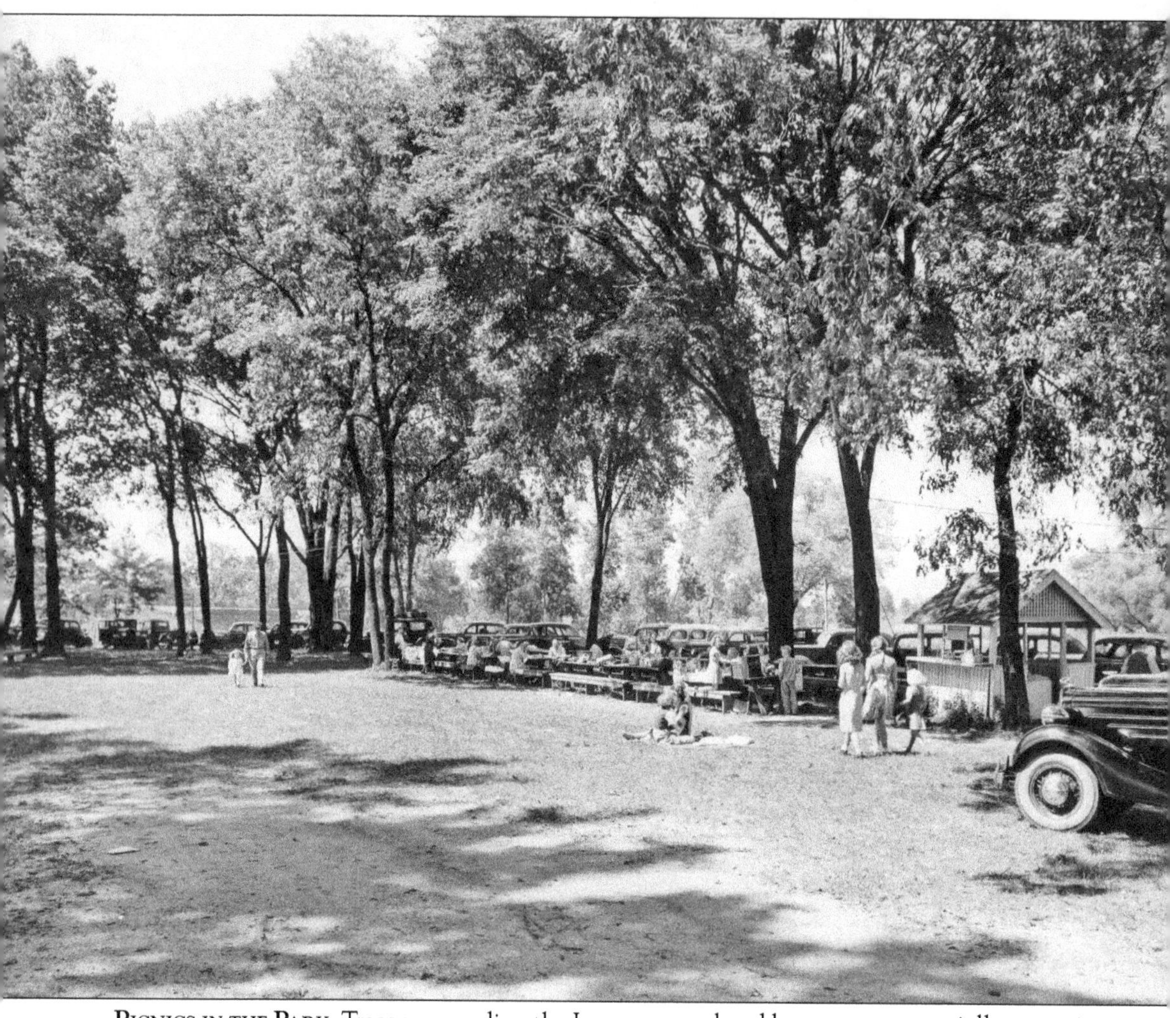

PICNICS IN THE PARK. Trees surrounding the Longacre pool and lagoon were especially attractive to families and businesses interested in hosting picnics. With plenty of shade, tables, benches and outdoor ovens, the picnic areas were frequently used for events and daily outings. (Perry Township/Southport Historical Society.)

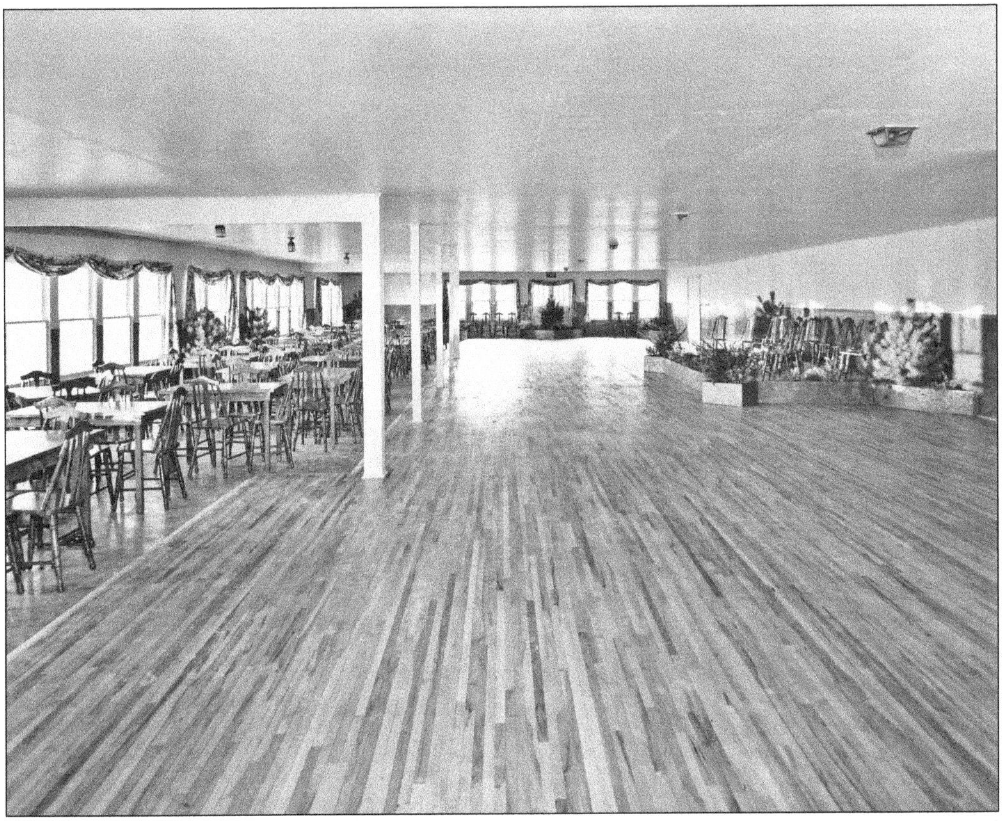

INSIDE THE POOL HOUSE. The Longacre pool house served multiple purposes. The building included a dance pavilion, maintenance structure, and second-story apartment housing a maintenance employee. Events would frequently be held inside, including wedding receptions and other parties. (Perry Township/Southport Historical Society.)

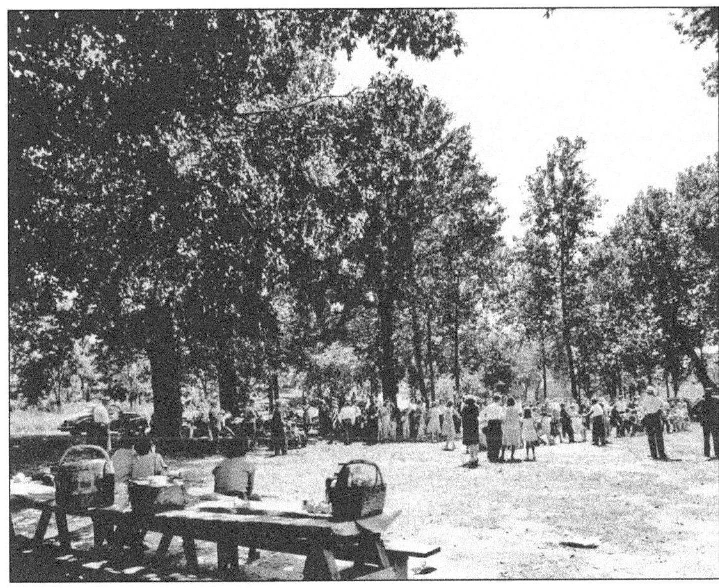

LONGACRE RECREATION AND PARKS. Lick Creek made its way through the playgrounds at Longacre, and play equipment was available for children at the playgrounds. (Perry Township/Southport Historical Society.)

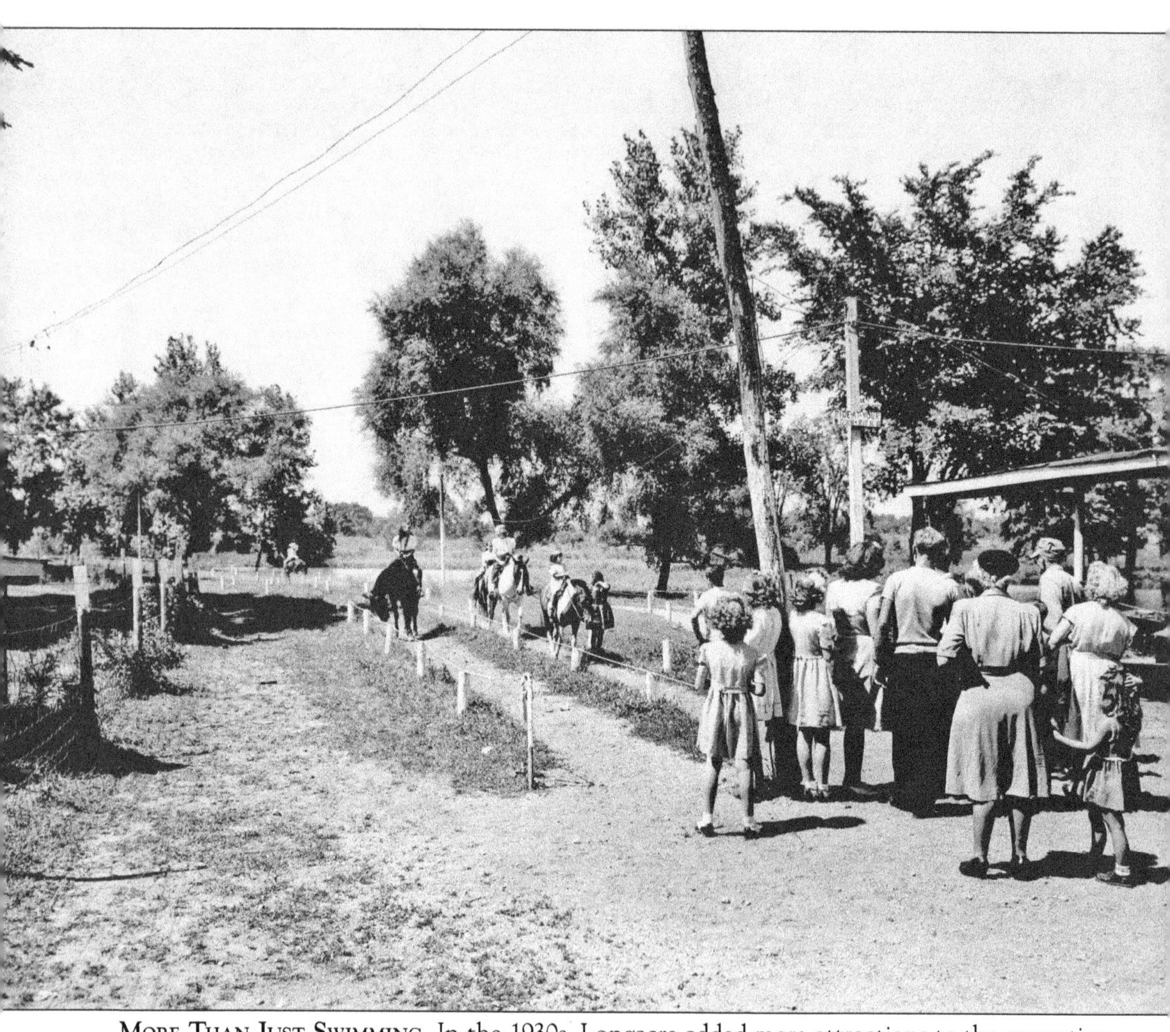

More Than Just Swimming. In the 1930s, Longacre added more attractions to the recreation area. Different aquatic sporting events were held at the pool throughout the summer, but other activities were also available outside of the water, including pony riding, baseball games, mini golf, and picnicking. (Perry Township/Southport Historical Society.)

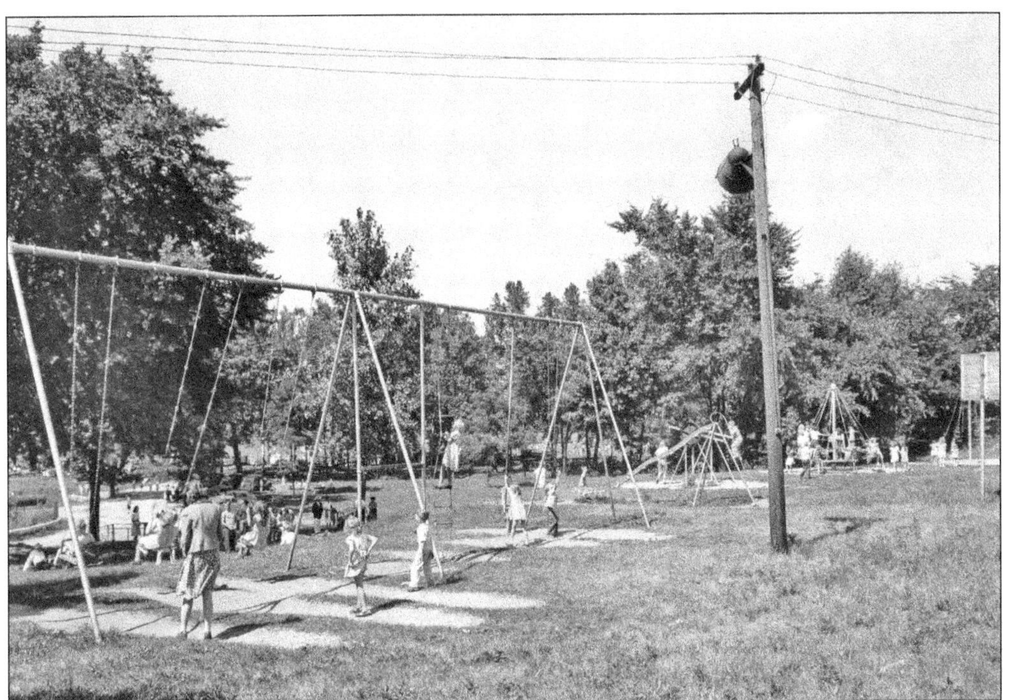

Longacre Recreation. Longacre Park also included a baseball field, a golf driving fairway under lights, tennis, croquet, pony rides, horseshoes, and basketball. Water polo matches were held during the 1930s. A putt-putt course was added much later. In the 1960s, Dodrill developed the park into an early prototype of mobile home parks with well-spaced lots and paved and lighted streets. (Perry Township/Southport Historical Society.)

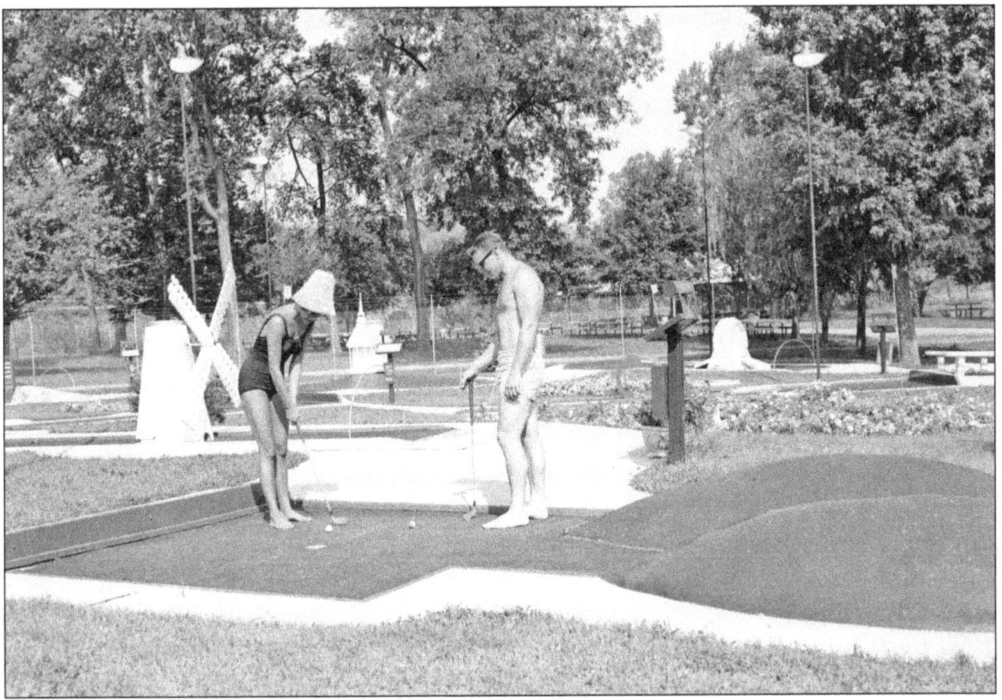

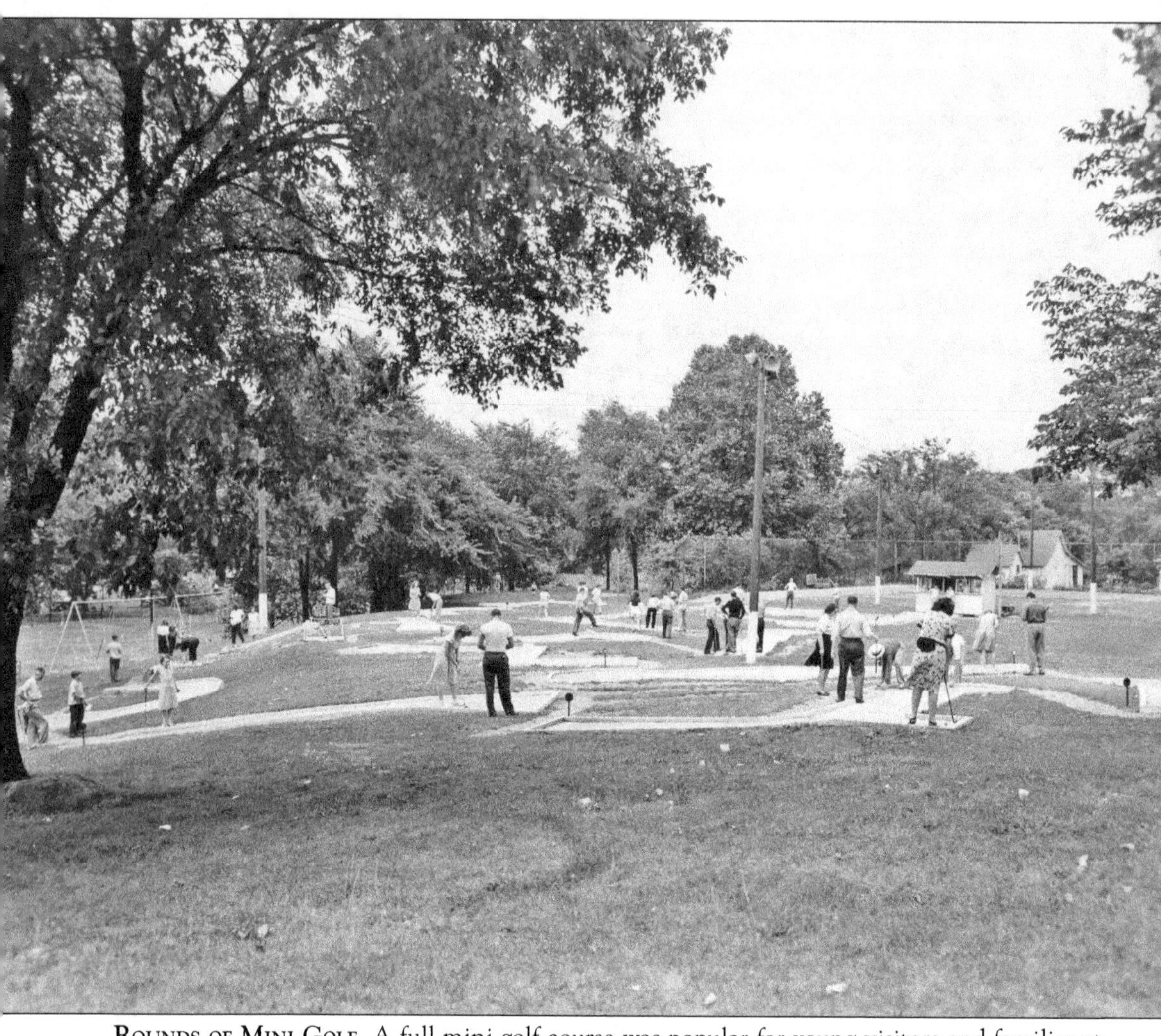

Rounds of Mini Golf. A full mini golf course was popular for young visitors and families at Longacre. Many swimmers would dry off while playing a round of putt-putt nearby the pool, and other out-of-water activity breaks on the grounds included lunchroom times and free Sunday night movies. (Perry Township/Southport Historical Society.)

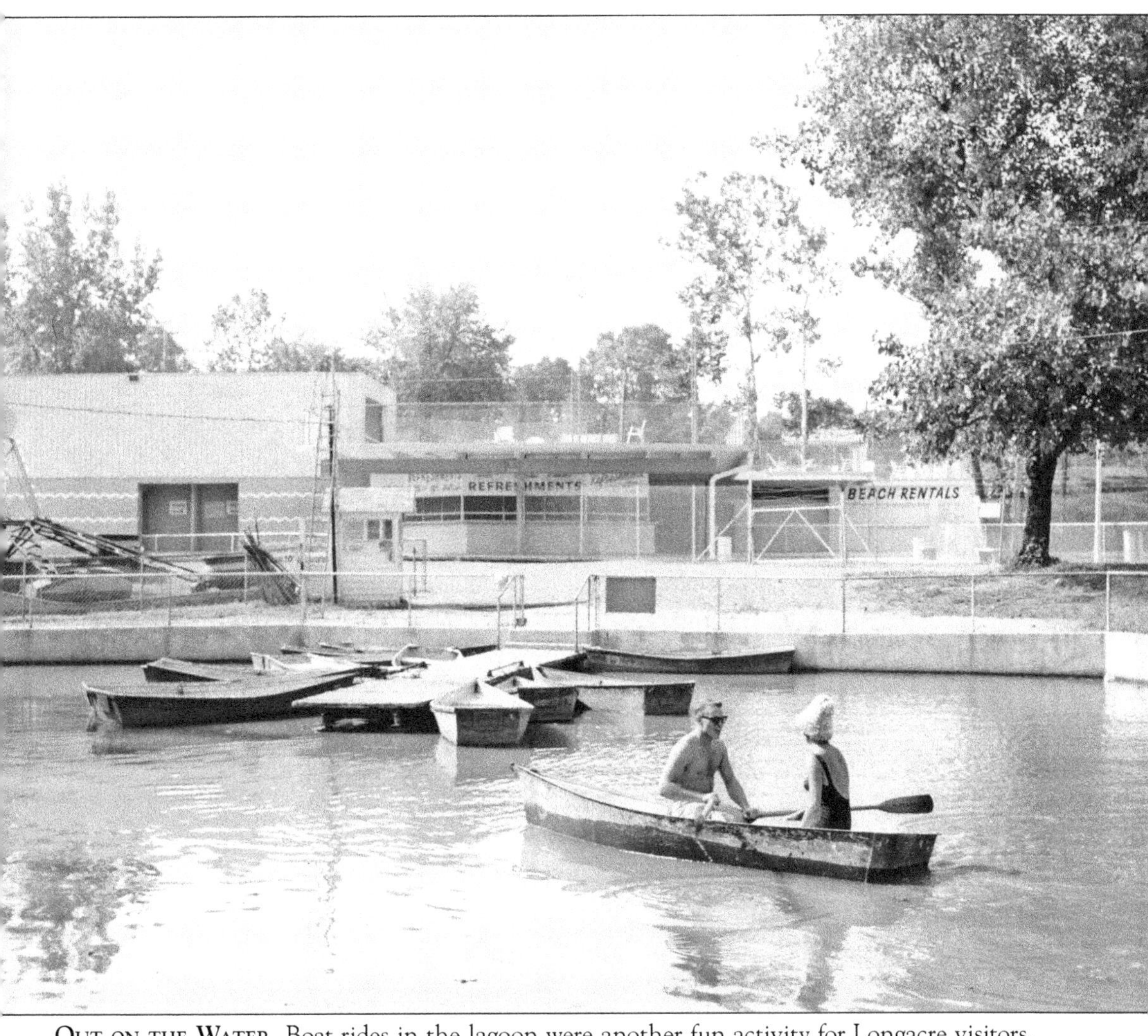

Out on the Water. Boat rides in the lagoon were another fun activity for Longacre visitors. Paddleboats and small canoes were available to use by patrons already, and because of the lagoon's large size, it was easy to have space while on the water. (Perry Township/Southport Historical Society.)

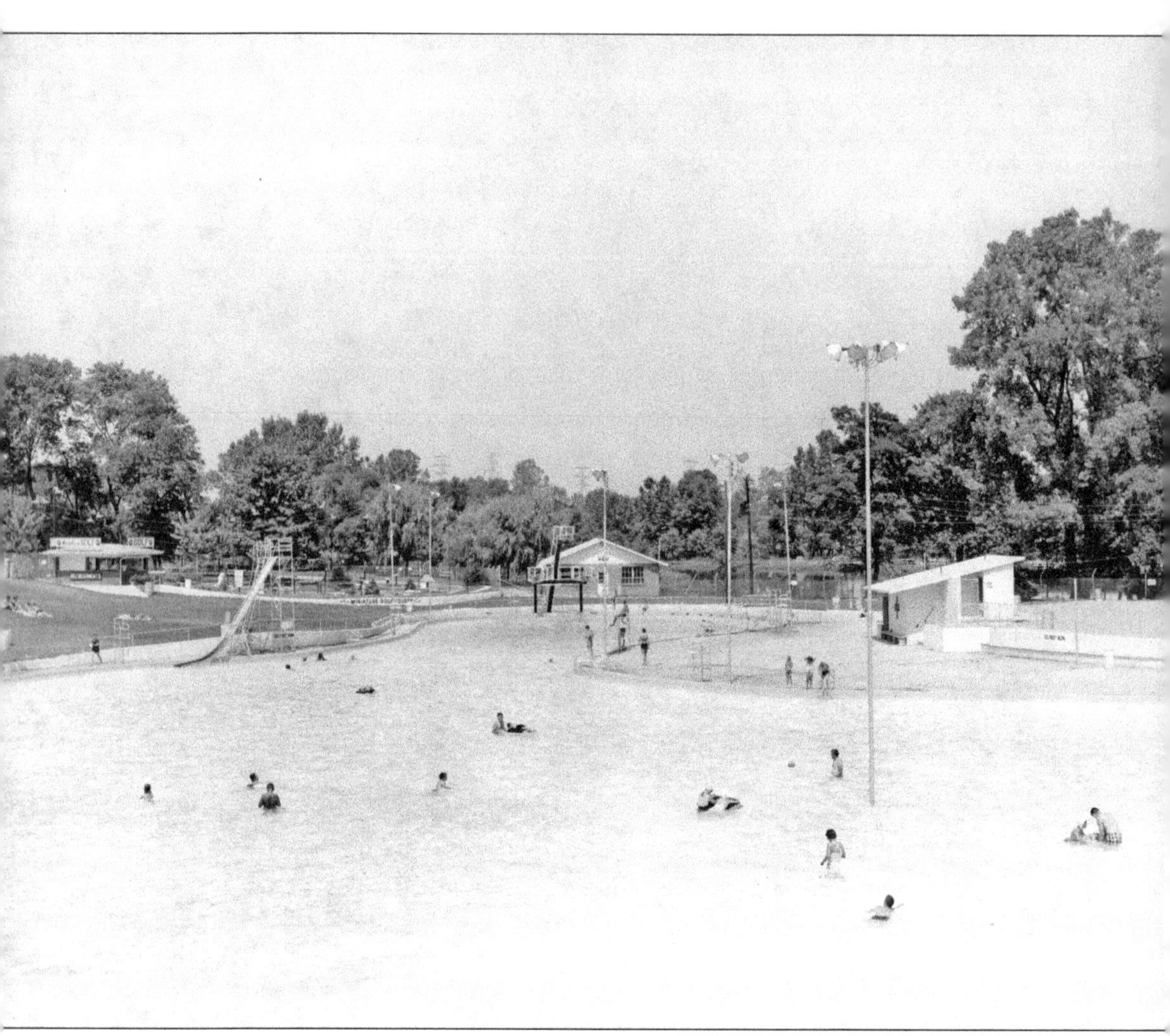

LONGACRE POOL. The pool was the showpiece of the park at 400 feet long and 185 feet wide at the widest point in a kidney shape giving it more of a natural swimming hole appearance. The pool was, in fact, natural. It had a concrete-reinforced wall around it, but the bottom was part of the natural springs, fed by Lick Creek with depths between 2 and 13 feet with no filtration system. It would not be fully concreted until the 1950s. (Perry Township/Southport Historical Society.)

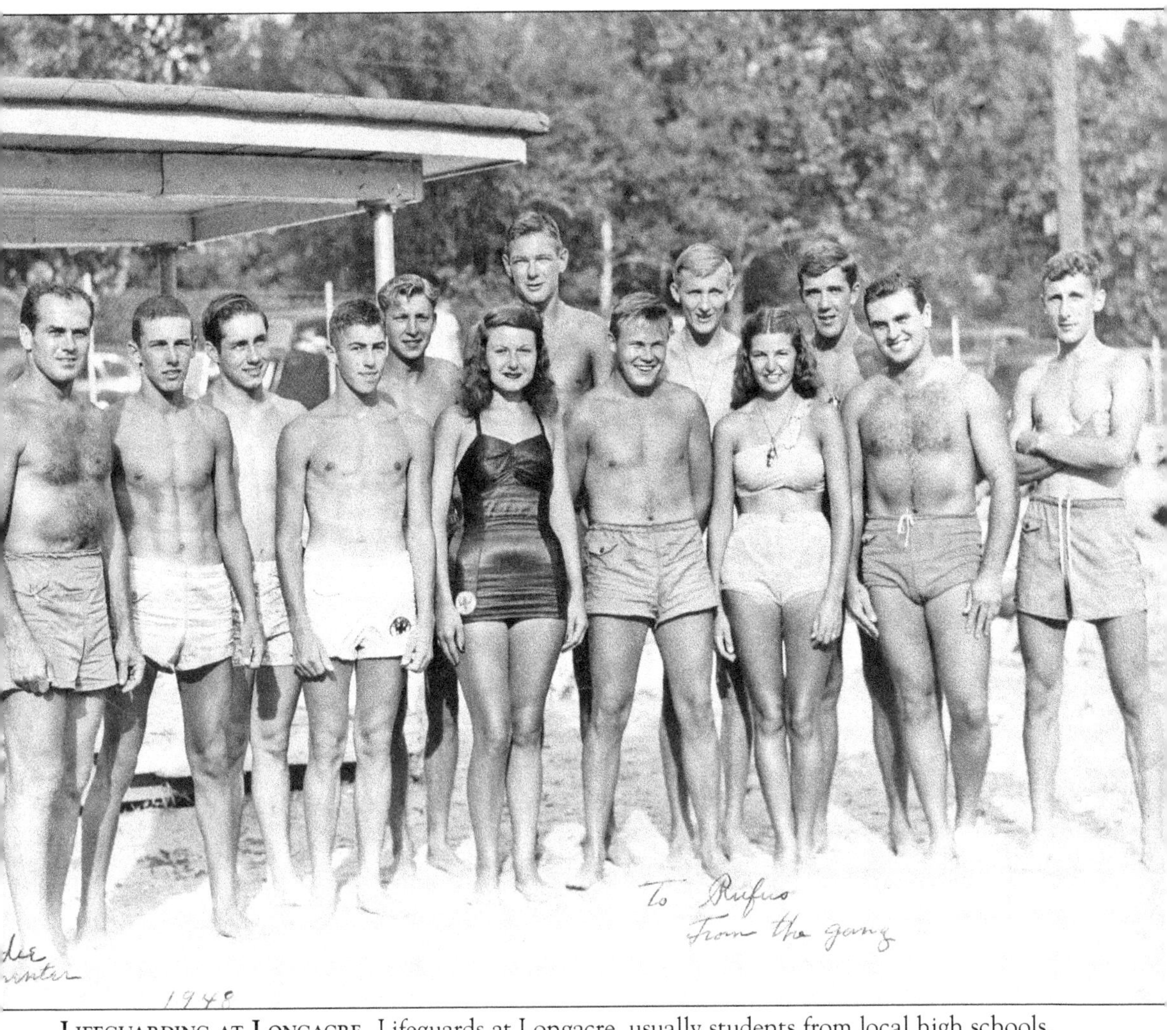

Lifeguarding at Longacre. Lifeguards at Longacre, usually students from local high schools, were trained and hired to keep their eyes on the water and those in it. On several occasions throughout Longacre's history, lifeguards were required to rescue drowning swimmers from the water. (Perry Township/Southport Historical Society.)

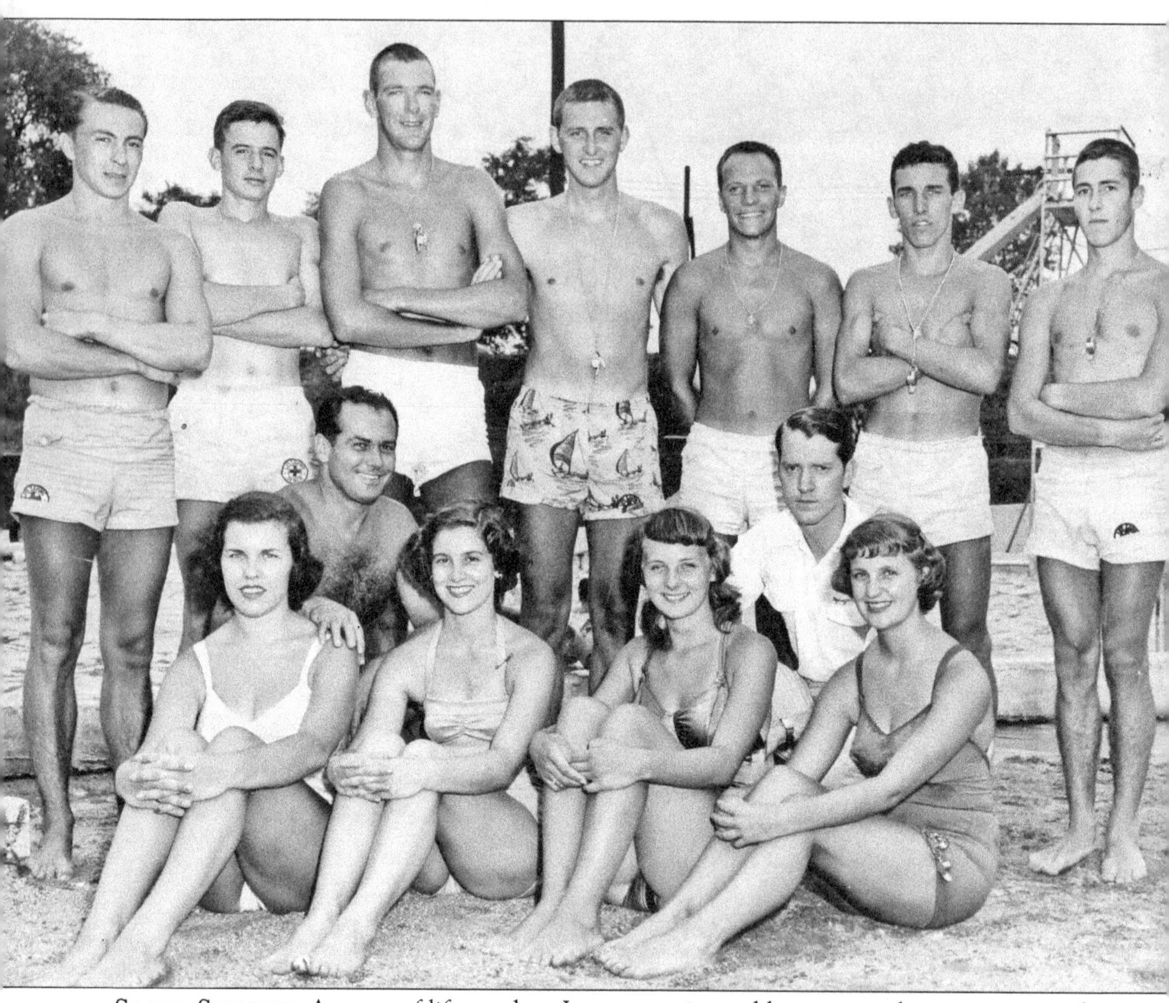

Senior Summers. A group of lifeguards at Longacre, pictured here, spent their summers at the pool. Many lifeguards were also seniors in high school, and their last summers while in school were spent with friends while on duty at the pool from Memorial Day to Labor Day. (Perry Township/Southport Historical Society.)

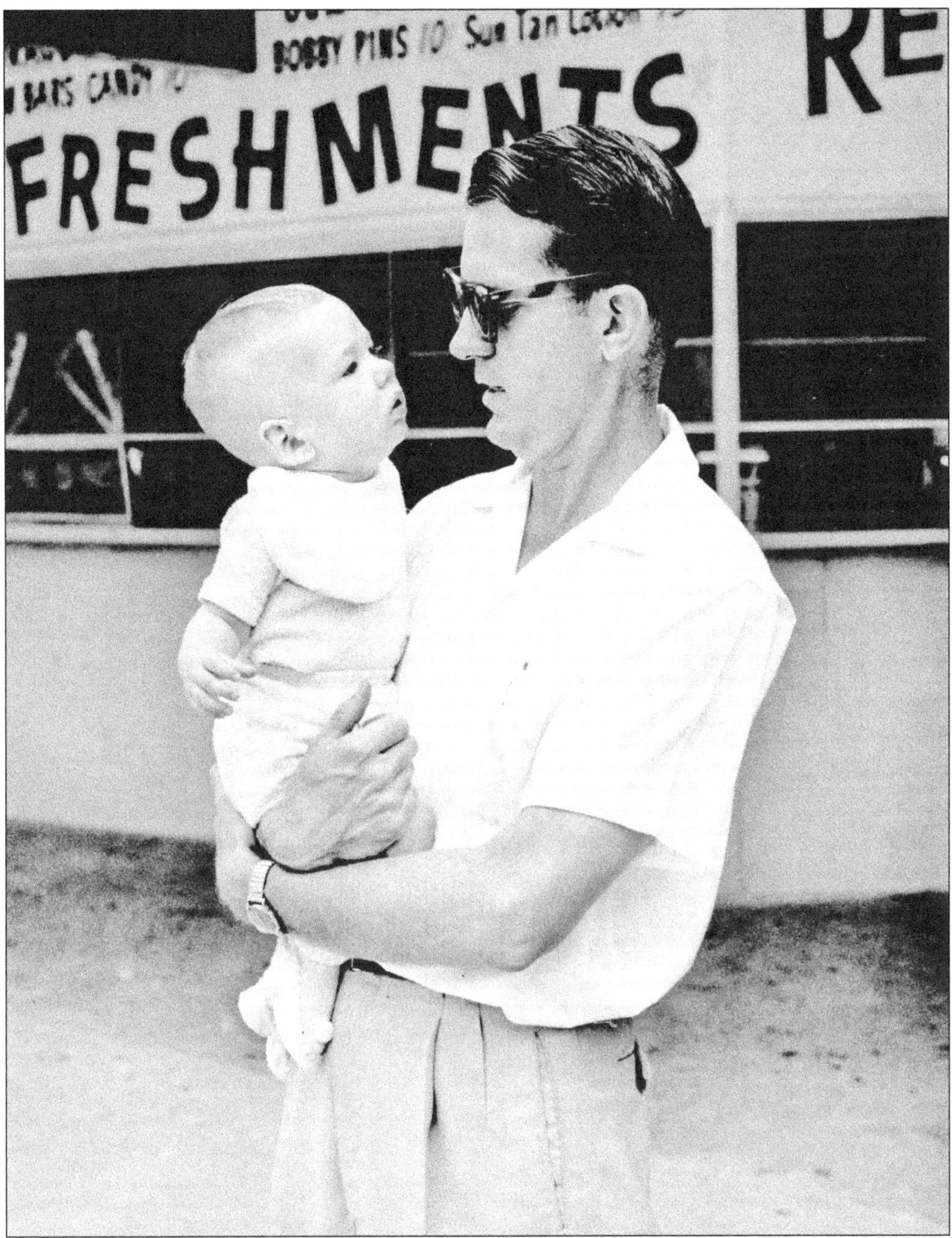

Family Time. Dodrill is seen here holding his son outside of the pavilion. Dodrill, whose wife called him a deeply religious family man, was a hard worker and was extremely dedicated to Longacre. Keeping the pool up and running was a family operation, and the give Dodrill sons helped their parents during the summers. Mobile home parks, which the Dodrills were planning to construct around Longacre, were relatively new when they decided to transform their property. (Perry Township/Southport Historical Society.)

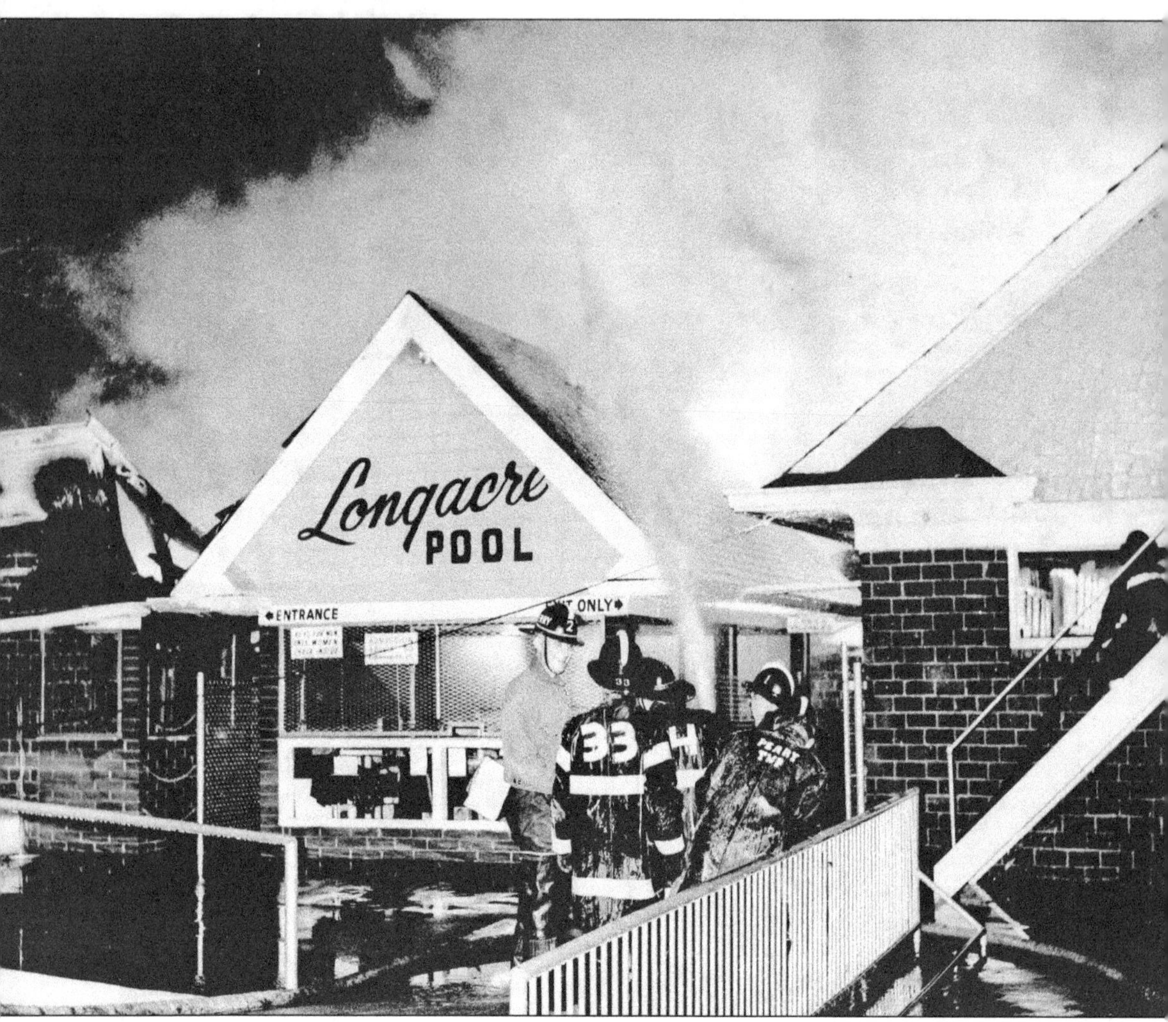

Fire at Longacre. The Longacre bathhouse caught fire in 1960. The blazes were so extreme that all of the firefighters in the township and those surrounding were called upon to assist in extinguishing it. The fire proved to be extremely destructive, but the bathhouse was later rebuilt. (Perry Township/Southport Historical Society.)

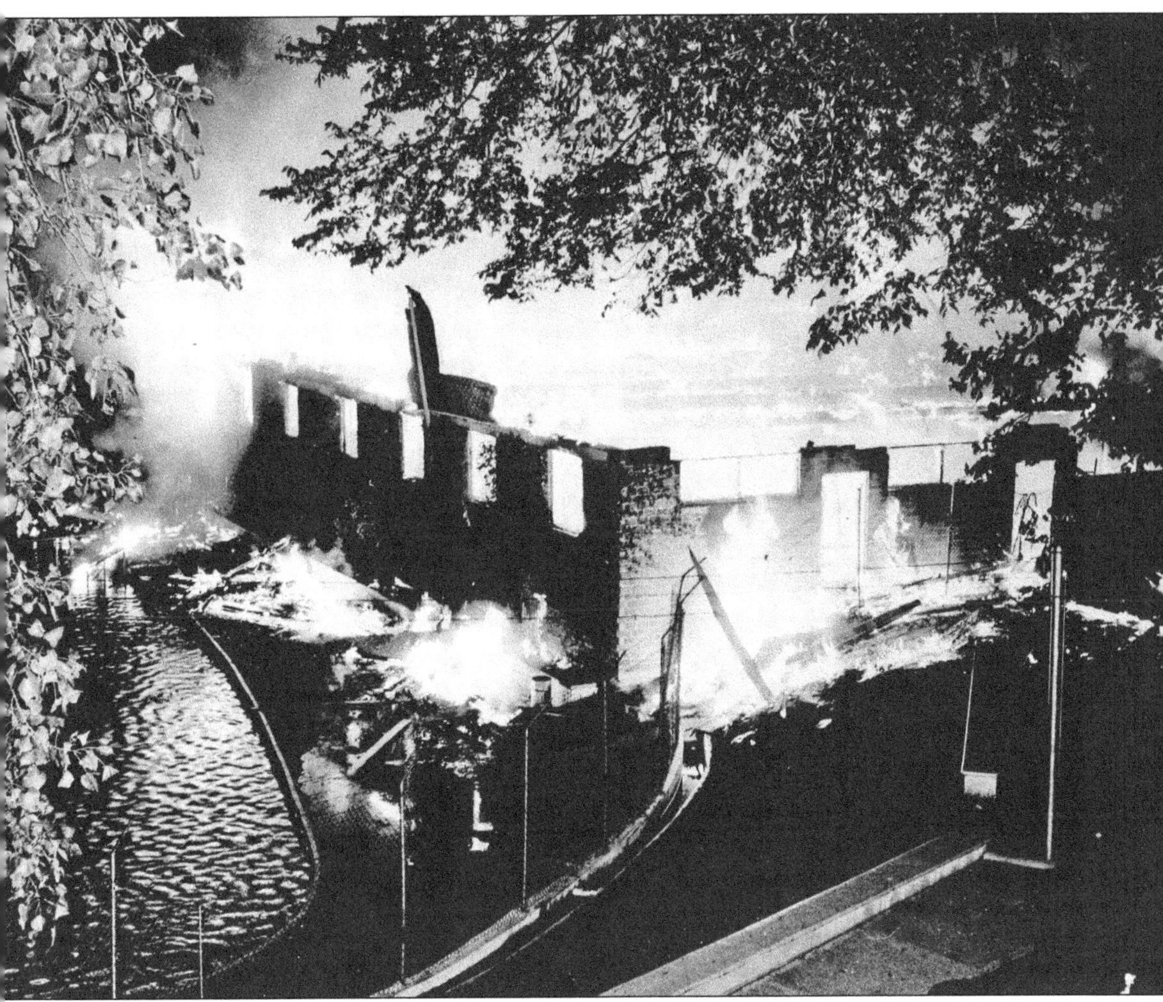

Pool House Destroyed. The deputy sheriff at the time, Robert Montgomery, said that the fire started on the ground floor of the building, which contained the lifeguards, lounge, and all electrical master switches. A snack bar and dressing rooms for men and women were also located on the ground floor. The fire was likely started by a shirt circuit, and total damages were estimated to be at $100,000. The pool remained open at the time, but swimmers had to go to and from the park in bathing clothes. (Perry Township/Southport Historical Society.)

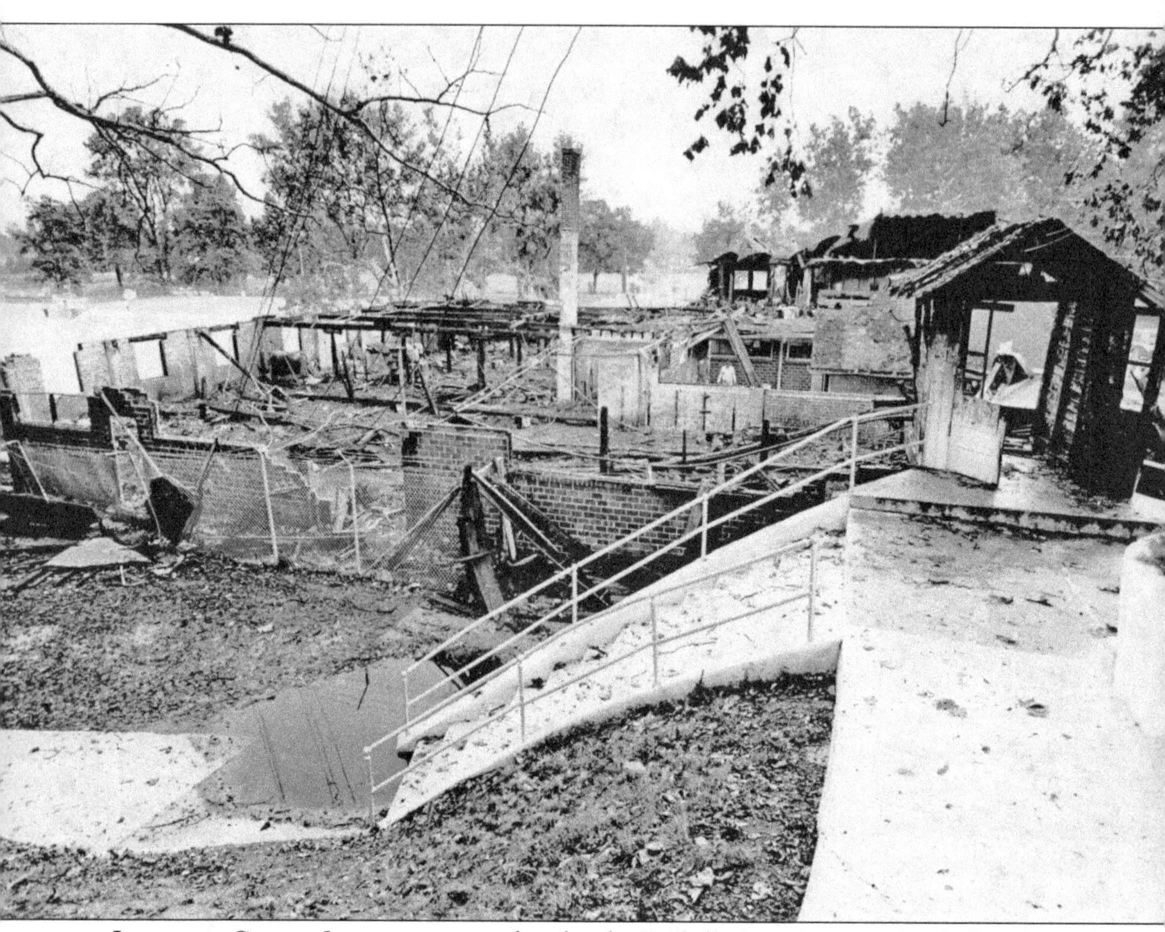

Longacre Closes. Longacre operated under the Dodrills from 1948 to 1972 before the park was converted into a mobile home park. The upkeep of the mobile home park was challenging, however, and the Dodrills sold the property and moved to Florida shortly after. (Perry Township/Southport Historical Society.)

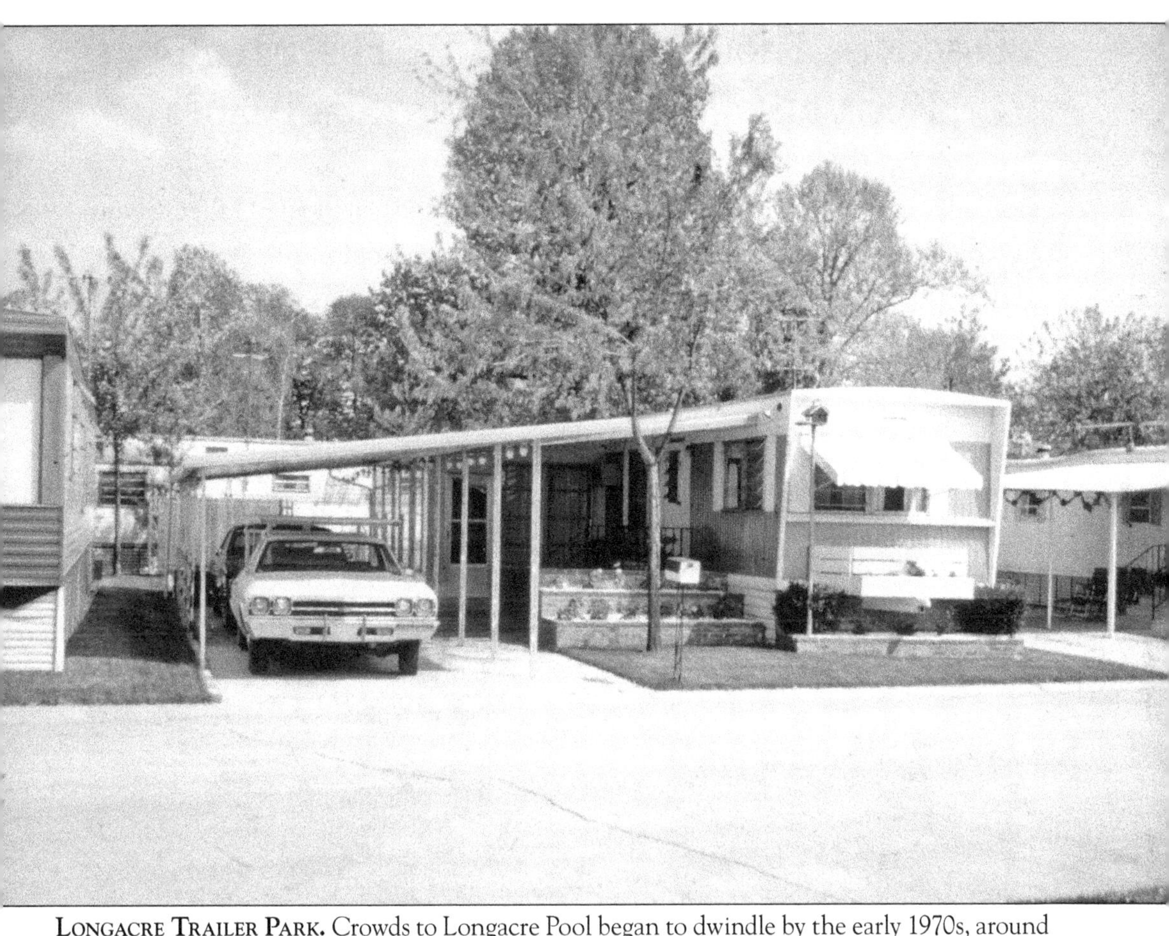

LONGACRE TRAILER PARK. Crowds to Longacre Pool began to dwindle by the early 1970s, around the time homeowners installed air conditioning and more neighborhoods pools became readily available. After Dodrill sold the park in 1972, the pool was open to residents only and eventually removed in the late 1970s. Longacre Mobile Home Park and the original lake are all that remains. (Perry Township/Southport Historical Society.)

www.ingramcontent.com/pod-product-compliance
Lightning Source LLC
LaVergne TN
LVHW081551100826
845153LV00004B/363

* 9 7 8 1 5 4 0 2 3 5 4 2 8 *